Cleanth Brooks and Allen Tate

For Mrs Bradford with warm regards, Alphonse Christmas 1998

Cleanth Brooks
and Allen Tate

☙

Collected Letters, 1933–1976

Edited by Alphonse Vinh

University of Missouri Press
Columbia and London

University of Missouri Press, Columbia, Missouri 65201
Printed and bound in the United States of America
5   4   3   2   1   02   01   00   99   98

Library of Congress Cataloging-in-Publication Data

Brooks, Cleanth, 1906–
    Cleanth Brooks and Allen Tate : collected letters, 1933–1976 /
  edited by Alphonse Vinh.
        p.   cm.
    Includes index.
    ISBN 0-8262-1207-7 (alk. paper)
    1. Brooks, Cleanth, 1906–   —Correspondence.   2. Critics—United
  States—Correspondence.   3. Tate, Allen, 1899–   —Correspondence.
  4. Authors, American—20th century—Correspondence.   5. Southern
  States—Intellectual life.   6. Poetry—Study and teaching.
  I. Tate, Allen, 1899–   .   II. Vinh, Alphonse, 1956–   .
  III. Title.
  PS29.B74A4   1998
  809—dc21   98-34156
  [B]   CIP

®™ This paper meets the requirements of the
American National Standard for Permanence of Paper
for Printed Library Materials, Z39.48, 1984.

Designer: Stephanie Foley
Typesetter: Bookcomp, Inc.
Printer and binder: Thomson-Shore, Inc.
Typeface: Palatino

In memory of the men I call my fathers

Cleanth Brooks

Allen Tate

M. E. Bradford

Russell Kirk

Kenneth Yearns

Contents

Acknowledgments

SO MANY PEOPLE have contributed to the creation of this book in ways small and great that I will not be able to thank all of them. But I would like to thank a few of those who have helped me along the way. First I would like to thank my editor, Beverly Jarrett of the University of Missouri Press, for believing in this project and for her amazing patience and fortitude with me. She has been always kind and generous in her support, and I would not have completed the project without her. I owe many thanks also to Jane Lago, Managing Editor of Missouri Press, for her invaluable assistance in the completion of the project.

A generous grant from the Wilbur Foundation allowed me to travel to archives and to reproduce much needed items. I am deeply indebted to the late Russell Kirk and wife, Annette, for helping me to obtain this grant.

I would like to express my deep gratitude to Mrs. Helen Tate for her permission to publish her husband's letters. Without her support, this book could not exist. I owe my thanks as well to the family of Cleanth Brooks for their unstinting kindness and support. I would like to thank in particular Cleanth's nephews Paul and Carver Blanchard, with whom I shared the great honor of caring for Cleanth during his last days.

I would like to thank Brooks's official biographer, Mark Royden Winchell, for the gift of his splendid life of Cleanth, which helped explain many references in the early letters. I am grateful to him as well for publishing a few of Cleanth's early letters to Tate in the *South Carolina Review.* I am grateful to John Michael Walsh, Brooks's bibliographer and former student, for his generous gift of a copy of his book to aid my own research. I depended heavily on his work to ensure the accuracy of my citations of Cleanth's writings.

Among others, C. Vann Woodward, Lewis P. Simpson, and Maynard Mack all helped me with their memories of Cleanth Brooks. I thank Vann Woodward for his friendship and support. To Lewis P. Simpson I owe a great debt for his kindnesses to me as well as for his insightful advice through letters and conversations. Many thanks too are owed to Louis D. Rubin, Jr., for his many precise and helpful suggestions in the revision of my manuscript. I am deeply honored that he was willing to read through the manuscript and make detailed notes and suggestions for its improvement.

To my family, my friends, and my associates I owe much in ways often difficult to cite tangibly. I especially want to thank my parents, Dr. N. X. Vinh and Mrs. Joan Vinh, my Grandmum Ruth Yearns (whose husband is one of the men I call my fathers—my grandfather Kenneth Yearns of Louisville, Georgia), my brother John, my friends Joseph and Rhonda Johnston, Anthony and Elizabeth Harrigan, Harry Hogan, the Snowden family, Bishop William Millsaps and his wife, Martha, Tam and Chris Carlson, Dale Richardson, George Poe, John Cummings, Caroline Langston, Vasilii Rudich, Cindy and David Robinson, Deal and Carver Hudson, Kevin and Paula Burzio, my goddaughter Tessa, my kum Steven Subichin, my godfather Father George Lardas and his matushka Ann, my dukhovnik Father Victor Potapov, Charles and Tunky Summerall, Mrs. M. E. Bradford, Cliff Bates, Maria Jessica Pitz, Laura Gray, Alan Solomon, Patrick M. McSweeney, Rob Robinson, Tony and Susan Lundy, Linda Hicks, and my late landlady Sennie Harris.

Thanks are also in order for the invaluable assistance I received from the library staffs of Vanderbilt University, the University of the South, Princeton University, and Yale University.

Finally, I wish to express my warm affection and heartfelt gratitude to M. E. Bradford, Marion and Dot Montgomery, Dolores Moyano Martin, Tommy Nixon of Durham, and my beloved sister Kathleen Brady. Last but not least, I wish to thank my dear friend and mentor, the late Cleanth Brooks. His friendship, his good talk, and his companionship are things I will always miss dearly.

Editorial Note

THIS COLLECTION INCLUDES all of the known letters exchanged between Cleanth Brooks and Allen Tate during their long and enduring friendship. It is possible that additional letters will turn up—in a very few places one refers to a letter from the other that has not been found—but for the most part the correspondence as reproduced here seems to be complete.

Unless indicated otherwise, the original letters are all typed and signed. When they are not typed, the designation OH, for original holograph, appears to the left of the return address. In some cases, the return addresses may indicate the letterhead of the stationery used rather than the location of the writer at the time. The addresses of the receiver included in the more formal business-letter format of some of the letters have been dropped. The absence of a return address indicates the absence of one on the original letter. When letters are undated, or clearly misdated, estimated dates have been provided in square brackets.

Obvious typographical errors have been silently corrected. Punctuation has been standardized in a few places where the lack of a comma or a period might lead to confusion, but none of these changes in any way affects the writers' style or intent. All ellipses in the letters are in the originals. Each letter is reproduced in its entirety, with no material written by either Tate or Brooks deleted, although notes written by a third party (for example, Tinkum Brooks) on the same sheet of paper have not been included.

Cleanth Brooks and Allen Tate

The Passionate Partisans: An Introduction

Louis D. Rubin, Jr.

THESE LETTERS, exchanged between Cleanth Brooks and Allen Tate over the course of more than forty years and edited for publication by Alphonse Vinh, constitute one of the more feisty and enjoyable documents in the history of twentieth-century American letters. They chronicle the active involvement of two leading participants in the literary and critical wars during an era when the way to read and to teach poetry in the English language was being profoundly recast. The two correspondents, both southerners, both graduates of Vanderbilt University, had as much to do with the nature and the impact of that change as anyone on the literary scene.

In the 1930s and 1940s, they were controversial figures, leaders of a critical and pedagogical revolution, and as such, anathema to their elders. In their later years, as so often happens, in turn they became targets for all who set out to overturn the dominion of what a younger generation viewed as the Repressive Establishment. What is so interesting about their letters to each other is the sense of what was involved in the process—a process which both reflected and helped to bring about significant changes in our culture.

Tate was the older, by some half-dozen years. Born in Kentucky in 1899, he arrived at Vanderbilt immediately after the First World War, and as a precociously well-read undergraduate became part of the remarkable literary group known as the Fugitives. During the early and middle 1920s, in company with John Crowe Ransom, Donald Davidson, Merrill Moore, Sidney Mttron Hirsch, and later Robert Penn Warren, Andrew Nelson Lytle, and others, he helped to publish a poetry magazine, *The Fugitive*, which drew considerable attention as a vehicle for the poetry of modernism, southern-style. In the late 1920s he played a shaping role in the formulation of the Agrarian symposium *I'll Take My Stand: The South*

1

and the Agrarian Tradition, in which twelve southerners called upon their native region to reject industrialization and urbanization and adhere to the traditional ways of the southern community.

Meanwhile he was building a considerable reputation for himself as poet and critic, and in the 1930s was an active and influential figure in our national letters. Tate freelanced in New York City, wrote several popular biographies of Confederate leaders, subsequently taught in Tennessee, North Carolina, and at Princeton, served a term as consultant in poetry at the Library of Congress, then in 1944 became editor of the *Sewanee Review*. In 1946 he moved to New York City as an editor for Henry Holt and Co. In 1951, at age fifty-two, he became professor of English at the University of Minnesota, his first teaching appointment with academic tenure. Most of his best work, including several collections of critical essays, a small but much respected body of poetry, and a novel, *The Fathers* (1938), was written during the 1930s and 1940s. When he retired from teaching in 1972 he moved to Sewanee and then to Nashville, where he died in 1979.

Brooks, born in 1906 in Murray, Kentucky, arrived at Vanderbilt in 1924. Although too late to become a member of the Fugitives, he studied with Ransom and afterward became very much a partisan of the modernists and what eventually came to be known as the New Criticism. Graduate study at Tulane and as a Rhodes Scholar at Oxford was followed in 1932 by an appointment to the faculty at Louisiana State University in Baton Rouge. It was there that he began writing and publishing the essays on modern poetry and on the English metaphysicals that earned him a reputation as a rigorous contextual critic. With his friend Robert Penn Warren, who joined the LSU faculty in 1934, he developed the *Southern Review* into a widely read and influential literary quarterly.

In 1938 the first edition of *Understanding Poetry*, edited by the two of them, was published, and over fierce resistance by old-line historical and philological scholars came to dominate its field and to focus the teaching and reading of poetry into an emphasis upon the actual text of the poem, rather than upon biographical, historical, theological, ideological, or philosophical relationships.

The books that Brooks wrote during this period, *Modern Poetry and the Tradition* (1939) and *The Well Wrought Urn: Studies in the Structure of Poetry* (1947), established him as one of the major critics in the language. Meanwhile in 1942 the *Southern Review* was discontinued, ostensibly because of the straitened wartime finances at LSU but in actuality because of opposition within the university, and thereafter Warren departed for the University of Minnesota. In 1947, after spending several terms at the University of Chicago, Brooks accepted an appointment at Yale University, where he taught until his retirement in 1975. During the Yale years, while continuing his writings about poetry and criticism, he began to shift his interests to the fiction of William Faulkner, about whose work he eventually wrote four books. *William Faulkner: The Yoknapatawpha Country* (1963), the first of Brooks's books on the Mississippi novelist, remains one of the seminal works of Faulkner criticism. He served a two-year appointment as cultural affairs officer at the American Embassy in London, held several visiting professorships, and remained professionally active until his death in 1994 at the age of eighty-seven.

To understand the nature of the correspondence between Brooks and Tate, it is necessary to keep in mind the circumstances of their arrival upon the American literary scene. As southerners they had been born into a region that was only beginning to extricate itself from the defeat of the Civil War. They grew to manhood at a time when powerful regional pieties still very much served to set the South apart from mainstream American experience and attitudes, but also when the provincialism and isolation that had hampered the participation of young southerners in the nation's cultural and intellectual life were receding.

The practice of letters in the South of the late nineteenth and early twentieth century was, with few exceptions, genteel, polite, and an affair of surfaces. The young men and women who began writing poetry at about the time of World War I and shortly thereafter were in revolt from the pervasive ideality of their elders, and they saw much to admire and emulate in the literature of modernism as propounded by Eliot, Pound, and their followers on both sides of the Atlantic. They found their role as youthful rebels against the then Establishment exhilarating.

As with much of the best literature and thought of the era, what the young southerners were writing and thinking was a response to the cultural shock of the Great War, and the chasm it had exposed between the optimism and ideality of the nineteenth century and the mindless slaughter of trench warfare. The result was a pervasive suspicion of high-sounding abstractions and an abiding skepticism about the way that mass public opinion could be manipulated through cynical sloganeering, clever advertising, and facile appeals to emotion. The New Criticism itself, with its insistence upon close reading and abhorrence of abstractions, constituted just such a reaction to the impact of 1914–1918; it wanted the poem to focus upon the exploration of the complexity of human experience in language, not try to simplify it through the evocation of stock emotional responses.

A delightful air of conspiracy pervades the earlier letters of this collection. Tate and Brooks considered themselves enlisted, together with Ransom, Warren, Davidson, Lytle, and certain others, in a Movement—though they did not call it that—aimed at overthrowing the literary and intellectual domination of the Brahmins who controlled the academy and at advancing the cause of the New Poetry and of those who believed in it.

At the same time, they remained involved, emotionally and imaginatively, with the community in which they had grown up to a considerably greater extent than they realized. However much they may have been dissatisfied with the genteel surfaces of southern cultural and intellectual life, and made common cause with the literary modernists, they found little that was congenial in the social and ideological allegiances of the urban Northeast. Not even Allen Tate, whose family background and rearing was perhaps the least settled and conventional of all the Nashville group, found the ways of the metropolis permanently to his liking.

The Agrarianism that all of the group came to espouse, and of which Brooks, though too young to take part in the Agrarian symposium *I'll Take My Stand*, was a loyal adherent, was in certain important respects an effort to reconcile the implicit contradictions between their literary and intellectual allegiances on the one hand, and the circumstances of their birth and rearing on the other. In calling for the South to reject the blandishments of urban industrial society, the Agrarians were censuring the materialism of the business and industrial South of the twentieth century as well as the corporate-dominated metropolitan society of the industrial Northeast, declaring their continuing loyalty to the South's historical identity, opposing the growing commercialization of the arts, and making a case for the continuing importance of the literary imagination. It was a willed assertion of an identity with the everyday southern community by a group of young writers and academics whose literary and intellectual interests had served to distance them from that community. Misunderstood, in part by some of the group themselves, as a book about economics, *I'll Take My Stand* was a pastoral rebuke to the dehumanizing, materialistic forces of mass society, of a kind with such works as *Walden* and Emerson's "American Scholar" address.

Much nonsense has been written about the relationship between Agrarianism and the critical approach known as the New Criticism. Tate, Brooks, and the others have been labeled Tory Formalists, elitists, male chauvinists, crypto-Christian apologists, racists, semi-Fascists, and the like. Tate's habit of taking exaggerated public stances, his romantic adherence to the Confederate tradition, and Brooks's reflexive response to facile criticism of the South by outsiders, together with both men's general suspicion of easy ideological prescriptions, have made them the target of considerable abuse.

Even some who are sympathetic to their literary views have acquiesced in the Formalist label, despite the fact that in the context of its use it involves some deft tactics of guilt by verbal association. Certainly the aesthetics of the New Criticism emphasized the achieved "form" of the poem—the words and images, the lines and stanzas, the ways they relate to each other, the primacy of what is actually printed on the page—as distinguished (though not ultimately separate or separable) from the "content," which is to say, the philosophical, theological, political, sociological attitudes and referents. To that extent the approach might be said to be "formal." But the connotations of "formal" thereby evoked are made to include such terms as "mannered," "ceremonial," "gentlemanly," "arm's length," "impersonal," "rigid," "cold," "hierarchical," "liturgic," "aristocratic," and the like—in other words, the opposite of whatever is "informal," "warm," "friendly," "open," "demonstrative," "democratic," and so on.

Now it is undeniable that there are instances in which the assertions of aesthetic and literary sensibility have coincided with social, political, and theological attitudes. In response to T. S. Eliot's proposed formula for civic and private virtue—in politics, Royalism; in religion, Anglo-Catholic; in literature, classical—John Ransom proposed an alternative transatlantic wording: "In manners, aristocratic; in religion, ritualistic; in art, traditional." Yet politically Ransom was a committed New Dealer and Fair Dealer. The truth of the matter is that there was and is nothing in a taste for complexity in poetry, or a belief in the need to begin with the actual poetic text and to keep returning and referring to it, that logically prescribes a commitment to a political, social, or religious program.

That, like Ransom, Cleanth Brooks was culturally an elitist, that he disliked whatever was tawdry, cheap, sentimental, or crude in mass culture, and that he was hostile to simplistic depictions of human nature whether in poetry or prose, says nothing whatever about his politics. Brooks too, like Ransom, was something of an Anglophile, although unlike him a High Church communicant, but that did not prevent him from regularly voting Democratic in national elections.

In point of fact it is impossible to discover any consistency in political views within the southern group. What united them was a common attitude toward poetry and a deep consciousness of their southern origins—and not much else.

The letters in this collection begin with the year 1933, several years after Brooks and Tate first came to know each other. Brooks had just gone down to Baton Rouge to join LSU's English Department. Agrarianism was still very much on their minds. The devastating economic Depression of the early 1930s had brought Marxism to the forefront among many intellectuals as an alternative to finance capitalism, particularly in New York City and the urban Northeast. It held little attraction for the southerners, however. Their involvement in Agrarianism led them to look for a public forum for their views, and Tate's acquaintance with Seward Collins, publisher of the *American Review,* resulted in invitations to various of the southerners to write for it. As the decade wore on, however, Collins and his magazine began to exhibit Fascist sympathies, and Tate and his friends severed their ties with him.

Meanwhile Robert Penn Warren had joined Brooks at LSU, and the two of them were soon editing the *Southern Review,* which while it published a few Agrarian writings was principally a literary quarterly. John Crowe Ransom had left Vanderbilt for Kenyon College, where his editorship of the *Kenyon Review* provided another, almost totally literary organ for what was by the early 1940s becoming known far and wide as the New Criticism. After the LSU administration killed off the *Southern Review,* Brooks was approached about taking over the editorship of the *Sewanee Review* at the University of the South. He turned it down, but in 1944 Tate, having secured an agreement that contributors were thenceforth to be paid for their writings, accepted the editorship. After several years Brooks went to Yale, and Tate to New York City and then to the University of Minnesota.

The urgency about jobs, publication outlets, and the like, so prominent in the earlier letters between Tate and Brooks, is largely missing from the later correspondence. By then, the New Criticism and its leading practitioners were solidly established on the literary and academic scene and needed no specific organ for promulgating their views, which in any case had long since diverged. As writers they had come to focus their attention almost exclusively on aesthetic and cultural issues.

All now held tenured teaching positions. They had taught a generation how to read poems. New modes of viewing literature, and new causes, allegiances, and heresies, some of them highly inimical to their own ways of thinking and feeling, were now moving onstage, but they could even so take satisfaction in the knowledge that the lesson of close reading had been learned. Whatever might be done with poems after they had been read *as* literary artifacts—and wild and weird indeed have been some of the doings—it was no longer possible to ignore or to sidestep the actual words and images of the poem itself. For what was ultimately of most importance about the approach to literature they had advocated was not a critical theory; it was a *method for reading poems.*

However much the two men whose correspondence follows shared important goals and loyalties and admired each other's work, they were in disposition and personality very different. Tate was the youngest son of a dominating mother who impressed her children with her quasi-aristocratic Virginia family background and felt that she had married beneath her. He was bequeathed an abiding sense of having been cheated by history of his rightful estate. Moved about from place to place in what was a largely unhappy childhood, he was precociously well read, and when as a college student at Vanderbilt he began to come into his own, he was quick to set up as a poet, enter the critical wars on the side of the modernists, and thereafter to see himself as a defender of the Old South, the Confederate tradition, and the classical virtues. His poetry was intense, confessional, packed with literary allusions and references, and seemed wrung from a controlled sensibility located somewhere close to the edge of chaos. As a critic he tossed out brilliant observations about literature, society, and the South almost in passing; he could get at the crux of a complex argument and, without being reductive, identify the true issue. The single novel that he wrote is a small masterpiece of imaginative historical re-creation.

A fiery controversialist, he was quick to pass judgments, impatient with mediocrity, and given to taking extreme stands. He took to the politics of poetry like a duck to the coastal marsh, and in his heyday he was a powerful figure in the literary world. To young people he was extremely generous; he liked to advance their careers, and he relished the possession of the influence that made it possible for him to provide the help and further the causes he advocated. At the same time he could hold grudges, and when down on someone he could be considerably less than scrupulous in his choice of weapons. He was a born manipulator, adept at dissembling, and greatly partisan in his likes and dislikes—as will quickly become obvious to anyone reading his letters who possesses independent knowledge of some of the persons and situations involved in them.

The abiding theme of his writings was the need for order and the search for it. From a youthful zeal for the Old South and its Lost Cause he moved into an ardent fealty to Roman Catholicism. His private life was disordered and chaotic, filled with contradictions. He was married four times, the first two to the same woman; there were also numerous affairs. He was chronically in financial straits. Very little of the literary largesse whose distribution he was able to control ever accrued to him; he died a poor man. In his lifelong and uncompromising devotion to the literary imagination he never wavered.

What will be obvious in these letters is how very much Cleanth Brooks admired him. Tate represented for Brooks the totally committed, dedicated practitioner and standard-bearer of the causes that he believed in so intensely himself, the belles lettres and the South. The ardor and impetuosity that Tate brought to their common loyalties, and the acuteness and discernment with which he wrote and thought, held a lifelong appeal for Brooks.

In his own way Brooks was as passionate a partisan, and as ardent a controversialist, as Tate, but they went about their campaigning, and their lives, very differently. Brooks was the son of a Methodist minister, and although he became a devout Episcopalian, there is little or no sense of the tempestuous soul-searching that characterized Tate's religious experience. Audacious in his intellectual life, in his domestic arrangements he was orderly and conventional. His marriage to Tinkum—Edith Blanchard—was secure and lasting. From the outset, once he discovered where his interests lay, Brooks set out to pursue an academic career, while Tate, for all his years in the classroom, taught principally because he could not earn his living as a writer.

As a literary scholar and critic, Brooks was both imaginative and highly intelligent, but in no way bombastic or flamboyant. When he took his stands—and he did not flinch from taking them—he remained courteous, reasonable, and temperate. He was thoroughgoing, persistent, and even dogged in making his points and supporting them. There was not an ounce of vanity or pose in his makeup. He was without personal malice, whatever his intellectual and professional contentiousness. His patience with students and younger writers was legendary; he was always ready, even eager, to answer their questions and explain his ideas.

He *was* disputatious. No small part of the problems that the *Southern Review* ran into, and that eventually brought about its demise, had to do with the resentment that Brooks stirred up in his efforts to reshape the teaching of literature at LSU, and to reform what he and a group of Young Turks rightly believed was the complacency and mediocrity of the university curriculum as a whole. The knock-down, drag-out battle that ensued made powerful enemies for Brooks and his friends; in the eyes of the LSU administration he was a troublesome dissident.

The move to Yale in 1947 only intensified Brooks's always powerful loyalty to the South. It was not that he did not have important reservations about numerous aspects of southern life himself. But let an outsider, particularly if ill-informed and given to generalizations, venture to asperse the South, whether Old or New, and Brooks was quick to answer back. His distinguished work on the fiction of William Faulkner is to an extent undercut by his insistence upon defending the South against hostile criticism. He was impelled to assert, for example, that in his pursuit of a plantation and a dynasty the character Thomas Sutpen in *Absalom, Absalom!* is "on all fours with the robber baron of the Gilded Age building a fake Renaissance palace on the banks of the Hudson"—which may be true, but Faulkner was writing about a slaveowning cotton planter in Mississippi, not railroad and oil tycoons in New York.

Brooks's allegiance to his native heath never diminished. We were driving together in Scotland several years before his death, and we passed a spot where a witch burning had once taken place. "I'll say this for the South," he declared. "It has many sins to atone for, but it never burned witches." The point is that Brooks no sooner read the historical roadside marker than he immediately and reflexively saw an opportunity to praise the South, not so much vis-à-vis Scotland, with which he had no particular quarrel, as by inference New England, which in its time had also burned witches.

In the correspondence that follows, one will find relatively little critical discourse such as characterizes Brooks's and Tate's correspondence with Ransom. The letters are mainly about career matters, joint projects, comments on each other's writings, the doings of mutual friends and acquaintances, and the like. A portion of the correspondence has to do with their professional relationships with each other as editors, Brooks for the *Southern Review,* then Tate for the *Sewanee Review.* There is a certain amount of comedy, however unintended, as when during Tate's tenure at the *Sewanee,* Brooks wrote a poem and submitted it for publication. Although as a young man Brooks had published a few poems, this was his first in many years, and Tate was clearly at a loss about how to respond. At length he concocted a report on the poem, supposedly written by a reader. Eventually he did publish the poem (see Appendix A).

In 1973 Tate wrote a note, entitled "What I Owe to Cleanth Brooks," for a symposium edited by Lewis Simpson (*The Possibilities of Order: Cleanth Brooks and His Work* [Louisiana State University Press, 1976]). "This small, mild-mannered man, so perfect a gentleman that one cannot understand that he has faced Eliot's 'horror and boredom,' is in my opinion, formed over more than four decades, the foremost American critic," he declared.

Brooks was greatly moved. "Why shouldn't I say it now—we are both old enough—," he wrote, "that from a very early period you were my special hero as man of letters and that you remain one of the three or four people from whom I have learned most."

They were friends and fellow warriors for almost fifty years. However unlike each other they were in personality, they were united in the defense of poetry. Their letters to each other constitute the record of their long, hard-fought campaign.

*Cleanth and Tinkum
Brooks, circa 1934–1935.*

Allen Tate. (Photographic Archives, Vanderbilt University)

Andrew Lytle (left) and Cleanth Brooks, summer 1989.

Cleanth Brooks and Robert Penn Warren, 1985.

Allen Tate's seventy-fifth birthday party at Sewanee: Tate with Brooks (top) and William Wimsatt (below).

1930s

Route 6
Clarksville, Tennessee
December 14, 1933

Dear Cleanth:

Collins[1] is turning over to us his April number for poetry and essays on poetry, and it seems that I have been elected to edit it. Won't you write us something? We want to run two long reviews, one by Warren[2] and the other by you. Red is doing recent books of poetry and will give some opinions of the present state of the art. We hope you will do the same thing for the criticism of the last two years or three—or set your own limits. Of course most of the criticism that you will examine will be in the metaphysical school; and that will be your point of view fortunately. In fact, this special number of *The American Review* is to be devoted to the metaphysical school; we hope to make its critical claims better known and to group the poets together for reference in one place. Our list of poets includes Yeats, Eliot, Putnam,[3] Auden, MacLeish, Bishop,[4] etc. All

1. Seward Collins (1899–1952) was the publisher and editor in succession of the *Bookman* and the *American Review*. The latter published many works by the Southern Agrarians during the 1930s.

2. Robert Penn ("Red") Warren (1905–1989), a poet, novelist, and critic, was one of the key members of the Fugitive poetry group and its successor, the Southern Agrarians. He contributed to the first Southern Agrarian symposium, *I'll Take My Stand: The South and the Agrarian Tradition* (New York and London: Harper and Bros., 1930), and with Brooks coedited the *Southern Review* from 1935 to 1942. Brooks and Warren went on to collaborate on a series of influential college textbooks that embodied the literary theories of the New Criticism. He was the first poet laureate of the United States and won Pulitzers for both his fiction and his poetry.

3. Howard Phelps Putnam (1894–1948) had been a friend of Tate's since they met in New York during the twenties. He was considered a major poetic force during the twenties and thirties, and his poems were widely anthologized.

4. John Peale Bishop (1892–1944), a West Virginia–born poet, essayist, and novelist, was another close friend of Tate's and served as poetry reviewer for the *Nation*. After Bishop's death, Tate edited his *Collected Poems* (1948) and *Collected Essays* (1948). Although never formally a member of the group, Bishop was sympathetic with the aims of the Southern Agrarians.

the criticism will be done by our group here except the essay which we hope you will write.

Should you consent to do it, will you need any books that are hard to get in Baton Rouge? Or magazines? If you will send me a list I will try to get them all to you early in January. We must have all the material in hand before the first of March.

Red has not finished your essay and thesis, but promises to bring it here when he comes to spend Christmas.

With best regards,
Yours,
Allen

I should add that your essay should be about 3300 to 3600 words. Payment at one cent a word.

Route 6
Clarksville, Tenn.
Mar. 14, 1934

Dear Cleanth:

I've asked Red to send your essay to you in order to avoid delay. I wish there had been more delay, for I fear you may have begun your revision of the article. I want to ask you if we may use a chapter of your thesis. I have just read it, having got it from Red yesterday in Nashville. I won't go into it in detail—I think it is a fine piece of work.

I suggest that we use your Appendix B, on *Axel's Castle*[1]—I think a better title would be simply "A Note on Symbolism and Conceit."[2] May we do this?

I should like to see combined with it your remark elsewhere about the public being in the Ivory Tower. That could be condensed, and put into the text or in a brief footnote. It is one of those brilliant commentaries that show first-rate critical insight.

It might also be possible to use some stuff from the chapter "Modern Conceit," to point up the connections; I have in mind particularly your quotations there. This could be done if you used only a stanza or two from [Yeats's] "Sailing to Byzantium." (Macmillan would not let you quote the poem entire anyhow.)

1. Edmund Wilson's collection of essays on symbolism was published in 1931. Wilson (1895–1972), best known as a literary critic, journalist, and pundit, was a close friend of Tate's.
2. "A Note on Symbol and Conceit," *American Review* 3 (April–October 1934): 201–11; reprinted with additional material as "Symbolist Poetry and the Ivory Tower," chap. 4 of *Modern Poetry and the Tradition* (Chapel Hill: University of North Carolina Press, 1939).

I think on the whole that we ought not to exceed twelve pages, and I think this length could be met, in spite of the additional matter from other chapters, if you cut your quotations from Wilson down to the bare minimum that will make your point.

One reason why I am urging this instead of the paper you wrote is that it is an independent study, not a review, and you show your real powers better. Moreover, this paper will parallel Ransom's beautifully;[3] they will reinforce each other for being written independently. I assume that you have copies of all this; so I don't send it on. Please let me hear from you soon. I suppose Red told you that the issue had been postponed till May; so if you can get the thing done by April 1st, there will be plenty of time.

Best regards,
Allen

[OH]   Louisiana State University
                                                                 Baton Rouge, LA
                                                                 April 19 [1934]

Dear Allen,

I hope that the article I submitted was satisfactory. I write now, however, not about that but about the series of articles which you have been running in *The New Republic*.[1] I have found them most interesting and very good indeed. In particular, I liked the second one. But in your third I feel that you might have used I. A. Richards[2] to support your position instead of considering him on the other side.

I agree with your position in the third article entirely; but I feel that Richards agrees with it too.

I speak here with a good deal of diffidence. I am not sure that I understand Richards. I certainly do not completely understand him. But I have made a very earnest attempt to understand him—I have read his *Principles* at least a dozen times in the last four years—and in so far as

3. John Crowe Ransom (1888–1974), an editor of the *Fugitive* and a leading member of the Fugitives and the Southern Agrarians, founded and edited the *Kenyon Review*, which became under his direction a major vehicle for literary criticism during the 1940s and 1950s. A contributor to *I'll Take My Stand*, he taught both Brooks and Tate at Vanderbilt and became their lifelong friend. Tate is referring to Ransom's "Poetry: A Note in Ontology," *American Review* 3 (May 1934): 172–200.

1. "Three Types of Poetry," *New Republic* 78 (March 28, 1934): 126–28, 180–82; (April 11, 1934): 237–40.

2. The English critic I. A. Richards (1893–1979), whose *Principles of Literary Criticism* (1925) and *Practical Criticism* (1929) influenced Brooks, later became a friend of both Tate's and Brooks's.

I do understand him I find him on your side. Understand that I feel that the compliment is to *him*, here. But I think that his support is worth something—and as regards most of the New York critics—is of some strategic importance. In the review I sent you[3] I think that you will find my interpretation hinted, at least; and perhaps there is no need for me to try to amplify it here. I should like to make the following comments, however.

In the first place I think that Richards has reduced the subject matter of poetry to "non-science" rather than "non-sense." Poetry, I feel sure Richards would say, is not "a tissue of lies." Poetry uses fictions. And fictions "may be used . . . to deceive. But this is not the characteristic use in poetry. The distinction which needs to be kept clear *does not* set up fictions *in opposition to verifiable truths in the scientific sense* . . . we may either use words for the sake of the references they promote [scientific use], or we may use them for the sake of the attitudes and emotions which ensue. Many arrangements of words evoke attitudes without any reference being required *en route* . . . But usually references are involved *as conditions* for, or *stages in*, the ensuing development of attitudes, yet it is still the attitudes not the references which are important (that is, I take it, though Dante's beliefs are indispensable to his poetry, it is not the beliefs as such which are primarily important in the poem). It matters not at all in such cases whether the references are true or false. Their sole function is to bring about and support the attitudes which further response." *P. of C.*, pp. 267–8. Moreover, the statements which I quoted in the review: "The use of fictions, the imaginative use of them rather, is not a way of hoodwinking ourselves, it is not a process of pretending to ourselves that things are not as they are," seem to me to indicate that Richards—whatever we may think of his terminology—is really driving at what you have said: namely, that the statements of the genuine poet are neither true nor false.

Perhaps I do Richards more than justice, but I feel that his mysterious statement about the *Waste Land* and belief can only be interpreted (to put it in our words) as a compliment to Eliot that he has not done what Tennyson did—made poetry a sort of vehicle for inferior scientific generalizations about life. I think the statement is unfortunate because it implies that Eliot is the first poet to have avoided this error, whereas the greatest poets have always avoided it. But I think this is the only interpretation which agrees with Richards' general thesis as I interpret it. Richards, in general, I think is trying to steer a course between the Scylla

3. See "Metaphysical Poetry and the Ivory Tower," *Southern Review* 1 (summer 1935–spring 1936): 568–83; reprinted with revisions as chapter 3, "Metaphysical Poetry and Propaganda Art," of *Modern Poetry and the Tradition.*

of the Marxists—poetry is a sort of inferior science—and the Charybdis of the Ivory Tower.

I do not like Richards' utilitarianism but I must admit that he has made it rather broad. He gives poetry a "use," it is true, but all of us who regard poetry as valuable also give it a use. I believe that his use turns out to be a restatement of the value of poetry—not as a means to ends, as scientific description is a means, but as a value or use which would include contemplation. He attempts to show the importance of contemplation and to relate it up to our other activities. I do not think, however, that he reduces poetry to a tool.

What makes me think that Richards is to be interpreted thus is ultimately his own taste—the fact that he has seen the "use" in poets with whom the practical men have had nothing to do. His taste seems to me excellent. And his attack on critics who will not respect their terms seems to me thoroughly sound. I have had much difficulty with his terminology and I read him at first looking for flaws—I still do. The whole is beginning to make sense now, however. I think many of his points are obvious ones, the obviousness of which has been obscured by his terminology and qualification. I have sometimes become disgusted, but I think that his care and his attempt to be thoroughly consistent are probably the causes.

I apologize for so long a letter—and a letter which may seem rather silly. I am very much interested in your critical position: and I am very much interested in developing my own.

Moreover, I have had in mind for some time a contribution to the Communist poetry controversy which involved a use of Richards. Some of the Communist critics[4] have been using him. Many of them have a holy reverence for science and most of all for psychology. I think that there might be some strategic value in using Richards to dynamite this position: unless my interpretation is badly off. I think that he could be used to show that it is the Marxists who are founding their view of poetry on bad psychology. As I pointed out in the review, I think that they are guilty, in his terminology, of "message-hunting." And it is just this message-hunting that is the essence of the Platonic view of poetry. I think that his statement that "it is never what a poem *says* that matters, but what it *is*" comes close to your statement that "the stanza is neither true nor false; it is an object that exists."[5] And for the benefit of those who attach great importance to scientific statement, one could follow up by giving a broadside of exposition of the above statement in psychological terminology.

4. Brooks was thinking in particular of Max Eastman (1883–1969) and Granville Hicks (1901–1982), two Marxist critics of the 1930s who often published in *New Masses*.
   5. From Tate's "Three Types of Poetry."

I think that I shall work up such an article and send it along to you for your comment. Do not let me impose on you, however, and don't hesitate to be quite candid in your criticism.

Later when you have time, and if you think it worth doing, I should like to submit my MS to a publisher. I should appreciate any suggestion on that point which you could give. Some rather important revisions will have to be made, I know, but I do want to begin prospecting at least.

Give my regards to Red and to John Ransom if you see them. I hope to get up to Nashville this summer. In the meantime I wish that I could persuade some of you to come down to Louisiana again. Your last stay was so short that it was hardly a visit.

Please remember me to Mrs. Tate.[6]

Cordially,
Cleanth Brooks

May 9 1934
[Clarksville]

Dear Cleanth:

I am sending you your check for the essay in the *American Review.* We could pay only $2.40 a page. I hope your copies reach you soon and that you like the issue.

I suppose I didn't tell you that I liked the essay a great deal, and that the others did too.

I have been trying to answer your fine letter as it deserves. Maybe you didn't hear about our automobile wreck, which lost us nearly a month. We weren't seriously injured although Caroline had a badly twisted shoulder. We are just getting organized again.

I agree with you about Richards to some extent. But I do think that we must take into consideration the method of arriving at a conclusion no less than the apparent validity of the conclusion itself. For this reason I think Richards has chiefly a negative value such as you find in him for the refutation of Marxian criticism. But I must go into this at length to make it clear, and that I can't do this morning. I wish you would come up here this summer, so that we could talk. It is hard for me to write letters.

With best regards,
yrs,
Allen

Remember me to C.W.P.[1]

6. Tate had married Caroline Gordon (1895–1981), the novelist and short story writer, in 1924.

1. Charles Wooten ("Pip") Pipkin (1899–1941), the founder along with Brooks and Warren of the *Southern Review,* was its first senior editor. As dean of the LSU Graduate

Route 6
Clarksville, Tenn.
August 7, 1934

Dear Cleanth:

I'm a mighty poor correspondent, and now I write about a special matter. The *Va. Quarterly* is getting up a tenth anniversary number for next March, and they asked me for suggestions. I pointed out that in the ten years of their magazine the South has led in two arts, fiction and verse, and that they ought to have special essays on them. I urged you for the poetry as the only writer who knew enough to do it and who is not identified with any special group. They will almost certainly ask you (I got Stark Young[1] to support my suggestion), and I hope you will consent. Otherwise the article will be written by somebody whose high standard is Masefield. I'm trying to get them to let Red write on fiction.

We've heard repeatedly that you are coming up here this summer. Your friends eagerly await your arrival. At this moment I am in Nashville staying with John [Crowe Ransom], and expect to be here another week; but here or at home I will expect to see you.

We're distressed that Red is leaving us but rejoice at his good fortune. It sounds like a fine job. You people are lucky to get him.[2]

Best regards.
Yrs.
Allen

2374 Forrest Avenue
Memphis, Tennessee
December 12, 1934

Dear Cleanth:

I have read your essay very carefully and I think it is a fine piece of work. I expect to be able to talk to you about it during the holidays though it is still a little uncertain whether we shall be able to come down.

School, he had been responsible for hiring Brooks as an assistant professor at Baton Rouge.

1. Stark Young (1881–1963), a novelist and drama critic best known for his Civil War novel *So Red the Rose* and for his drama criticism published regularly in the *New Republic*, was a contributor to *I'll Take My Stand*.

2. Warren told Brooks that he was "fired" by Vanderbilt in 1934, and he held that view to the end of his life. Edwin Mims, the chairman of the Vanderbilt English Department, had led Warren to believe that several courses were reserved for him to teach in the coming term. Instead, Mims gave the job to someone else, thereby forcing Warren out of Vanderbilt. He subsequently joined Brooks at LSU, where he taught English and coedited the *Southern Review*.

I write this to ask permission to send the article on to *The New Republic*. I doubt if Cowley[1] takes it, but if he doesn't I feel sure that Collins will. Won't you wire me yes or no?

I agree with everything you say as far as you take it. But there remains one great objection to Richards. If poetry is merely a balancing of emotion (I don't do it justice that way), if it's the fusion of heterogeneous matter into a unity, what is the metaphysical status of the section of reality represented by the poem? Richards avoids this, but by implication he would say that in the long run the poem cannot be "true" because of those embarrassing pseudo-statements, and that the poem has "value"— a strictly pragmatic value—because it orders our minds, or something like that. Now I think we must go farther, and we must discard Richards. It is simply that the great poem *is* a section of reality, and, being that, represents reality as a whole: that is, through it we are initiated into a qualitative whole which of course extends indefinitely. And of course, this is "useless." That is the point at which my three essays ["Three Types of Poetry"] stopped, but they would not have stopped there had Cowley wanted to give me a chance to ward off the attacks that followed. He didn't want to give me this chance.

We'll talk it all over. Meanwhile, best regards.

Yrs ever,
Allen

Feb. 20, 1935
Baton Rouge, La.

Dear Allen:

Malcolm Cowley sent me back the other day the MS. of the article on "Propaganda Art and the Ivory Tower," evidently the copy which you sent him some months ago. He was quite polite and the comments which he made on the article, taken together with his "Note on Marxian Criticism" which appeared in the *N.R.* for January 30, make me think that he has not yet seen the way to a direct and satisfactory answer. He has asked me for a review of Richards' new book *On Imagination*[1] (which by the way is most interesting).

In my reply to his letter I pointed out that I thought that an answer to my article would have to (1) either show that I had misused Richards or

1. Malcolm Cowley (1898–1989), a lifelong friend of Tate's and Brooks's, served as literary editor for the *New Republic* from 1929 to 1934.

1. "The Poet's Fancy," Brooks's review of *Coleridge on Imagination* by I. A. Richards, was published in the *New Republic*, November 13, 1935, pp. 26–27.

(2) show that Richards on the matter of belief is essentially wrong. His comments do not touch on these points. I wonder if you have sent the MS. on to Collins. If so, I want to write to Collins about it, for I think that it is worthwhile to make the attack soon.

Lambert Davis[2] has taken my article for the *Va. Quarterly* and is running it as it stands.[3] I hope that you will like it and will be in substantial agreement with what I say, though I am far from satisfied with it. Fortunately, the topic did not come up in conversation with Fletcher[4] while he was here last week. If it had, I am not sure that the conversations would have been so pleasant as they were. I have not yet seen his article on the same subject in the *Westminster Magazine.*[5]

Red sends best regards,
Sincerely,
Cleanth

2374 Forrest Avenue
Memphis
February 23, 1935

Dear Cleanth:

I meant to write you about your article. I had, until a week or so ago, expected to see Collins at a conference in Cincinnati. But that was postponed till late in March. I will therefore send the article to him today. I agree with you that it should be published right way, and I feel sure Collins will do it.

Cowley is simply incompetent in these matters. He is vague and journalistic. I must get Richards On the Imagination right away. Red said too that Fletcher was mild. He came down on Memphis like a wolf on the fold, and gave us a good deal of trouble. I very much fear that he used his article to pay off secret grudges. He has no critical standards; it is all personal; that is, he asks whether another man's poetry, if it is different from his, is good enough to threaten the reception of his own with the public. That's as far as it goes. I have never asked my friends to

---

2. Lambert Davis (1905–1993) was editor of the *Virginia Quarterly* from 1933 to 1938. He then worked as an editor with various publishing houses before serving as director of the University of North Carolina Press from 1948 to 1970.

3. "The Modern Southern Poet and Tradition," *Virginia Quarterly Review* 11 (1935): 305–20. The essay was later revised into a chapter of *Modern Poetry and the Tradition.*

4. The poet John Gould Fletcher (1886–1950), who had been involved with the Imagist movement in England, subsequently became a Southern Agrarian and contributed to *I'll Take My Stand.*

5. "The Modern Southern Poets," *Westminster Magazine* 23 (winter 1935): 229–51. This article was very critical of Tate's poetic method.

admire my work; some of them, Ransom for example, don't admire it; but in Fletcher's case, I get extreme private admiration and public attack. I'd rather it were consistent.

I am very anxious to see your article. I had decided not to write mine, but at the last minute, three weeks late, I did something very quickly (one day) and sent it to Davis. It may have got there too late. It is about the profession of letters in the South.[1] A profession that doesn't exist. Best regards,

Yrs ever,
Allen

Southwestern College
Memphis, Tennessee
March 17, 1935

Dear Cleanth:

I have had the *Va. Quart.* by me for two days and I've been reading and pondering your essay. To tell you the truth, I can find nothing wrong with it. Naturally I don't know whether some of this feeling is due to the high seriousness with which you discuss us, and to the extreme accuracy of your commentary upon my own intentions. Whether the group in general and I for my part are as good as you think, I do not know. I hope we are. But I am sure you have laid bare the workings of our minds in poetry. The function of the imagery in my Alice[1] I could not have described nearly so well myself. Of course I should like to hope that your essay will be the basis of any future discussion that our work may receive from other hands. I think it will.

There is an extraneous matter that gives me extreme satisfaction. Davis is kind enough to tell me that every suggestion I made to him last summer bore fruit in this issue. Of the people I suggested you were the youngest and, to him, the least familiar. I am enormously pleased that your paper should have turned out to be so brilliant a performance.

I suppose you have heard the echoes of Fletcher's recent outrageous behavior about this issue of the *Va. Quart.* Ostensibly because they refused Davidson's[2] article he demanded that we withdraw at the last minute. His pretext was that Don's article contained the agrarian

---

1. "The Profession of Letters in the South," *Virginia Quarterly Review* 9 (April 1935): 161–76.

1. "Last Days of Alice," *New Republic* 66 (May 13, 1931): 354.
2. The poet, essayist, historian, and musicologist Donald Davidson (1893–1968) was one of the original Fugitives and a leading member of the Southern Agrarians.

doctrine, and that the *Va. Quart.* enticed us in to get our literary papers; using us, in short, but not doing anything for us. Fletcher's heroic position was expressed in the usual terms of unspeakable abuse, in which some degree of naïveté indicated the presence of less heroic elements in his attitude. It occurred to me that he had not been invited to contribute. I fear he made some impression on Don. John and I told him to go to hell. He demanded of John a signed statement that he would never again have any commerce with the *Va. Quart.* He has behaved badly before, and although his latest message indicates a softening spirit, he has done his work too well, better than he evidently supposed.

Yours ever,
Allen

[Handwritten] Have you heard from Collins? He has had your essay for some time.

Southwestern College
Memphis, Tennessee
January 13, 1936

Dear Cleanth:

I've been nearly batty the last few days, and I didn't get a chance to tell you that both Agar[1] and I liked your essay very much and that it has been sent on to Houghton-Mifflin. We did take the liberty of changing a word or a phrase here and there, but if you prefer your original version at these places you can easily restore it in the proof.[2]

The point of view and the argument were just right. We should have wanted the essay alone, but it happens that it offsets beautifully Belloc's[3] Catholic statement and protects us from a suspicion of popery.

Best regards,
Yrs ever,
Allen

---

1. After earning his Ph.D. from Princeton, Herbert Agar (1897–1980) moved to England in 1929 to serve as the London correspondent for two Kentucky newspapers. He spent the rest of his life there and became literary editor of the *English Review*. He and Tate coedited *Who Owns America? A New Declaration of Independence* (Boston: Houghton Mifflin, 1936), in which English Distributists and Southern Agrarians addressed issues having to do with their respective societies' encounters with modernity.

2. Brooks's essay was published as "A Plea to the Protestant Churches" in *Who Owns America?* It first appeared as "The Christianity of Modernism," *American Review* 6 (November 1935–March 1936): 435–46.

3. Hilaire Belloc (1870–1953), a versatile writer and man of letters, was one of the English Distributists and a contributor to *Who Owns America?* He was associated with the English Catholic Revival and closely linked to G. K. Chesterton.

[Baton Rouge]
March 27, 1936

Dear Allen:

Your letter appeared in the *Tribune* the morning of March 25 on the editorial page.[1] I am getting a copy and sending it to you right away. Red and I have been terribly busy for the last week, and I am dashing off this note in haste, realizing that it should have been sent two days ago. I am almost sorry that the matter turned out this way, but the paper, though it is incredibly stupid, did give the letter a prominent place.

By the way, your article has been set up,[2] and we think it is excellent. I quite agree with Andrew[3] in that it is probably the best single thing you have written. I say this with a sharpened sense of what you have written in the past, for I have just been going over your *Reactionary Essays*[4] for the last day or two. They are altogether excellent, and I had not realized how very fine some of them were. Many thanks to you for the book.

Best regards from Red and myself to you and Caroline.

Cordially,
Cleanth

The Log Cabin[1]
Monteagle, Tennessee
October 25, 1936

Dear Cleanth:

I've read your fine essay twice,[2] and if I were not in a hurry to get it back to you, a third reading I am sure would make it seem even better. It is beyond any question the finest interpretation of the poem yet written;

1. The reference is to Tate's open letter of March 22 to Grace Lumpkin (1892–1980), a Marxist sympathizer whose novels written in the 1930s depicted social injustice in her native South. In an interview with Seward Collins published in *Fight* (1936), Lumpkin accused the Agrarians and Distributists of "fascist" sympathies. Tate's rebuttal to Lumpkin's charges was also published in the March 1936 issue of the *New Republic*. At the time of this quarrel, both the Agrarians and the Distributists were sympathetic to the ideas propounded by British economist C. H. Douglas, as was Ezra Pound, but Douglas's Social Credit ideology was not a part of the Agrarian worldview.
2. "The Function of the Critical Quarterly," *Southern Review* 1 (winter 1936): 551–59.
3. Andrew Lytle (1902–1995), editor, novelist, essayist, and social critic, was an important member of the Agrarian group and a contributor to *I'll Take My Stand*. He continued to espouse the Southern Agrarian viewpoint in talks and writings throughout his life.
4. *Reactionary Essays on Poetry and Ideas* (New York: Charles Scribner's Sons, 1936).

1. Tate often stayed at "The Log Cabin," Andrew Lytle's house. Visitors to Lytle's Monteagle residence often remarked on the extraordinary personality of this house.
2. "The Waste Land: An Analysis," *Southern Review* 3 (summer 1937–spring 1938): 106–36.

I don't see what else any other critic can do. I question only one or two minor points, on the margins.

You have covered every difficult question. I believe you have left one large question open; but that could be an essay in itself. I mean the significance of the eclectic symbolism drawn from the widest sources of our tradition. Of course Milton did the same thing, but the focus was quite different.

Such a discussion would include commentary on the last lines of the poem, which I still find unsatisfactory. The Sanskrit words may very well, as you say, convey the most ancient truths of Aryan culture, but they are remote from our immediate experience: wouldn't Milton have gone straight to the Christian tradition instead of circumventing it? Of course, Eliot's reasons for going round the long way could be pretty easily divined, and I think you are the man to do the job.

Why should you worry about a place to publish the essay? Perhaps you have heard of a magazine called *The Southern Review*.[3]

By the way, Montgomery Belgion[4] wants to see the magazine. Why not send him copies of two or three of your best issues? He would help the magazine in England. Address 27, Lawn-road Flats, London, N.W.3.

Remember us to Tinkum,[5] and regards to everybody.

Yrs, ever,
Allen

We decided that if we tarried long in Louisiana, we would spend what little money we hope to have before we ever got to Mexico. But we'll be coming through for a few days.

Monteagle, Tennessee
April 5, 1937

Dear Cleanth:

This letter is wholly confidential, and I hope you will reply to the question that I am raising with equal frankness.

I heard from Red recently that Howe[1] had been in Baton Rouge, and that the poetry textbook had been discussed. Naturally Howe wants it as soon as he can get it, and he has already been as patient as Job.

---

3. Tate's joke refers to the fact that Brooks was one of the editors of that quarterly.

4. Montgomery Belgion (1892–1973), an English journalist and author, served as an editor of London's *Daily Mirror* during this period, 1935–1937.

5. Edith Amy Blanchard Brooks (1911–1986), Brooks's wife for fifty-three years, was known throughout her life by this childhood nickname.

1. Mark Antony DeWolfe Howe was an editor with Charles Scribner's.

I don't see how we can all get together long enough to complete the work. You and I could, but Red will never be permitted again to spend that much time in Tennessee if I am in the neighborhood. And I cannot finance a trip and a long stay in Baton Rouge. It would take us two months, and I think it is futile to try a real collaboration apart. The pieces would never fit together.

Last summer when I told Red I thought you ought to join us, my real purpose then, as now, was to turn over to you my part of the work and to resign from it. I fear otherwise the book will never be done.

I am explaining this to you confidentially before I take any steps about it with Red or with Howe. Your consent to the plan is naturally quite necessary before it can be carried out.

Howe advanced me three hundred dollars, and I should undertake to transfer, with your consent, my debt to you, and to pay it before next January 1st, or to make a similar arrangement to pay it to Howe directly. I imagine the former plan would appeal to him more than the latter because it would allow him to recover the money through royalties in the ordinary way.

I do feel that something must be done soon. Red and I could have worked at the book the last two summers, but he had to go off to the West Coast every time. His summer teaching wouldn't have interfered, it was the family visit.

The pressure of my money obligation to Howe is prompting me to this suggestion. It can't run on indefinitely. I do dislike losing my part in the book because I am convinced it will be a gold mine. But whether you accept this arrangement or not, I shall lose it; Red and I can never get together.[2]

The new *Southern Review* is very fine, almost your best number. Isn't Wade's destruction of Brooks perfect and beautiful?[3] Wade is getting better all the time. I read the piece five times with mounting envy.

2. The relationship of the project mentioned here to Brooks and Warren's *Understanding Poetry* is not clear. Joseph Blotner, in his biography *Robert Penn Warren* (New York: Random House, 1997), notes that on July 22, 1936, Warren received $150 from Henry Holt and Co. for his share of an advance on future royalties for *Understanding Poetry*, and that at the same time Warren and Tate were "anxiously awaiting word on a poetry text they had sent to a publisher sometime before" (157). Tate's letter suggests that Scribner's had accepted Tate and Warren's textbook and paid them an advance on it. One can only surmise that Tate and Warren, after sounding out Brooks about joining them, abandoned plans for the Scribner's text in favor of *Understanding Poetry*.

3. John Donald Wade (1892–1963), a literary biographer and essayist, a contributor to *I'll Take My Stand,* and a close friend of Donald Davidson's, founded the *Georgia Review* in 1947. In the issue of the *Southern Review* Tate mentions, Wade severely critiques Van Wyck Brooks's *The Flowering of New England* (1936), for which the latter garnered a Pulitzer. Van Wyck Brooks (1886–1963) was a powerful literary critic during the 1920s and 1930s.

We are going to Benfolly[4] on the 25th, and we hope you and Tinkum will come up this summer for a good visit. You all are among the very few of our very good friends who have not been there. We enjoyed hugely the Christmas reunion; we look forward to a better, calmer one in the very near future.

Yrs ever,
Allen

Of course Red will tell you that I have responded enthusiastically to his own enthusiastic plan of getting together this summer. We have exchanged, at this time of year, exactly the same kind of letters for two years,—no, three years, '35, '36, '37. He doesn't know even now that he won't be allowed to come up here.[5] Strange—we know these things better than he does.

April 7, 1937
901 America St.
[Baton Rouge]

Dear Allen—

Your letter came in this morning, and I hasten to write you about some of the points involved. I obviously would regret very, very much your pulling out of the book for two reasons: the fact that the book will be terribly weakened if you are out of it; and second, the fact that in such a case I would definitely feel that I was reaping where another had sown. I hope that some arrangement will occur to us by which we keep from doing this, even though I realize the difficulties of trying to do the book while we are separated and though I realize fully the difficulty of our all three getting together.

As to the plans that you suggest—providing that we can't work out some solution which will keep you in—I think that the first, that of transferring the debt to me, is by all means the best, but in that case I wouldn't hear of your paying the money back to me. The three hundred could be taken out of my share of the royalties. You have certainly done far more than that much work on the book already. *I wouldn't consider coming on the deal on any other basis.* Such an arrangement at least wouldn't

<hr>

A highly impressionistic interpreter of literature and culture, he remained a lifelong opponent of Tate in his approach to literature.

4. Benfolly was the nineteenth-century country home purchased for the Tates by Allen's entrepreneurial brother Ben. During the Tates' sojourn there, many writers and artists enjoyed the convivial hospitality offered at the rustic retreat.

5. What Tate meant was that Emma (Cinina) Brescia, Warren's first wife, would not allow him to visit the Tates in Monteagle.

penalize you any further than losing the possibly large royalties which the book might pay, and if it should be a gold-mine, I would be amply paid any way. I say this before going any further because I want this point clear if you should decide to get out. Meantime, I want to urge again that we try to work out some other solution. For one thing, Tinkum and I now have an apartment with an extra bedroom. I don't need to tell you how much we would love having you and Caroline visit us for as long as you would stay. That might solve the problem of a long stay in Baton Rouge. C[inina] could hardly carry Red off from Baton Rouge—at least in term time.

(Excuse the change to handwriting—but I can't get at the typewriter just now.)

Incidentally, whatever happens with regard to the book, do come and stay with us whenever you can.

There is also, Allen, the possibility of working at the book by twos—even if all three could not get together for any length of time. I believe that we could get a pretty close collaboration in that way. I know that such a play would be more awkward than our working it out together on a basis of all three, but I believe that we are close enough together on most points to get relatively fine coordination even at that. I think that it would be disastrous for the book, for you not to continue with it; and I am sure that, under the circumstances, I should feel pretty much like a rat if the book should actually make money. My own feeling would be that you ought to stay with it in whatever capacity you may choose. If you did no more than go over the material worked out by Red and me, making alterations, cuts, and additions, the book would be far the better for it—we should be asking your advice on all sorts of things, anyway, even if you retired from the book formally—and I see no reason why you should not have your share in the profits—if any—too. To sum up, I believe that we could work out some sort of plan for a division of labors and for collaboration by pairs, if not all together; and in the second place, even if such a plan were not feasible, I believe that you ought to remain in to go over our work, to suggest revisions, alterations and extensions, and to give the work a final check and revision.

I am not sure that I haven't stated this very awkwardly. But you know me well enough to know what I think of you and what I think of your work, and to know that I sincerely hope that you won't retire from the project. On any basis, you deserve your part of whatever profits may accrue. And I am very sure that the book done by Red and myself would not be the book that it would be with you in it.

Obviously, I have not (and shall not) say anything to Red about this; but I do urge you not to retire from the plan, and I am hoping that you will reconsider. But in any case, drop the idea at once of paying back the money advanced to you; that would be thoroughly unfair to yourself, and I couldn't consider carrying on under such terms.

There is very little news to write. We see very little of Cinina these days though our relations with her are quite cordial. Tinkum has had her work hours lengthened and I am hoping that we can arrange for her to stop it. Work with me—on articles or books—would be far more pleasant. Incidentally, I believe that Tinkum has a very interesting book in her experience in relief work through the last six years. I don't think she will write it, but if she did, there would be at least one book of that sort with an agrarian point of view. She has a mass of splendid material— not only for its "human" interest, but powerful evidence for the agrarian idea. (She has been working principally with negroes and whites pulled off the farms of the old Feliciana parishes above here by the Standard Oil Co., and now stranded.)[1]

Tinkum wrote Caroline a brief note just after we had started to read *None Shall Look Back*.[2] It is a powerful and beautiful book. I hope that we will get a chance to talk with her about it later. For the moment, a brief word [will] have to suffice. It's splendid. (By the way, I see from *The Publishers Weekly* that it's selling well.)

Red and I are working slowly at the new text-book,[3] hoping to finish it up, and I, meantime, am at work on Yeats' *Vision*.[4] I sent my commentary on *The Waste Land* to Eliot, and got back, somewhat to my surprise, a prompt reply. He says, after stating his usual position to the effect that the author cannot help much, "it seems to me on the whole excellent, and very much better than H. R. Williamson's which went to rather fantastic lengths." He goes on to say that he thinks such an essay valuable if it does not set up to represent the author's method of composition—a matter I had already taken care of.

I'm afraid that I can't use the statement publicly. (I had promised to consider private whatever he cared to say.) But if I publish the essay, at least I won't have to fear his sawing off the limb behind me.[5]

1. Tinkum Brooks possessed a fine literary gift, as all her family and friends knew. Before his own death, Brooks arranged for a private edition of his wife's letters written during the Brookses' stay in England in the early 1960s. Her correspondence with the writer and close Brooks friend Katherine Anne Porter is being prepared for publication by the University of Missouri Press.

2. Gordon's novel was published in 1937.

3. *Understanding Poetry*.

4. "The Vision of William Butler Yeats," *Southern Review* 4 (summer 1938–spring 1939): 116–42.

5. Brooks published the letter Eliot wrote him with commentary as "The Wasteland: A Prophetic Document," *Yale Review* 78 (winter 1989): 318–33.

I appreciate the invitation to visit you all. Tinkum and I hope to take it up this summer. In the meantime, do come down if you can. Best regards from both of us to Caroline. The Christmas meeting remains a very bright spot in our memories.

Cordially,
Cleanth

By the way, if you have occasion to write further confidentially about the book, you might address me at 901 America St. I got to the mail before Red did when your last letter came in and so the question was not raised. But otherwise, there would be natural inquiries about what the news from you was.

The Log Cabin
Monteagle, Tennessee
April 19, 1937

Dear Cleanth:

I have been pondering your letter. You will know how I appreciate what you say of my value to the book, and how thoroughly aware I am of the exact nature of your scruples about accepting my proposal. But you see what my position is: if we can't get together for real collaboration, you and Red will be doing all the real work, and I should not be entitled to an equal share of the profits if I merely looked over the work after it was done. Perhaps after all we had better wait until this summer and see what Red is going to be able to do. I am sure he will be able to do nothing, but then at least the situation will be developed and I can make him face it.

It would be fine if we could come to Baton Rouge and stay with you and Tinkum, but nice as it would be for us it would be hard on you all. We have Nancy,[1] you see, and then too even though staying with the Warrens would be impossible, Miss Emma would make a scene of it if we stayed with you all, and Red would be terribly on the spot. And as I say we haven't the money to finance a trip and a visit.

The other day I received a nice note from Howe. He seems contented with the delay; so there is no outside pressure upon us. I do think, though, that we ought to get busy very soon.

I am delighted that Eliot liked your exegesis. I was sure he would. You are much better on the *Waste Land* than anybody else, Matthiessen[2]

---

1. Nancy (b. 1924) was the only child of Tate and Gordon.
2. F. O. Matthiessen (1902–1950), a literary critic sometimes linked with the New Criticism, published a study of Eliot titled *The Achievement of T. S. Eliot: An Essay on*

included. You haven't had anything of your own in the SR for a long time. Can't you go ahead and print it?

The little quarterly *Purpose,* in London, has just reprinted, with acknowledgment to the *SR,* my reply to Kenneth Burke.[3] I've told the editor, Desmond Hawkins[4] (who does the fiction each quarter for *The Criterion*), that he ought to make an arrangement with you all to exchange contributions for simultaneous appearance. There's a very nice essay by George Barker.[5] *Purpose* is a little tinged with Social Credit, but on the whole it is steering a course not unlike that of the *SR* . . . I sent him the MLA poetry program from the *A[merican] R[eview].* Maybe he will reprint it.

Aff. regards to you and Tinkum from us both,

Yrs.
Allen

Benfolly
Clarksville
June 24, 1937

Dear Cleanth:

I enclose a carbon of a letter to Howe. I hope you can persuade him. The text is a fine piece of work. What shall I do with the portion of the ms. that I have? I'm not quite clear about it—shall it be sent to Howe or returned to you? If to Howe, maybe you'd better wire me.

We hope devoutly that you and Tinkum will come up to see us. We'll be away from July 15th to August 4th; but any time before or after that period we'll be right here waiting for you all.

Red and Miss Emma came through Middle Tennessee like a bewildered Kansas tornado. It is increasingly impossible to talk to Red. He is doing so many things he can't put his mind on any of them. Ford[1] wanted to write an article, maybe two, for the *SR,* but Red just stared at him vaguely, and at last suggested that he read and review 49 novels

---

the *Nature of Poetry* (New York: Houghton Mifflin, 1935). He was a professor at Harvard from 1929 to 1950.

3. "Mr. Kenneth Burke and the Historical Environment," *Southern Review* 2 (autumn 1936): 363–72; *Purpose* 7 (April–June 1937): 75–83. The literary critic and philosopher Kenneth Burke (1897–1986) was also labeled a New Critic. His signature criticism is to be found in *The Philosophy of Literary Form* (1941) and *A Grammar of Motives* (1946).

4. Desmond Hawkins (b. 1908), English novelist, critic, and broadcaster, was literary editor for the *New English Weekly and Purpose Quarterly* from 1935 to 1945.

5. The English poet George Barker (1913–1991) early attracted the admiration of Yeats for his *Thirty Preliminary Poems* (1933).

1. Ford Madox Ford (1873–1939), the English novelist and founder of the *English Review,* was a friend and mentor to both Tate and Gordon.

for the fall issue. Ford replied mildly that he reviewed only books that he admires. After all Ford is one of the great men of letters in the world today, and I do think that Red oughtn't to have suggested such a routine job to him. I'm really upset by it. Couldn't something be done? Red didn't mean anything unpleasant; he just didn't know what he was saying. At that moment he was surveying mankind from China to Peru, sub specie Californiae, and doubtless had one eye on the question: Will Miss Emma take me off to the bedroom before or after lunch? She by the way was like a sucking dove, and played a piece of high politics. She knew what we'd think of the California trip; so she disarmed me by saying that if she hadn't got Red away from Baton Rouge, where so many people made demands on his time, he would never finish his novel.[2] It just occurred to me that one might get away from Baton Rouge a little this side of San Francisco.

The trek to the coast certainly authorizes me to set up as at least an assistant to Tiresias.[3]

Our love to you both,
Yrs.
Allen

By the way, if you want to change anything in my review,[4] do so. It's bad. The difficulties I labored under I've reported to Albert.[5]

901 America St.
Baton Rouge, La.
June 28 [1937]

Dear Allen—

I was out of town Saturday when your letter arrived and accordingly didn't get to read it until this morning. I appreciate your kindness in ,writing to Scribner's. Hold the MS there, for the time being. I expect to hear from Red in a few days, and then we can decide what to do.

---

2. Warren was working on his first novel, *Night Rider* (Boston: Houghton Mifflin Co., 1939).

3. Tiresias was a Greek mythological figure who prophesied the fall of Troy. In his notes to *The Waste Land,* Eliot suggests that in effect the poem is what Tiresias sees.

4. Tate reviewed R. P. Blackmur's *From Jordan's Delight* in *Southern Review* 3 (summer 1937): 192–98.

5. Albert Erskine (1911–1993) was the business manager of the *Southern Review* when it was edited by Warren and Brooks. He later worked as an editor for several publishers including Reynal and Hitchcock before joining Random House in 1947. He spent the rest of his career there, working with such notable novelists as William Styron, Robert Penn Warren, William Faulkner, Ralph Ellison, and Cormac McCarthy. He was briefly married to Katherine Anne Porter and remained a lifelong friend of both Brooks's and Warren's.

By the way I wrote Finney[1] at Sewanee several days ago about the deficit. I should have heard from him by now. If I do not receive word by tomorrow, I shall get a check to you at once. We can manage the matter here whether or not Sewanee comes in on the matter. At any rate there's no reason in keeping you waiting longer.

I am sure that you are right in your interpretation of Red's attitude in his suggestion that Ford do the semi-annual fiction chronicle. I shall write Red at once about the matter of soliciting an article from Ford. I'm sure that Red was not meaning to exclude the possibility of other articles but was merely seizing on the chance to get the fiction chronicle— a tough assignment and one which we may have to revise—into expert hands.

There are several reasons why Red should have been in a daze when you saw him, and it is worth while stating them here. We had fairly slaved for weeks—night work as well as day—trying to get the manuscript of the textbook in shape before Red had to leave. We finished Thursday evening about five, and Red—having found out our mistake in the date of the Ransom dinner that afternoon—decided to leave for Nashville that night. In addition, he had suffered with terrible headaches almost continually for four days before he left; and besides this, there were a thousand things to do incident to getting off: the cow to place, and the chickens, and the house to rent, and packing to do. As Cinina remarked one day when I was there for lunch: "I've made the decisions, Red, and thought out what we'll do. Now you'll have to see about them."

I tell all of this to indicate the enormity of what Cinina was to do that evening. John wanted Red to come up that evening so as to get to see him for a little while the next day before he left. And Red might have gone on the train. He could have slept on the way up, seen John, tended to his errands there, and returned while Cinina stayed here. Moreover, money was not a consideration, for I am sure that Red could have turned in an expense account. It was Miss Emma who suggested that they start out that night driving through.

I was so tired myself after we finally stopped work that evening that I could not have faced the trip. Red, with other worries, lacking sleep the previous nights, and with his headache I knew was bound to be much more tired.

Albert [Erskine] and Tinkum and myself fairly gasped when we heard that they were actually going to start that night. I still don't see how Red made it. I'm sure that Cinina just couldn't see Red's going to Nashville

1. James Finney was vice chancellor of the University of the South.

alone. She had invitations from all of us here to stay while Red went up by train. The car could have stood some work on it, and Red could have got a little rest.

I suppose that you heard how Miss Emma got her rest before the trip. A week or so before they left, Cinina came down with the yawns, and was put to bed by her physician because she needed rest and quiet. His orders (as reported by Cinina): Stay in bed, eat what you like, and read all the detective stories you want to. Cinina did.

I hope that my writing all this does not seem too petty and nasty. (You forget how bad Cinina is after you get away from her for a little while, and your conscience begins to worry you a little.) But Red was so obviously completely used up that it made me furious to see Cinina rush him off when nothing could be served by it except her own jealousy.

I hope that Red has a good summer, but I think that it will be most remarkable if he accomplishes anything. He obviously had no interest in going to California, and told me as much. He talked of going to Mexico; he might have taken a place very cheaply on the Gulf Coast where it is cool and where he would have been bothered by no one. There is an old decayed summer resort across the lake from N[ew] O[rleans] which I pointed out to him, and which he seemed interested in. I'm afraid that California will make its own demands with Cinina in charge.

Tinkum and I do hope to pay you and Caroline a visit in August. If, later, it's not perfectly convenient, let us know; but we are anxious to see both of you. And when you have time let me know more details of the Ransom matter. I have not yet heard from Red. I saw the notice in *Time*[2] and thought it was pretty sniffy, but I'm sure that it will do more harm to Vanderbilt than to Ransom and its intention may have been perfectly favorable to him.

Love to both of you,
Cleanth

Note to you in your capacity as assistant to Tiresias: Tinkum says that C[inina] volunteered not long ago in a burst of beerish confidence that she indulged herself no more than once a week.

---

2. The June 21, 1937, story in *Time* about John Crowe Ransom's departure from Vanderbilt to assume a position at Kenyon College in Ohio mentions his differences with Vanderbilt's Chancellor Kirkland, who did nothing to keep the university's most celebrated man of letters. Vanderbilt's treatment of the Agrarians makes it rather ironic that they are sometimes referred to as the "Vanderbilt Agrarians." In fact, Vanderbilt fired Warren, let Ransom go to Kenyon College, denied Tate a graduate scholarship, and isolated Davidson at the university.

[OH]

Sunday
901 America St.
Baton Rouge
[late autumn 1937]

Dear Allen—

I've intended writing you for weeks, but my natural laziness has made me put [it] off again and again. Some of the incidents that seemed to call for immediate comment are now some weeks past—and some of them I have already expressed my opinion on through Red's communications.

In the first place, I'm very sorry about our loss of your article. It was a mix-up that was thoroughly unfortunate for us but one in which we must share the blame. We should have acted more promptly—but you already know something of the difficulty of getting the machinery here moving rapidly.

Then two: I hope that we can still persuade you to do the Dollard book,[1] first because we ought to reply to it, for the Yale Press' benefit, if no other, and in the second place, because you are the only person that we have to do it. But I can understand why it may seem a dreary task. Maybe later you'll change your mind.

Item three: *Time*'s review of your book and Caroline's.[2] Perhaps I took them too seriously, but the reviews made me thoroughly furious—not the stupidity so much but *Time*'s special variety of stupidity—the male equivalent of *Harper's Bazaar*'s stupidity or *Vogue*'s stupidity. My first impulse was to write in to *Time* and Red and I talked over the matter of the form which the letter would take. We finally had to give up. The opportunity of scoring off *Time* before *Time*'s own audience is rather slim.

On soberer thought, it is entirely likely that the reviews may actually do more good for sales than harm. The review of Caroline's book was especially outrageous. Incidentally, please tell Caroline that Tinkum and I thoroughly enjoyed *The Garden*.[3] I think that *Aleck Maury*[4] on the whole is still her finest. But the last book in some ways has something more difficult and more interesting—the writing is mighty fine. Good going.

Item four: Have you seen John's piece on Shakespeare's sonnet?[5] If not, you will see it in a few months, for we are publishing it in the *Review*.

1. John Dollard, *Caste and Class in a Southern Town*. See Donald Davidson's response to this work in *American Review* 9 (summer 1937): 152.

2. See the review of Caroline Gordon's *None Shall Look Back* in *Time*, March 1, 1937, p. 70, and "Allen Tate," *Time*, November 1, 1937, p. 38.

3. *The Garden of Adonis* (New York: Charles Scribner's Sons, 1937).

4. *Aleck Maury, Sportsman* (New York: Charles Scribner's Sons, 1934) remained Brooks's favorite among Gordon's novels. Faulkner also held it in high esteem.

5. John Crowe Ransom, "Shakespeare at Sonnets," *Southern Review* 3 (winter 1938): 531–53.

About ten days ago John sent it in, and I read it with misgivings. Red and Albert [Erskine] felt [the same] at once on the same day, and Red and I then got down to write John a detailed criticism of it. In brief, we felt that John was defining the sonnet very arbitrarily, even pedantically; secondly, that in separating Shakespeare from the Metaphysicals (on the basis of the sonnets, and certainly, on the basis of the poetry in the plays) he was doing violence to the facts; and last, that it was [his] strategy to use Donne as a stick with which to beat Shakespeare. (This summary does not represent, however, the particular objections or their order.)

Red and I obviously stated the objections as tactfully as possible, but we made them specific and suggested examples. (I thought of your comments to Albert and me [during] the summer on the subject of steering John off the article repudiating Agrarianism.)[6] John answered the other day, kindly and apparently with an attempt to be honestly objective; but, though he had made minor revisions and agreed that certain objections are valid, he said that he thought all the main matters stood. There is nothing to do but publish. The article is certainly publishable—John always has something interesting and fruitful to say—and we certainly aren't worried about any ill-effect on the *Review*. Not to publish would be to wound John's feelings, I am sure, and perhaps to breed some misunderstanding. But I hate to see the appearance of the article for John's sake. And the article will obviously appear in his volume whether we publish it or not. The only issue was that of steering John off it altogether. I'm sorry that we failed to do that, though I am not very much surprised. But perhaps you've seen the essay already. And perhaps it is much better than Red and I think it is.

We had a very delightful visit from Katherine Anne [Porter] a couple of weeks ago. We went to New Orleans on the spur of the moment and hardly expected that we would be able to bring K.A. back. I saw L.S.U. beat Auburn 9 to 6 yesterday in a beautiful game. Auburn, incidentally, I believe, is a far better team than Alabama. They beat Ga. Tech. worse than Alabama did, beat Tennessee worse, and should have beaten Tulane instead of only tying them. I heard that game (in the early season) on the radio, and Auburn should have got one of the two field [goals] which she tried. Alabama beat Tulane only by a field goal.

Tinkum and Albert and I have been working on a parody on *The Waste Land* in the *Southern Review* office, and the [deed] has been buried in a MS on social science which we hope will remain interred in the filing

6. In later years, Tate said he had been able to persuade Ransom not to publish an essay repudiating his former Agrarian views. See, however, Ransom's "Art and the Human Economy," in *Beating the Bushes: Selected Essays, 1941–1970* (New York: New Directions, 1971).

cabinet. At present we have only a few scattered fragments, but you can see the relevance of the following:

> O keep the Pip[7] far hence that's friend to men
> Or with his nails he'll dig it up again—

and Albert has made a really fine contribution by suggesting that the last section deal with the lost MS under the heading "What the Dunder Said."

I haven't forgotten the promise to send the *Vision*[8] to you and Caroline. Katherine Anne has it at present, but I'll send it up to Ben Folly when she has finished it. Best regards to Caroline and to Nancy, and Tinkum sends her best. We are hoping that you all will really come down this winter. I trust that the Harvard trip won't sidetrack that.

Cordially,
Cleanth

901 America St.
[Baton Rouge]
March 27 [1938]

Dear Allen,

This is the letter which I have been intending to write you for the last three months. I'm a very poor correspondent at best—and for the last several months any spare time that I have had has gone in on the Holt textbook or on my critical book.[1]

Perhaps it is just as well that I have waited so long to write, for I want to tell you of the Cinina-Brooks feud that broke out in all but riotous form last fall, and it is perhaps just as well to have waited long enough to get a little perspective on it. Briefly, Tinkum got kicked, and slapped on both cheeks by Miss Emma, and though we have seen her a few times since and ostensibly the wound is healed, relations have been mighty formal and chilly.

The evening started off innocently enough. The Warrens came by early in the evening, and after a while left to go to a wedding reception. President Smith's[2] daughter had been married that evening but Tinkum

---

7. The reference is to Charles Pipkin.
8. "The Vision of William Butler Yeats."

1. In addition to working with Warren on *Understanding Poetry*, Brooks was writing his first critical book, *Modern Poetry and the Tradition*.
2. James Monroe Smith, a Huey Long appointee, was president of LSU from 1930 to 1939. During Smith's administration, the university underwent a large academic expansion and the *Southern Review* was established. His career ended in disgrace when he was imprisoned for embezzling university funds.

and I, feeling that we were not in any way intimate with the family, decided not to go. Perhaps Cinina felt that we were making a silent criticism of her by not going with her—I don't know. At any rate, when she returned to our apartment an hour or so later, she was spoiling for a fight. I suppose extra drinks in the interval also had something to do with her mood.

Tinkum and I suspected nothing, however. Everyone was apparently very jovial—ourselves, our other guests who had stayed with us away from the reception, and Red and Cinina themselves. Anyway, just after they came in, Tinkum gave C. a playful pat on her seat when she leaned over. C. proceeded to kick the hell out of her. Tinkum still suspected nothing, thinking that C. was merely playing and had not realized how hard she had kicked. Tinkum then moved across the room, and C. followed her, and standing over her, dared her to hit her again. Perhaps Tinkum should have realized by now that C. was really angry. Anyway, Tinkum tried to pass it off by smiling and tapping her on the cheek. C. then proceeded to box her jaws. I didn't see what happened, and I don't think that poor Red did. The other guests saw everything, however. Needless to say, the party broke up in a hurry.

C. called us the next day, and though Tinkum was anxious to let the matter drop, insisted on making an apology. I think that it would be difficult to take such an apology seriously in any circumstances; but C. didn't even come with clean hands. After she had got her apology said and her explanation—too much drink and a morbid fear that people didn't understand her or like her—she insinuated that she liked us really a great deal more than some other people did whom we thought liked us. The people apparently included you all and perhaps other Nashville friends. At the moment that you begin to think that you could pity her, she does something really revolting. Since then we have seen very little of Cinina, avoiding social meetings as much as possible. Our relations are superficially friendly, and I hope that they will continue to be so, but they remain merely formal.

I'm genuinely sorry for Red—but we've been over that before. As a matter of fact, it seems very [much a] pity, in a way, to be recounting such an affair to you—I hope that it does not sound too petty. Perhaps that's the worst thing about her: she does not even let one's possible quarrel with her rest on a basis of any dignity.

I'm glad that you like the textbook so far. Red and I have felt pretty discouraged sometimes in going over proofs. It has been a hasty job and much of the writing seems very sloppy. I hope that we can get some sales. Holt finally seems in earnest after appearing lukewarm over it for a year and a half.

By the way, I'm now engaged in trying to rewrite the chapter on the Fugitives for my book.[3] I've rewritten the first four chapters thus far, and the present one will be Chapter V.

The first four represent basically the Three Revolutions in Poetry plus the *American Review* article on the symbolists. I have expanded a good deal, however, trying to give a more logical presentation, and supplying more illustrations. The first chapter deals with theories of metaphor since the Restoration, insisting finally on the fact that figurative language is the only way that certain things can be said—contrary to critics from Dryden to Housman who uniformly imply that it is not a necessary means for communications at all but an illustration or an ornament. Chapter two illustrates some of the uses of witty metaphor, coming finally to the point that wit is not antithetical to seriousness but is in reality the sine qua non of real seriousness. Chapter three attempts to state a definition of poetry. Chapter four attempts to relate symbolism to metaphysical poetry—with the claim that ultimately the two poetries are one. Chapter five treats the Fugitives; six is the Waste Land essay (with a few minor revisions); seven is the essay on Yeats's system, which is now complete.

I have decided to make my case for the moderns before attempting to suggest the changes in the account of the history of English poetry which an acceptance of the moderns implies. Chapter eight will therefore be an account of the death of the Elizabethan drama, an account which will take it as merely one aspect of the decline of metaphysical poetry. (The essay is substantially complete.) Chapter nine will be a rapid restatement of the history of the tradition with illustrations from some of the major 18th and 19th century figures. For example, I am claiming that Swift's greatest prose was attacked in the same terms as Donne's poetry was attacked and for the same reasons. I am taking Pope as fundamentally a sentimentalist—the interest in Thomsons' *Seasons* as comparable to the last generation's interest in Imagism, etc. (This chapter is now on paper but is still in very rough shape. It is the most controversial part of the book—will be with the academic brethren at least. I don't think that I am saying anything very radical in it, but it will be interesting to see the reaction. I believe that it is really necessary, for unless one calls names and gives instances, many people will never notice how much of a readjustment the earlier part of the book involves.) There will probably be a chapter ten,[4] but there may not. In any case, there must be, I'm sure, some kind of epilogue.

3. "The Modern Poet and the Tradition," in *Modern Poetry and the Tradition*.
4. Chapter 10 was titled "Notes for a Revised History of English Poetry."

I'm having a great deal of trouble in the rewriting. I'm very stale—I have continually the feeling that I'm repetitious. Consequently, I should like to ask you to use the blue pencil liberally when you look it over.

Just now the attempt to rewrite the chapter on the Fugitives has sent me back to your poetry—and prose. I believe that I am much closer to the center of the poetry than I have ever been before but I feel far from confident about writing on it. I don't know how fair it is to ask your help—what I am going to do is to send you what I have written in due time and ask you at least to indicate the places that I have gone astray. I don't mind confessing that your poetry has been more difficult for me than almost anyone else's!

By the way, the violently hostile reaction to your preface,[5] which you mentioned in your last letter to Red, is interesting. It certainly goes to prove that Communism and Liberalism are religions and that their communicants are capable of genuinely religious rage. It is something of this sort that I detect in some of the outbursts against your work.

I wish that you and Caroline were to be down this way this summer. I hereby extend a cordial invitation. Incidentally, I assume that Miss Emma won't be here then—Red indicated the other day that his summer plans were vague but that he did not expect to be here.

Give my best regards to Caroline. Tinkum asks to be remembered to both of you.

As ever,
Cleanth

112 Arden Place
Greensboro[1]
April 30, 1938

Dear Cleanth:

I've been a scandalously long time getting round to answering your excellent letter of more than a month ago. I have read it repeatedly with two resulting emotions, interest and amazement.—We had heard back in February from the Radfords[2] something of Miss Emma's latest

---

5. Brooks is referring to the preface to *Reactionary Essays on Poetry and Ideas*.

1. Tate and Gordon had both accepted teaching positions for the spring 1938 term at the Woman's College of North Carolina. They stayed until 1939, when Tate accepted an appointment at Princeton.
2. Manson and Rose Radford were Tennessee friends of Tate's. Manson Radford was a poet and Gordon's cousin.

outbreak—or is it still the latest? Of course, it was much more disgraceful than her attack on Caroline, and much more without excuse. Caroline did tell her that we all thought she ought to treat Red better, and I suppose she had a certain right to resent it, if that right remained after she had pointedly asked Caroline why she wasn't liked. Again, her outburst at Benfolly was not witnessed by casual acquaintances; it took place within the family, so to speak. There is no doubt that she told the truth when she said in her apology to Tinkum that she had a morbid fear that people didn't appreciate her. That gets pretty close to the poor girl's main trouble. And by the way, in telling Tinkum that people didn't like you all as well as she was liked, she repeated a definite pattern of defense that she long ago developed. In the scene at Benfolly she told us that we had no friends, that I particularly was generally hated, and that moreover she and Red were better married than Caroline and I, because it was well-known that the Tates were about to get a divorce. I remember distinctly the horror in Red's face when she said that. He of course knew that she had made up the tale and had been talking it around; and had foolishly exposed herself. The Radfords reported something that you omitted, but it sounds characteristic and true—that Miss Emma told Tinkum that you all had been influenced by the evil Tates, who were responsible for all the woes of her life.—I wonder what end the situation will come to. Even if Red is so infatuated as to believe that the Tates are responsible, and that you all are so weak-minded as to let us make up your minds for you, I don't see how that pretext will make his daily life any easier. To blame somebody else for the trouble doesn't remove it.

I am greatly excited by the near completion of your book. I hope you will send it on to me as soon as you have a carbon. The other day I was talking to Couch[3] over at Chapel Hill about it, and he is interested. He is not nearly so hostile as he thinks he is. He is just not very intelligent, and a little conversation tends to convince him how wrong he has been about us. I don't say that he will ever be right, about us or anything else; he will not be so pig-headed in the future. He is getting ready to publish an awful book on contemporary literature by Grant C. Knight. I am sure that he would see how much better yours is. Why not try him?

I'd be delighted to tell you about the discussion of my work, though I

---

3. William T. Couch (1901–1988) served as director of the University of North Carolina Press from 1932 to 1945. Some 170 of the 450 book titles published during that time dealt with the South, making that press an important regional publisher. Couch resigned from the University of North Carolina Press in 1945 to direct the University of Chicago Press and later served as editor in chief of *Collier's Encyclopedia*.

am sure that you know more about it than I do. I was disappointed that your essay on Yeats wasn't in the Spring *S[outhern] R[eview]*.

Well, while we're having this sub rosa correspondence I may as well offer you a brief meditation on K.A. and Albert.[4] Of course Albert, being young and merely sophisticated without experience of the world, doesn't know that La Belle Dame sans merci has him in thrall. It's a nice state to be in—what man wouldn't want to be in it for a few months? But married to her? No! I predict that in less than two years K.A. will get the wild mustang look in her eye, and charge off, perhaps gathering in another Albert, and in less than a wink Albert I will be as if he had never existed. We've known K.A. for going on fifteen years, and she has gone through this same pattern five times. She always comes out of it with a kind of moral virginity, ready to try it again because she forgets that she has tried it; but the men lie gasping on the sand. What has become of them all? Somehow they are never heard from again. As soon as the relation becomes solid, and of predictable permanence, she runs off. Like her heroine, that is to say like herself, at the end of one of her long stories, she flies off to seek Truth, which is another way of saying romantic irresponsibility. The most romantic and the most charming woman in the world, but one of the least interesting. I say that because nobody who is completely predictable is finally interesting.

We've just about decided to go to Connecticut for the summer. Caroline will be starting the actual writing of her new book, and she wants freedom from family responsibility. I will have finished mine (unless God smites me) by the middle of June,[5] and I want to be near the proofreading.

I'm still not convinced that we'll all ever get together to write our book on modern poetry. I saw Wheelock and he wants it next spring. Maybe I'd better write you this in a brief note to the SR office. I will do so in a day or two.

Give our love to Tinkum. We miss you and wish we might get together soon. Maybe we can in September.

Yrs.
Allen

4. Albert Erskine and Katherine Anne Porter (who was twenty-one years his senior) were married on April 19, 1938, in New Orleans, with the Warrens attending as the sole witnesses. They divorced in 1942 after having lived apart for several years. Tate, knowing the couple, was quite prescient in his prediction of the eventual dissolution of their union. Erskine eventually found marital happiness with his third wife, Marissa, with whom he had a daughter.
5. Tate's only novel, *The Fathers*, was published in New York by G. P. Putnam's Sons in 1938 and in London by Eyre and Spottiswoode in 1939.

[Baton Rouge]
June 20 [1938]

Dear Allen,

This is a letter which I have been planning to write you for weeks. The delay has been caused by petty interruptions incident to teaching in summer school and trying to keep up with *The Southern Review* manuscript pile now that Red is away. But primarily I have delayed because I have wanted to get the MS of my book in a little better shape to send you.

First, with regard to Albert's marriage. I thought that something was up long before the marriage itself—obviously. But I still didn't think that the marriage would actually take place up until a short time before it actually did. Albert kept his own counsel, and we saw little of Katherine Anne. After her first visit when she spent a few days with us early in the fall, she was here only on a few visits to the Warrens, and our relations with Miss Emma were such that we saw very little of K.A. and almost none of that alone. Albert told us about it the week before the marriage took place. I need not tell you what I think of the match. Perhaps it will work out very beautifully—I hope that it does—but it seems to me that the odds are hopelessly against it. But I am sure that it will go nicely for awhile. Both of them seem happy now.

In the same way I thought that Red was going to Italy sometime before he told me that he was leaving—a few days before he left. I don't think that Red really wanted to go. (I may be quite wrong.) Miss Emma, however, has been vowing to go for a long time, and though I know little of the details I think that she is to do some study while in Italy.

By the way, we have very good reason to believe that trouble has already broken out between the Erskines and the Warrens. But both sides are keeping mum; and Albert may be depended on to keep silence about it. As Tinkum remarked to me a few days ago, Albert's relation to Cinina is even more puzzling than Red's; for one often feels that Red is trapped. But Albert gave us a long defense of her—no recriminations on you all or us, but arguments to the effect that she really had a great deal of good in her, etc.

I wish that you and Caroline and Nancy could come down and see us for awhile. I know that your plans are made to go to New England but the town is very quiet and almost deserted as far as we are concerned. It would be delightful to have a week of good talk. Perhaps you will be able to come later on.

I am sending you a bundle of MS soon. Much of it you have already seen; some you have not. I am particularly anxious for you to look over

Chapter V which has the material on you and Red and John and Chapter VII which has the essay on Yeats.

But, if it is not imposing too much, I wish that you would go over, if only very hastily, the old material which is largely in the first four chapters. There are a good many additions here and rearrangements. I have gone over some of it so much that I am completely stale on it. Consequently, it needs the blue pencil badly. I am conscious that I have frequently fallen into a sort of jargon which is very bad. Suggestions for cuts and even sentence-structure would be mighty helpful. I can't ask you to take the time to treat it as you would a freshman theme, but as far as my feelings are concerned, don't hesitate to treat it that way, wherever you see faults.

A further complicating factor has been the difficulty in envisaging my audience. I have tried not to write down too far, but I have wanted to be plain enough so that I might appeal to a little wider circle than merely the converted. The result, I'm afraid, is a pretty bad compromise.

The Oxford Press wrote that they simply couldn't see the audience for the book. I had asked for a candid opinion, in order to save time. Scribner's has asked for a reading, as has Holt. I have thought that Harcourt might be interested because of the Eliot material and perhaps Macmillan, because of the Yeats! But I would give my chances at these places up like a shot if I thought that I could get anything like early publication at North Carolina. But you'll be best able to advise me after looking over some of the MS. itself.

I hope to see John Ransom on his way to Texas or on his return.[1] I've written him asking him to stop off. Best regards to Andrew [Lytle] if you see him, and to Caroline. I hope you have a most pleasant summer. Your last piece for the Review is fine.[2] The new number is about ready to go to press.

Cordially,
Cleanth

901 America St.
Baton Rouge, La.
[July 1938]

Dear Allen,

I wrote you a letter a month ago which I am sending along with this one. Foolishly, I mislaid your address, and so haven't been able to send it.

---

1. Ransom taught that year in the summer program of the University of Texas.
2. "Tension in Poetry," *Southern Review* 4 (summer 1938): 101–15.

John Ransom stopped by on his way to Texas this last weekend and gave me the present address. The letter of June 20 deals with some general matters and particularly with the MS. This one will largely concern itself with John's visit. But first, one or two matters of later date. (1) I found Caroline's ms. of her story only a few days ago in the manuscript pile which I had allowed to grow larger than I should have. It's highly interesting and is now on the way to Red.[1] She ought to have a report on it soon, but this [is] to report that it's been received. (2) At the last minute, I decided to rewrite Chapter I of my poetry ms. It was pedantic and repetitive. I've lightened it somewhat and shortened it. I'm afraid it's still too heavy. I hope that you will slash away at it and the other chapters. The ms. itself I am sending by express tomorrow.

We met John in New Orleans early Saturday morning, and drove him out to Baton Rouge. He had the day with us and left the next morning. The visit was most pleasant. We talked about the *Kenyon Review* and John's work at Kenyon and the visit which he had with you all and the Agars.

The most intensive talk occurred, however, Saturday night. We got off on the question of economic determinism, Albert and I attacking it and John and Duncan Ferguson[2] (whom I believe you met here) defending it. John mentioned the essay which you had suggested he not publish— the one you mentioned last summer. We went on from there into a consideration of modern poetry and the general relation of science and poetry.

In general Albert and I argued the position taken in *God without Thunder*[3] and Ransom, the position taken in Max Eastman's *Literary Mind*! I was not totally surprised in view of our conversation last summer. Moreover, I find it difficult to believe that Ransom was not taking the position he did to some extent for the benefit of the talk; partly, perhaps, to see what he would say, partly to pose certain questions which may have been troubling him and to see if convincing answers could be given. The talk was good and highly enjoyable. John seemed to enjoy it very much himself. But I was left with the uncomfortable feeling that John was reversing some of his earlier and sounder judgments.

1. Gordon's story, "Frankie and Thomas and Bud Avery," was published in *Southern Review* 4 (spring 1939): 696–712.

2. Duncan Ferguson, a painter and instructor at LSU, was a member of an art group called the New South.

3. Ransom's *God without Thunder* defended the need for Christian orthodoxy from his unorthodox stance as an agnostic. Ransom's father, like Brooks's, had been a Methodist minister. Ransom held on to his father's ethical values while rejecting the metaphysical underpinnings of his religious faith.

By the way, he mentioned the book which O'Donnell[4] proposed several years ago, and seemed to feel enthusiastic about taking it up again. He suggested that maybe some of the chapters might appear in the *Kenyon Review*.[5] I think that it's a good idea—and if the *Kenyon Review* couldn't handle all of them, there is always *The Southern Review*, though John in this case ought to have first choice. But, as John said, to get the book under way will require another meeting. May it be soon.

We are looking forward to *The Fathers* and are mighty happy to see it announced. Katherine Anne has left for Olivet. Best regards from all of us.

Cordially,
Cleanth

West Cornwall, Conn.
August 3, 1938

Dear Cleanth:

I've had your ms. about ten days, but only yesterday completed my reading of it. I've been submerged in the proofs of *The Fathers*, which I finished Friday. The book is on the press today.

Your book is very fine. I've made only a few marginal notes here and there. Of course, of the more general, theoretical chapters, your discussion of the decline of tragedy is the most brilliant and original. But it seems to me that there, or earlier in the book, you ought to produce a pretty solid exhibit of Hobbes' doctrine by direct quotation; your argument is revolutionary, and it ought to be documented to the hilt. I have the general impression that the first three chapters ought to be condensed a little. There is some repetition; but a second reading convinces me that condensation will be difficult; everything you say is necessary as the chapters are at present organized. I do think that you could save a little by making your argument more direct, omitting references to similar views except, of course, in the one place where you are citing Ransom, Eliot, Richards, and myself as foreshadowing your own view. Elsewhere I would go entirely on my own, if I were you.—You already know how much I admire your Yeats and Eliot. The Yeats is the best technical criticism of the sort that I've seen.—In your chapter on the other contemporaries, I believe that Frost ought to be moved up to the front of the essays and made to precede Red, John, and me, for two

4. George Marion O'Donnell (1915–1962), a poet, short story writer, and critic, taught at LSU and later at Yale. He was a contributor to *Who Owns America?*

5. The book Ransom was alluding to became his seminal *The World's Body* (New York and London: Scribner's, 1938).

reasons: first, chronology; second, he is not such an extreme example of the new revolution as we are. I am possibly not a good judge, but I think your discussion of me is quite perfect. How in God's name did you get inside the twin poems as you did? It gave me a little gooseflesh, and it still does. I suppose other poets are as conscious of their symbols as I am; but you are just as conscious. In so far as I can tell, you have stated with deadly insight the exact purpose and function of all the symbols of those poems.—I don't think you are so good on Red, but then you may be: how do I know? If I were you, I would rewrite the Ransom section, putting it entirely in your own terms, and only noticing Red's essay[1] as support.

In short, I think the general structure of the book excellent. I should think that a week tinkering would put it into final form.

I'm so delighted with what you say of me that I should like to see it printed as a separate essay. Maybe a paragraph to lead off, and another to close, would be enough to make it stand alone. It is likely that [Lambert] Davis would publish it, and of course there's John's new magazine.[2] Even the *Yale Review* might sniff at it, at least.

There was one minor criticism that I forgot. Don't take it too seriously because it may represent only a hobby-horse of my own. It seems to me that your whole theory of poetry is opposed to the prevailing theory of communication as the function of art. You use the term communication very frequently. And yet you state your view at other times with perfect accuracy as a theory of creation, the poet being a maker of objects that have reality of their own. Your argument would convince me that Hobbes accelerated the common-sense, and the wrong theory that art is a medium rather than a reality. Couldn't you just check this in your ms? It wouldn't require any real rewriting.

In sum I congratulate you on a fine performance.

I believe the first person to try is Couch at Chapel Hill. He is awfully stupid, and he should be warned that the stenographer of the professor of sociology would not be a competent reader of the ms—least of all the Professor of English, a fellow named [George R.] Coffman and a perfect blockhead. If I were you, I would suggest readers myself: Ted Spencer at Harvard, Mark Van Doren,[3] etc. It would seem to me proper to point

1. "John Crowe Ransom: A Study in Irony," *Virginia Quarterly Review* 11 (January 1935): 93–112.

2. Ransom had recently founded the *Kenyon Review*. He had proposed to the board of the new quarterly that they hire Tate as his associate editor, but he had to retract his proposal because the board could not afford the salary of someone of Tate's stature.

3. Theodore Spencer (1902–1949) was an authority on Renaissance tragedy and metaphysical poetry. Mark Van Doren (1894–1972), a critic, essayist, and poet, was literary editor for the *Nation* during the 1920s and taught at Columbia from 1920 to 1959. He won a Pulitzer for his *Collected Poems* in 1939.

out to him that the ordinary professor of English has as stock in trade the views that you are opposing, and would automatically say no, even if he understood what you are talking about.—I will make this point in my letter to him. Please wire me the day you send him the ms.

If my novel sells, I may have a chance to put the book over with Putnam's. And there's Scribner's. But I believe your best chance is Couch, and I suggest him first.

I wish we might see you and Tinkum. We join in love to you both. And give our love to K.A. and Albert.

Yrs.
Allen

Just got a letter from Red. It sounded like a pep talk. He's evidently having a fine Eyetalian summer.

The Southern Review
Baton Rouge, Louisiana
Aug. 9 [1938]

Dear Allen,

Tinkum has just heard from Rose Radford, and we feel quite envious that we were so far away from the week-end gathering that you all had. Rose's news about your book is fine, especially the very large pre-publication sale. It looks as if it ought to go wonderfully well.

The news about your strenuous work in finishing up your MS makes me feel a little bad about unloading my own bulky manuscript on you. But I am extremely anxious to hear what you think of it—particularly about the chapter on the Nashville group. I must get the MS. typed over and off on its rounds to the publishers this month if possible. School starts early this year.

Albert has had his tonsils out, but is recuperating rapidly, and K.A. has returned from Olivet. We hope to get a little vacation on the Gulf Coast later this month.

Best regards to Caroline and yourself,
Cleanth

901 America St.
Monday [August 1938]

Dear Allen,

Your letter was very, very gratifying to me—especially because I believe that you are always willing to be candid with me. I have planned now for a long time to dedicate the book to you, with your permission.

But I didn't think it fair to send the MS. to you with the word that I intended a dedication. I feel free now to do so. Again, be quite candid— there may be some perfectly valid reason for my not doing so. Don't hesitate therefore to say.

Naturally, I was much elated to have your good word about my treatment of your poems. I think that I shall take your suggestion and prepare a copy of the material in essay form to send the *Va.Qu.* By the way, Lambert Davis is no longer at *Va.* He has taken a place with Bobbs-Merrill and *Va.* has not yet announced his successor. If they had a great deal of intelligence there I think that you by this time might have had an offer trying to lure you away from North Carolina. But I don't credit them with that much intelligence. Presumably the editorship will revert to a board.[1] (Incidentally, if you were at *Va.*, and with John's *Kenyon Qu.* and the *S.R.*, we might have the queer spectacle of the agrarians being charged with running a monopoly with concealed interlocking directorates.)

I think the suggestions you make [are] very helpful. I agree that the section on Red is not so good as that on you. I shall make another try there, though, as I see it, Red's very fine poetry being more accessible to the reader, does not allow the critic a chance for much display of his critical wares as critic. But there are other things wrong with it, and I intend to work it over somewhat.

I am tempted to omit Frost altogether. I had not intended to mention him originally. The reference grew out of a conversation with Red in which we agreed that Frost apparently considered himself as doing another sort of thing than what you all do; but that his best poems really revealed a similar structure. I intended, therefore, to use him to make the following point: even a man like Frost, at his best, far from representing the normal structure of poetry measured against which the Nashville Group and Eliot are to be regarded as eccentrics, shows in a tamer form the same structure. But I don't think that this point emerges in the book as written, I'm not sure that it would be wise to state the point more obviously, and I expect that it would be best to move Frost up, or omit him. If the point I have used him to illustrate is thoroughly clear, his poetry comes as a sort of anticlimax at the end of the chapter.

I agree about Hobbes. I'm not sure just yet where to put the exhibit, but a good deal of direct quotation from Hobbes is necessary and must go in.

I am tempted to cut some of the material out of the earlier sections and use it in the back of the book as notes or short appendixes, in something

1. After Davis's departure, Lawrence Lee became editor of the *Virginia Quarterly Review*.

of the manner of Matthiessen's *Achievement of Eliot*. What do you think of this, the section on Frost might go, and a short note that I have on Dr. Johnson's use of the term "metaphysical" poets.

Do you think that the ninth chapter, "Notes for a Revised History of English Poetry," pulls its weight? I hoped that it might infuriate some of the academic brethren, but it may be too sketchy even for a sketch.

I look forward to going over the marginal comments. (By the way, send back the MS. collect by express.) I shall try to get a clean MS ready immediately then, and send it on to Couch as you have suggested. But in the interval during which the readers are going over the MS. I hope to make some stylistic revisions, so that on acceptance (when and if it occurs) I may send in a thoroughly corrected copy.

I also intend to clarify the point about communication. I shall let you know at once when I send in the MS. to Couch.

I have already written you a short note in which I told you that I had heard the good word about the advance sale on *The Fathers*. I look forward to the book with great interest. You remember that I read about 140 pages of it last summer at Benfolly, and it was mighty impressive. I know that you must feel a different man with the MS. actually finished and the book on the way to its appearance.

Thanks for the word about Phelps Putnam, Leonie Adams, and Troy.[2] I shall get on the job at once and write to them. I shall also write to Schwartz.[3] You know the story of our adventures with Zabel. He was to review your book of poems in the group review in time for the press. Then we sent back the rest of it when it finally came in to him (including a long section on your S.P.)[4] for him to revise—and having let the MS. get out of our hands never did get it back. He must have had a siege of sickness, and I feel sorry for him, but I feel sorry for the magazine too. Our poetry reviewing was disrupted for three issues.

---

2. The poet Leonie Adams (1899–1988) lived with Tate and Gordon in Paris. She later married the critic and journalist William Troy (1903–1961). Adams, cowinner with Louise Bogan of the 1954 Bollingen Prize in Poetry, taught at Bennington College and then at Columbia University. Troy also taught at Bennington College; Tate wrote the afterword to a posthumous collection of Troy's essays edited by his Bennington colleague Stanley Edgar Hyman.

3. The poet, short story writer, and critic Delmore Schwartz (1913–1966) was editor of *Partisan Review* from 1943 to 1955. He had been a student of Brooks's at LSU.

4. Morton Zabel (1901–1964), a critic and literary scholar, served as an associate editor and later an editor of *Poetry* magazine. He had a distinguished career at the University of Chicago and was a fellow of Ransom's Kenyon School of Letters. He was a fine scholar respected by Brooks but was perennially tardy with promised articles. He did review Tate's *Selected Poems* in "Reactionary Poems," *New Republic* 92 (October 20, 1937): 315–16.

I hope that the Communist brethren will be satisfied when the Schwartz[5] appears and when my essay appears.[6] That they should have been able to deduce a quarrel from our tardiness in reviewing your S.P. is distinctly amusing. It throws so much light on their mental processes. It makes you think of a group of old gossips counting up the months on a girl. At least they must read the S.R. and notice what is in it and what is not.

There is very little news from these parts. Pip is away in Mexico. Summer school is over and the campus and the town deserted. Albert and Katherine Anne are to move into the apartment across the hall from us this week. It will be very delightful to have them so near. I am wondering what Cinina will think. I have an idea that she will create out of her lurid imagination a plot—a very nasty sort of plot on the part of the Brookses. It happens that Albert proposed the matter himself when he heard us rejoicing that our unpleasant neighbors across the hall were moving out. But this will be too simple for Cinina. I am afraid that the good resolutions which poor Red is undoubtedly having her make now will go by the board with a crash when she hears of the Erskines' new address.

With all regards and with love from both of us to Caroline and Nancy and to the Van Dorens.

Cleanth

The Southern Review
Baton Rouge, Louisiana
Sept. 2, 1938

Dear Allen:

I have just got back from a little visit to the Gulf Coast, which we and the Erskines spent in a cottage near Pass Christian. It was very pleasant and very restful, and there was lots of good food and good talk.

The other night I happened to be by the bookstore here, and they showed me an advance copy of *The Fathers*, paper bound, and I managed to pry it loose from them for one night. My reading was too hasty to get the full savor, but certainly it is a fine novel—very fine indeed. I am delighted also that the "trade" apparently thinks that it will sell. The

5. Delmore Schwartz, "The Poetry of Allen Tate," *Southern Review* 5 (winter 1940): 419–38.
6. This essay on Tate's work by Brooks was never published. Brooks did later publish "Allen Tate," *Poetry* 66 (September 1945): 324–29.

owner of the bookshop showed me a trade journal in which the book is described as having all the ingredients of a best seller; on the strength of this he had ordered several additional copies. This is, of course, no compliment in itself to the goodness of the book, but it would be mighty fine if a good novel could also sell heavily, and I hope that this will happen. In my hasty reading I was tremendously impressed with the power of the last third of the book and the tremendous dramatic quality. Heartiest congratulations.

I noticed in the reading a slip of tongue on page 129 or thereabouts where you refer to "Vieux Carré" where I think you must mean "Maison Carré"—the Square House of Nîmes. I imagine it is a slip of the tongue, and certainly a trivial one, but I hasten to send word of it in case you may want to have it corrected before many copies are printed off.

I have written to [Delmore] Schwartz, by the way, for the article on your poetry; and I am now typing off my section on your poetry to send to *The Virginia Quarterly Review.* I am looking forward to seeing your marginal annotations on my manuscript. I suggest sending it collect by express. When will you get back to North Carolina?

Best regards,
Cleanth

901 America St.
Baton Rouge
Oct. 31, 1938

Dear Allen,

I'm just finishing up my MS. I hope to have it ready to ship in two more days. I've cleared up the use of the term "communication" by rewriting—satisfactorily, I hope. I am sure that your criticism here is thoroughly well taken. I've also added material from Hobbes to two of the chapters, and I am sure that the chapter on the decline of tragedy is stronger for it. In addition, I've rewritten the section on Ransom, and made sundry small changes all through the work.

I've done very little revising, however, taking the work as a whole, and what I have done shouldn't have taken over the week's work that you suggested was necessary—but this fall I haven't been able to get going. There have been constant interruptions, and so I have used up two full months.

At any rate, it will be finished up by this evening, and here follows the occasion of getting off this note to you. Katherine Anne told me yesterday that she had just heard from [Ford Madox] Ford that he had been appointed an advisor to the Dial Press and had asked her if you knew of any books. He had obviously had books of fiction in mind, but she thought that he would be interested in mine, and would like to write telling him about it. Accordingly she got a letter off to him yesterday. Meantime, I had planned, of course, to send the MS to Couch the first day it was finished, and still think that this is probably the safest thing to do. What do you think? You will have a good idea also of what the chances for fairly prompt action from the Dial press would be. And the chances of Ford's interest in this particular book. Moreover, you may have already spoken to Couch. At any rate, I should like your advice. Will you wire me collect?

I hate to seem to bother you continually, Allen—and particularly with the sort of details which I ought to settle for myself. But time is a great factor in the local situation here, and I am anxious to lose as little time as possible in getting the book out. I know that much must be lost necessarily from this point on. By the way, the University of Oklahoma has asked for a reading, and I shall have them in reserve if some of my first choices don't go through.

By the way, I've changed up the fifth chapter. I've ended the chapter with the account of your poetry, and the material on Frost will go into another chapter which will deal with Frost, MacLeish, and Auden which Red has persuaded me to write. This chapter will not be ready for some time, but I hope to work on it while the readers are dealing with the rest of the MS. Its omission ought not to affect the fortunes of the rest of the book anyway. Readers can decide whether they want to recommend on the basis of the rest of the book, and if the chapter pans out it can be added (after the 5th chapter) at the publisher's discretion.

Tinkum gave me a clipping the other day from the Society page of the local paper. I don't have it by me to send, but it related that an esteemed leader of the city reviewed the poems of Ogden Nash, Dorothy Parker, etc. before one of the culture clubs, and was followed by another who "reviewed" *Cold Sky at Morning* by Maria Zaturensky and *Selected Poems* by Allen Tate. After this remarkable conjunction teas and canapés were served. I see by the *Sunday Picayune* that *The Fathers,* by this token, must be going really great guns in Boston and New York.

Owsley[1] is to be here tomorrow on his way to the Southern Historical Association's meeting in N.O. We all look forward to seeing him. Pip just

1. The historian Frank Owsley (1890–1956) was one of the contributors to *I'll Take My Stand.* He specialized in nineteenth-century southern history and remained a lifelong partisan of Southern Agrarian ideals.

returned from North Carolina the other day to report a very pleasant stay with you and Caroline. He says that you are going to begin another novel![2]

There is no news here. We wish that we could see you and hope that you and Caroline can head this way soon. Best of regards to Caroline and to Nancy. Tinkum sends love to all of you.

Cordially,
Cleanth

Greensboro
November 15, 1938

Dear Cleanth:

I'm mighty glad you sent the ms. to Couch, because since I wired you I have seen in the *N.Y. Times* a notice saying that the announcement of Ford's connection with the Dial Press had been premature. That must be why you haven't heard from him. Very likely he demanded at the last minute impossible terms, and out of senile vanity ruined the only sort of connection he has open to him and between him and starvation.[1]

I will be seeing Couch, I hope tomorrow, when I go over to Chapel Hill to make a speech. Couch has to be handled carefully as do all stupid and ignorant persons whose vanity is on their sleeves.

We got back yesterday from Nashville. Caroline had to go to East Tennessee, the Watauga country, to look at some scenes for her new book;[2] we arranged the trip so we could take in the football game. It was a whizz, and if you heard only the last quarter, you got a one-sided impression. I suppose you read about the razzle-dazzle of Tennessee, giving them the ball in midfield with the wind at their backs. That beat Vanderbilt, who would otherwise have played the quarter in Tennessee territory, and might have won, since they outplayed Tennessee all through the first half. Again, the game might have been a tie: Wood didn't actually make the first touchdown. I was directly opposite the goal line, and saw it, along

---

2. Although Tate talked about writing another novel and attempted one, his only completed novel was *The Fathers*.

1. Relations between the rapidly declining Ford Madox Ford and the Dial Press were coming to a close. The press offered Ford one hundred dollars per month to be its fiction consultant and yet kept its distance from him; it turned down a book proposal by him and showed no interest in the young writers he recommended. He subsequently wrote Burton C. Hoffman of Dial breaking off all ties to the press. Ford died in France in 1939. Tate, who was never as close to Ford as was Gordon, still regarded the veteran writer as the last great English man of letters.

2. *The Green Centuries* (New York: Charles Scribner's Sons, 1941).

with five thousand or so other people. Wood fumbled but the referee ruled that he was over before the fumble; but he wasn't and Marshall recovered the ball on the one-foot line; it would have been Vanderbilt's ball anyhow since it was fourth down. When Marshall went out of the game injured (he had started with two broken ribs), and Vanderbilt really quit since their offensive spark was gone, and a tie was out of the question. Tennessee is a great team, but better than Vanderbilt only in reserve power. Marshall is every bit as good as Cafego and Wood, but he's not on a winning team and doesn't get the publicity. I have a bet that Vanderbilt will beat Alabama.

We're planning a house party at Monteagle for the Christmas vacation. How fine it would be if you all and the Erskines would come! We'll write again about it in more detail. I'll be writing to Red.

Our love to you all,
Allen

[OH]   901 America St.
                                                              Baton Rouge
                                                              Dec. 8 [1938]

Dear Allen—

I am enclosing copies of a letter from Couch (which seems rather favorable) and of a report from his reader on the ms.[1] You may have already seen both from Couch himself, but I am sending the copies in case you haven't.

I am replying to Couch by saying that I am willing to waive royalties on an edition of 750 copies but would like for the contract to assign me 10% royalty on further editions (remote possibility that they are!). Perhaps I am making a mistake, but I don't think so. The academic line-up here is such that it will be very valuable to me to have the book out next year, if possible; and I think that the possibility of making anything out of the book is very slight anyhow.

I am also telling him that the additional chapter will deal with Frost, MacLeish, and Auden—three poets, not eight or ten.

It seems to me that Couch is not taking the reader's report too seriously —I suspect your good offices—and consequently I am playing down references to the reader's report in my letter to Couch. I am merely saying that I am too highly gratified at some of the things the reader says to care to burden Couch in this letter with a detailed defense of my method of

---

1. Couch went on to accept *Modern Poetry and the Tradition* for the University of North Carolina Press.

organization; that, in brief, I think that the reader has taken my title to imply a detailed survey of modern poetry—a valuable book to have, but one which I have not attempted.

Actually, I am a little peeved at the reader's report, particularly at "especially Conrad Aiken, whether they are adapted to Mr. Brooks' point of view or not." The last paragraph seems to indicate that he has missed all the points which he seemed to have grasped in paragraph two. But I am sure that one has mighty little to do, if he has time to be worried by reader's reports. I'm very hopeful that Couch will send in the contract. And my very real thanks for your good letter to his secretary on the ms.

Have you heard much about the Birmingham Conference. Pip has been pretty mum—pretends to deplore the foolishness in introducing the race issue. I suppose the University of North Carolina is full of talk about it. I felt that what occurred was perfectly predictable—judging from the people who dominated the meeting. Were *any* Agrarians asked?[2]

There's no news here. We run across the hall to see the Erskines from time to time and they to see us. It's really very pleasant living next to them. Red is hard at the proofs of his novel.[3]

I wish that I could see you. Best regards to all of you.

Cordially,
Cleanth

The Southern Review
Baton Rouge, Louisiana
March 4, 1939

Dear Allen:

I am behind again in writing to you. The notes which you had made on my manuscript were extremely helpful. Let me thank you again for having sent them. I know that you must have put in a good deal of time in going over the manuscript so carefully. Needless to say, I have adopted nearly all your suggestions; and with Red's help I have pulled the Frost section into some sort of shape.

A long time back I wrote telling you that I intended to dedicate the book to you if the dedication could come with no embarrassment to

2. Twelve hundred delegates, inspired by Roosevelt's New Deal, gathered in Birmingham, Alabama, in November 1938 to form the Southern Conference for Human Welfare, a liberal organization that advocated sweeping social changes for the South. The group was active between 1938 and 1948; its first chairman was Frank Porter Graham, president of the University of North Carolina. Herman Clarence Nixon, a contributor to *I'll Take My Stand,* later joined the conference, as did other prominent southern liberals.
3. *Night Rider.*

you. Perhaps I should not have asked at all but should simply have gone on to make the dedication. But I have asked, and since I have raised the question at all, I am anxious to get your candid opinion. Please be quite frank. My motive is the very simple one of gratitude, for you have undoubtedly taken more trouble with my work and have done more to help me get publication than any one else. On the other hand there may be very good reasons—of strategy, for example—why you should prefer me not making the dedication; and in that case I shall understand perfectly.

We enjoyed Rose [Radford]'s visit and hope that before very long you all will come this way, or we find an excuse to get to North Carolina.

Best regards to Caroline and Nancy.

Cordially yours,
Cleanth

[Greensboro]
March 6, 1939

Dear Cleanth:

I am sending you a copy of a letter to Dr. Read,[1] with the hope that you or Red will see that the girls get prompt replies. You will remember that the other girls I've sent you didn't hear from their applications until September. These three girls must hear as soon as possible, because if they don't get a scholarship there, they will have to look around for something else right away. I will appreciate it if you will give this matter your attention as soon as you have the time.

Regards,
Yrs in haste,
Allen

[OH]

The Women's College of
The University of North Carolina
Greensboro, N.C.
March 8, 1939

Dear Cleanth:

My feeling about your dedication is as simple as your desire to offer it: it would give me great pleasure. The older I get the less I feel the importance of "strategy" in these matters. All the good people are our friends and if we avoid praising them because they are our friends, we

1. William A. Read was chairman of the LSU English Department until his resignation in 1940.

have left for praise only the inferior people. Mark Van Doren and I have dedicated back and forth and written about each other; but in the long run the test of disinterestedness will not have anything to do with the fact that we are friends. I am not, of course, urging you to dedicate the book to me; I am merely trying to see it as an outsider.

Our love to you all,
Allen

Red must have told you the report that Arndt brought back here. I thought at first it was his fatuity; now I suspect that Pip's expansiveness is to blame.

[OH]   16 Linden Lane
Princeton
December 19, 1939

Dear Cleanth:

I appreciated your letter, and I have decided not to reply to the note that I sent you. Anyhow, he has probably forgotten by this time that he wrote it.

I am going to miss the good company in New Orleans. Laughlin[1] and the Schwartzes[2] make the first break in the journey here tomorrow night.

Have you heard what has happened at Yale? Bob Daniel[3] writes me that *Understanding Poetry* has been put in as the freshman text—600 copies per annum, to say nothing of the victory over Tinker and Phelps[4] that the change represents. It appears that the younger men virtually went on strike, and won.

Friday I go to the hospital to have my appendix removed. And that's how I expect to spend Christmas week. Drink an absinthe frappe for me.

Our love to you both,
Ever yrs,
Allen

1. James Laughlin (1914–1997), as a young would-be writer, was told by Ezra Pound "to do something useful." With the fortune left him by his family, he founded New Directions and published much of the best new literature of his time, including the works of Pound.

2. Delmore Schwartz and his first wife, Gertrude Buckman.

3. Robert Daniel (1915–1985) was an instructor of English at Yale from 1939 to 1944. He later taught at Kenyon College. A native of Tennessee, he had close family ties to the Sewanee community.

4. Chauncey B. Tinker (1876–1963), Sterling Professor of English and Keeper of Rare Books at Yale University and an authority on Matthew Arnold, and William Lyon Phelps (1865–1943), Lampson Professor of English at Yale, were the most formidable old-guard opponents to the adoption at Yale of *Understanding Poetry*. Ironically, Phelps had been the first to introduce a course on modern American literature at Yale.

1940s

[OH]

The Southern Review
Baton Rouge, Louisiana
Friday [January 1940]

Dear Allen—

I am sorry to hear about the operation, though I am sure that you are wise to go ahead with it . . . I sincerely hope that you will have a prompt and easy recovery. And I'm glad to hear that the Hardy piece will not be sidetracked by the operation.[1] Feb. 1 will be all right—we are anxious to have it.

The MLA meeting was exhausting but lots of fun, and the meeting with John [Ransom] and Mizener[2] and [Delmore] Schwartz here in Baton Rouge was most pleasant.

It's a pity that you and Caroline could not have come. Mizener impresses me as being a perfectly delightful person; he is much interested in the South, and more specifically, in the poetry and criticism that have been coming out of the South. Schwartz is a little more difficult to know but keen and brilliant.—But you saw them on their trip back and can judge for yourself.

I was glad to get your candid letter about the last number.[3] I'm very glad that you gave it, and I have been pondering it for the last several days and I agree about Simons' style,[4] and from what Schwartz hinted about [William Carlos] Williams (and from what he suggests), I imagine that I should agree . . . he is something of a nut. One of the difficulties in

1. Tate was working on an essay on Thomas Hardy that had been commissioned by Brooks and Warren. It was published as "Hardy's Philosophic Metaphors," *Southern Review* 6 (summer 1940): 99–108.

2. Arthur Mizener (1907–1988), a literary scholar best known for his biographies of F. Scott Fitzgerald and Ford Madox Ford, was for many years the Mellon Foundation Professor of English at Cornell. He was a lifelong friend of Tate's.

3. This letter of Tate's has not been located.

4. Brooks is referring to Hi Simons's " 'The Comedian as the Letter C': Its Sense and Its Significance," *Southern Review* 5 (winter 1939): 453–77.

choosing stuff on the basis of the work alone is that you may give more encouragement than is justified by picking a piece that in itself may be good, but the people attached to them were awful.

Red and I worked through a lot of Williams' stuff for nearly two years. I still think that the poems as poems are better than what usually appears. We thought too that we saw a definite growth. Perhaps we were quite wrong. Even if we weren't, perhaps Williams will produce so little good that it won't do any good to have published a few isolated goodish poems.

But that is a necessary wish, I guess. Mizener and Schwartz [who] I picked purely on their work turned out to be fine. As for the rest of the number, I believe it a little better than you allow. [John Peale] Bishop (whose criticism I usually don't admire particularly) seems better than usual; Miller weaker than usual; the Valéry, at least interesting.

I am glad that you like Zabel's piece. I expected the worst; instead we got something which seems to me really excellent on the whole. But, in any case, let me know what you think. Few enough people have any judgment, and fewer still will be honest with you.

At any rate, the drawer for accepted mss is about clear, and if the new things (on hand and commissioned) come in all right, I believe we have a fine number coming up: Ramsdell[5] of Texas is to review Sandburg's Lincoln and may the sparks fly! [John Donald] Wade is to do a piece on some of the new books about England; [Kenneth] Burke is to review Parkes' *Marxism: an autopsy*. The Mizener piece on Shakespeare's sonnets is excellent. And we've got a new batch of poems which I think are good. Even if many of our best people are tied up with the Hardy number, I believe we can make a good showing in the spring issue.

Poetry is hard as hell to get. Can't you send us some? We can get any amount of goodish stuff—but practically none that is really good. And one can't even depend on some of the young writers who have appeared before. They send in new groups that crumple up in the middle from which you can salvage no more than one or two that are usable.

We certainly want to see the piece on Faulkner by Coindreau,[6]

5. Charles W. Ramsdell was coeditor of LSU Press's History of the South series. His review of Carl Sandburg's *Abraham Lincoln: The War Years* (1939) was published in *Southern Review* 6 (1940–1941): 439–53.

6. Maurice Coindreau, a professor of French at Princeton and a translator of Faulkner, wrote the first Faulkner criticism published in France: "Lettres Étrangères: William Faulkner," *Nouvelle Revue Française* 236 (June 1, 1931): 926–31. The piece referred to by Brooks was not published in the *Southern Review*.

preferably in shortened form—but that could be determined later. Will you ask him for us? Love to Caroline from all of us.

As ever
Cleanth

Monday

P.S. I'm sorry I got to see so little of Thorp.[7] He is fine and I wanted to talk with him. [I'll] write about the Ford matter this week; I shall also send a copy of my paper.

Take care of yourself.

[OH]

16 Linden Lane
Princeton
May 29, 1940

Dear Cleanth:

I've owed you a letter ever since you sent me your M.L.A. paper, which I thought extremely fine.—All my writing (including letters) has been slowed up by Princeton,[1] or say by my reaction to the place. But I'm getting started again, and the Hardy piece, bad and fragmentary as it is, is a symptom of the resurgence.

The symposium that you all are planning with John sounds fine.[2] I suppose my piece will be in the Kenyon, though you and John must decide that. In April I read to this English Club here a paper on historical scholarship that infuriated the Department. (Incidentally, it has probably killed my chances for a permanent appointment at Princeton.)[3] The paper will be in the fall issue of the *American Scholar,* and will be the first gun of the S.R.-K.R. campaign. I read the same paper at Yale, with even more disastrous results. Stanley Williams,[4] I am told, left the lecture hall while I was reading.

---

7. Willard Thorp (1899–1990), a scholar of American literature and professor of English at Princeton, was a close friend of Gordon's and Tate's.

1. Tate was poet-in-residence at Princeton from 1939 to 1942.

2. The *Southern Review* and the *Kenyon Review* cosponsored a five-part symposium titled "Literature and the Professors." John Crowe Ransom and Brooks were in charge of dividing the contributions between the two journals.

3. This lecture, which so angered the old-school English faculty, who were mostly literary historians and philologists in the German academic tradition, was one of Tate's most brilliant pieces of criticism. It was published as "Miss Emily and the Bibliographer," *American Scholar* 9 (autumn 1940): 449–60.

4. Stanley Williams (1888–1956) was a professor of American literature at Yale from 1915 until the year of his death.

What has happened at Cornell? When I was there lecturing a month ago, the head of the department (Davis?) asked me all about you; you may imagine my response.[5] I made it somewhat against the grain, because I don't want to see you leave the South. My observation leads me to conclude that the fluidity of the South is better for us than the entrenched routine of the Eastern universities. In five years you would be a Cornell professor. Nobody could stand out against the inertia of the academic tradition in the East. However, I hope you get the offer; it may be the best thing possible for you under the conditions that seem to prevail at L.S.U. A letter from Red, written before the invasion of Holland, expresses anxiety about the general situation there. But what will happen to the *Southern Review* if you both leave?

I hope that Red is either already here or on the high seas. He may have landed the other day with a large group from Italy; but of course he would not be allowed to communicate with us. John says that he expects him at Gambier for this summer.

We are expecting to see you and Tinkum in September, when you come up for the English Institute at Columbia. Princeton will be your headquarters; we'll all commute to the meetings in N.Y.—We have decided not to go home this summer. Expense and loss of time decided the issue.

The Lytles will come here at the end of June for a couple of months. We had originally planned to go to them.

I suppose you know that *Understanding Poetry* was used by the younger men at Yale to change the Freshman English, which had been the same since Pottle[6] and Tinker put it in [in] 1790 [sic]. And do you know that *Modern Poetry and the Tradition* has sold more than forty copies at Princeton? You've seen Horace Gregory's crack at you: I feel that I am to blame.[7] He is not in your book; I figure in it; and he hates me. I haven't seen the Drew book[8] but doubt its merit; I saw an earlier book by her, which was very bad.

Write me the news. I am trying to stay away from the radio, but without much success. It seems to me very rash to assume that the allies

5. The Cornell English Department was seriously courting Brooks for a tenured position. He was offered the chairmanship of the department but declined because he did not wish to join a department that was evenly split about his candidacy.

6. Frederick A. Pottle (1897–1987), a professor of English at Yale, was the chief editor of the private papers of James Boswell.

7. Horace Gregory's unfavorable review of Tate's *Poems: 1930–40* was published in *Partisan Review* 8 (May–June 1941): 241–42. Brooks had made some sharp comments on Gregory's "Defense of Propaganda Art" in his "Metaphysical Poetry and Propaganda Art," chapter 3 of *Modern Poetry and the Tradition.*

8. Elizabeth A. Drew, *Directions for Modern Poetry* (1940).

are already defeated; the English seem washed up, but the French will beat the Germans in the end.

Love to you both,

yrs,

Allen

[Baton Rouge]

June 7 [1940]

Dear Allen—

It was fine to get your letter of a few days ago. I began an answer at once, but the pages which I had written have disappeared and so I am beginning again. Actually, I had planned to write to you again and again through the past three months, but too much work, and worse still, that form of *accidia* which descends upon you when you can't really get caught up with the work, got me. The letter never did get started until the other night.

I wish I could have heard the lecture that you gave to the Princeton and Yale departments. Ransom had written me earlier that you had given the bibliographers fits. And then Mizener wrote some weeks ago that you had startled some of the crustier Yale men. Mizener said some of them were heard to say afterward, "Mr. Tate was really a little rude, wasn't he?" I look forward to the next number of *The American Scholar.*[1] Your attack bodes well for our symposium. By the way, please don't hesitate to send in suggestions for it. At his last writing, John had suggested that we include among the contributors, two students. I think that the idea is good if we can get the right students. Have you any suggestions?

I have to thank you for the very handsome treatment of my book in the magazine *College English.*[2] But how did they ever happen to ask you to do an article? Nothing could have surprised me more than the sight of your name in it when I first saw it there. I knew that the magazine had tried to dust itself off of late, but their attempts had been rather floundering. To say what you said *there* is to put a bombshell into the very middle of the enemy.

What you say about eastern universities is most interesting. I knew from what Mizener had told me about Yale that the situation was bad there; and from the reading I do in the academic journals (which isn't

1. The autumn 1940 issue of *American Scholar* was the one that included Tate's "Miss Emily and the Bibliographers."

2. Tate's review of *Modern Poetry and the Tradition* was published as "Understanding Modern Poetry," *College English* 29 (1940): 263–74.

much) I knew that all the bigwigs in English were sterile enough. I did not know how much of a grip they had on Princeton. Your saying that a Cornell man asked you about me is rather strange. I've heard nothing from them directly and had supposed that my nomination was entirely out. Apparently they're still sounding me out—from a distance. Naturally, in view of the situation here, I would like to get an offer; but I would want to use it as a lever here.[3] Of course, if the University here leaped at the chance of excusing me for duty elsewhere, I might decide that I had been very lucky in having a chance to get away. As a matter of fact, as the situation is now, I think that the University would be disposed to meet almost any offer. But the acting president[4] may not be confirmed, and Red and I have scant reason to feel that the Dean of A. & S.[5] loses any love over us. After all, in choosing an acting chairman of the department a couple of months ago, the administration went over the heads, not only of three full professors but over the heads of Red and myself also.

I think that they are going to try to find a permanent head from the outside. I'm afraid that he will turn out to be a man from the top-flight of the second class, a Ph.D. who has written a dissertation on John Gower and published the due number of entries in M.L.N., and a man who has just enough glimmer of the light to lend tremendous prestige to all his wrong-headed actions. This is not the portrait of any particular man that the administration has in mind. It is simply my picture of what the composite choice of the department will turn out to be. I'm trying to get a personal meeting with the acting president in the near future to try to show him that he has a chance to do something really big if he wants to; but, that if he writes to a few big-wigs for recommendations, or, if he polls the department he will get just what I have described above. But I have little hope. As a lawyer, he has escaped the Ph.D. mill; but he wills good somewhat feebly, and I'm afraid that his most daring move will be that of keeping up with the Joneses; i.e., Harvard, Yale, Pennsylvania, etc.[6]

3. LSU did try to retain Brooks's services. He was made the first Read Professor of English just before deciding to leave for Yale in 1947.

4. Paul M. Hebert, who had been dean of the LSU School of Law, became the acting president in 1939.

5. Dean Frederick C. Frey had been at LSU since 1922 and was a possible candidate for the presidency.

6. Hebert's first choice for the chairmanship of the LSU English Department was, in fact, Brooks. Unfortunately, the polarized political situation in the department posed difficulties for his candidacy. In the end, Hebert chose a compromise candidate who was, as Brooks feared, an old-fashioned medieval English philologist, Thomas A. Kirby (1904–1993). Kirby served as chair of the English department for a record thirty-one years, retiring in 1973. Although he was an old-school philologist, Kirby was surprisingly open to the ideas of the Southern Agrarians and New Critics and was supportive of Brooks.

By the way, I heard a very amusing story the other day which I believe is authentic. It seems that I was put up for the headship—Red and I had thrown in our chips at the beginning, and so it is surprising to me that I was put up at all. The objection was raised, however, that my connections with you and John were so strong that I might be influenced by you two into doing radical things. Apparently, the objector was one of the members of the executive committee appointed to make the appointment. It was probably a dean, and I think I can guess which one. Remembering that it was a dean; i.e., a person who does not read books—you and John have every right to feel flattered. Your fame has spread a long way. By the by, the story is to be kept pretty close. It was told me under all sorts of vows of secrecy, and it is unusual enough to get itself traced back to the man who told my informant, if we are not careful.

I got a card from Red a few days ago. Apparently he had just landed in New York, and promises to write a long letter to me in the next few days. I'm sure that you've heard from him and perhaps have seen him. (In spite of Miss Emma, or perhaps even with a cordial and enthusiastic Miss Emma, I imagine that he has come. For Princeton is mighty close to New York, and I know that after a year's absence Red is mighty anxious to see you and Caroline.) In view of our English department situation here, I wish that he might come to Baton Rouge soon, but dare say that he won't come here until after the trip to Colorado.

Your Hardy piece was fine. And I hasten to sign you up for something else—in addition to the piece for the symposium. It seems to me that my estimate is correct. What about it? I don't mean to try to saddle you with an article which may not appeal to you; but I hope that you will decide to undertake it.

The invitation to stop with you and Caroline on our trip to New York is most welcome. We hasten to accept. But you all must not let us make a nuisance of ourselves. We have a sort of half-way engagement to see the Mizeners and we hope to see Manson and Rose [Radford]. But we shall certainly count on having two or three days with you and Caroline.

I hope that the Columbia Institute meetings will give us an opportunity for some real argument. I haven't seen Tindall's book,[7] but Blackmur[8]

7. William York Tindall, *D. H. Lawrence and Susan His Cow* (New York: Columbia University Press, 1939).

8. The literary critic R. P. Blackmur (1904–1965) was a colleague of Tate's at Princeton. He was often linked to the New Criticism, partly because of his close readings of poetry during the 1930s and 1940s.

says that it's bad. Daiches'[9] book I've read hastily and shall read again more carefully before the meeting. It has plenty in it with which you and I will disagree, though he is apparently pretty bright. Auden's abilities we know, but I am sure that his leftism—some of it undigested, I think—will put him far enough on the other side of the fence on many points. I could wish that matters would so come about that we might catch the Left on an exposed flank. But I'm looking too far ahead. As these meetings usually go, there isn't any real debate at all; and even if there should be some, perhaps the lines taken will be thoroughly different. Still, it would be fun if that sort of engagement developed. Having [that] possibility in mind, I was particularly glad to see your name on the program.

I haven't seen the Horace Gregory attack. Where did it occur? I want to look it up. As a matter of fact, the slurring reference to Gregory in my book was probably sufficient, had there been no other reason, to account for his attack. You remember I picked up his stupid statement that none of Shelley's faults could be put down to his propagandistic intent. Our best regards to you and Caroline and Nancy.

As ever,
Cleanth

Tinkum says not to sell the British short. They're far from washed up. But I'm fearful tonight that both Britain and France have waited too long to get ready. The news certainly sounds bad.

[OH]   [Princeton]
                                                                      June 20, 1940

Dear Cleanth:

I am wholly demoralized by the war, by accumulated words, by trips to the World's Fair. I am just back from the last of these.—I had a card from Red at Bennington, but that's all; I hear they intend to stay there a month or more. No, Miss Emma won't let him come here, I am sure.

The Hardy number[1] is fine. I was greatly pleased by the review in *Time*.[2] *That* ought to keep your enemies at bay. The frightful influence that John and I exert upon you and Red I had heard about before. Red wrote me that Bryant[3] was considered dangerous as prospective head because, being a Vanderbilt man, he might bring me there. I will keep your story quiet. I have a new one from my appearance at Yale. Chauncey

9. David Daiches (b. 1912), a Scottish-born literary critic, taught at New York University. His *The Novel and the Modern World* was published in 1939.

1. The summer 1940 *Southern Review* was the special Thomas Hardy issue.
2. "Wessex and Louisiana," *Time*, June 10, 1940, p. 92.
3. Joseph A. Bryant Sr. (b. 1899) was an American literary scholar.

Brewster Tinker was at the lecture. He said to someone, "Why doesn't somebody throw a stool at him?" Maybe we can throw some stools (pun) at him or his like in our attack.

I am now casting about for a spring-board for my article. The great initial trouble is that I can't bear to read the writings of these penguins. I'll have to do it.

We'll be looking for you all in September. The Lytles are due here next week. We're expecting Sam Monk[4] today.

Love to you both,
Allen

Do we need to attack the leftists? It seems to me they are as liquidated as the Confederate Army.

[OH]   *The Southern Review*
Baton Rouge, Louisiana
Monday [October 7] 1940

Dear Allen—

I should have written earlier, but my late arrival here has left me unusually harried. The consequence is that I owe letters all around.

Red and Albert thought your symposium piece was magnificent. Red said he thought it was one of the finest pieces of prose that you had writ-ten in the last several years. It *is* fine. By this time, of course, you will have received your proof.—But first we should have acknowledged it earlier.[1]

Kirk wrote me a week or so ago that he was giving up his claim on it. I replied at once, thanking him. He has apparently been confused by the arrival of the carbon copy and he wired this morning to ask whether we are using it after all. I have just wired, assuring him that we are—and I shall write him at once. Anyway, the matter is definitely cleared now.

Tinkum has written Caroline to tell both of you how much we enjoyed the visit. I had thought to add my thanks at that time. I do so now. It was thoroughly enjoyable and something that I needed very much. I *do* hope that you all can stop with us this winter.

When I arrived Red told me that the acting president, Hebert, had told him he intended to make me department head if I would accept. Since then I've seen him, and he raised the question once more. I named conditions, conditions which he indicated he could meet. What the next move will be, I don't know. He knows that he will have to fight all the

---

4. Samuel Holt Monk (1902–1981), a critic and English literature scholar, had been a friend of Tate's since their days at Southwestern together.

1. Tate's essay was published as "The Present Function of Criticism," *Southern Review* 6 (autumn 1940): 236–46.

old guard here—the various deans—in order to put me in. Maybe he'll get cold feet. But I think that he means business.

I really believe that the symposium is going to be a knock-out. We'll be out by the 15th.

Our best regards to Caroline and Nancy.

As ever,
Cleanth

We've made a point of trying to get Cinina off to a good start—at least on our side. It's been hard, but has worked so far. C. is obviously on her best behavior—but she nearly got out of control the other night. I'm afraid it can't last.

[OH]   [Princeton]
October 10, 1940

Dear Cleanth:

Yours of the 9th has just come, and I can't postpone even an hour my pleasure in the renewed prospect of your promotion. I would feel this of course if you were only a friend; but you are more than that. If you become the head, it will mean rout for the forces of darkness and victory for the light!—I hope you will wire me as soon as you know the final decision, I will be on tenterhooks.

A rather cheerful letter came yesterday from Red. He alluded vaguely to Iowa, but I took it as warrant for a lecture on his true course of action. I still feel strongly on that subject.

We'll see you at the M.L.A. I doubt if I can get off from C.B.S. long enough to come South; but we'll see.[1]

Allen

[OH]   Princeton University
Princeton, New Jersey
Nov. 29, 1940

Dear Cleanth:

Only a complete statement about "knowledge" or no statement at all will do. If Hook[1] wants his reply to appear in the winter issue, I can do

1. Tate was a frequent participant on a panel of distinguished men of letters hosted by Mark Van Doren that met weekly on CBS Radio to enjoy unrehearsed conversations about Western culture. A collection of these broadcasts was edited for publication by Van Doren as *The New Invitation to Learning* (New York: New Home Library, 1942). For Tate's contributions, see pp. 61–73, 194–205, 223–36, 327–38.

1. The philosopher and educator Sidney Hook (1902–1989) was incensed by Tate's "Present Function of Criticism." His response, arguing against literature as a special form

nothing. If you postpone it till the spring issue I will do an essay, *not as a reply* but merely taking off from his misunderstanding. Literature as knowledge is the main point. The rest of his essay is a quibble. He's all wrong about Belloc, and he makes his point about Richards by wilfully ignoring the intention of my point. My misstatement about the Third International gave him his chance.

I enclose for your momentary amusement a letter that might have been run as an answer.

These people have reached such a state of bigotry that all they can understand is their own point of view thrown back at them.

Please write me the gossipy letter that you promise.

Love to you all,
Allen

I am keeping Hooks' ms. since it's an extra copy.
Albert will regret working for Jay Laughlin.[2]

16 Linden Lane
Princeton
Dec. 26, 1940

Dear Cleanth:

You will probably have heard by this time that I can't get up to Cambridge. YOU MUST STOP HERE ON THE WAY BACK. Now do this. You won't be in such a big rush. And try to come by Saturday at dinner time, or even later; or Sunday, or Monday. In short, come.

Red asked me if you all could have the fiction essay for the spring issue. Yes: if you don't mind its coming out in my new book at the same time, or maybe a week before. It's scheduled for early April.

In haste,
Allen

The Southern Review
Baton Rouge, Louisiana
January 30, 1941

Dear Allen:

I've been expecting to write every day for a week but apparently I can't get the time. And I must not wait a moment longer, and so I am

---

of knowledge aside from its sociopolitical context, was published as "Late Mr. Tate and the Positivist Critics," *Southern Review* 6 (spring 1941): 840–43. Tate's response was published as "Literature as Knowledge: Comment and Comparison," *Southern Review* 6 (spring 1941): 629–57, and reprinted in Tate's *Reason in Madness: Critical Essays* (New York: G. P. Putnam and Sons, 1941).

2. Albert Erskine had left the *Southern Review* and moved to Connecticut, where he took an editorial job with James Laughlin's New Directions Press.

dictating this letter now. Are you ready to send in the essay on literature as knowledge? Or can we expect it in the next week? The only reason for getting it in soon is that I would like to send a copy to Hook. I shall simply say that we are running his communication and that this article will appear in the same number. If he cares, on his own volition, to say that he would like to change the tone of his communication, then I can send that to you and you will at least have time to do a footnote, if you care to, which would refer to him and his communication explicitly. I quite agree with you, and Red agrees of course, that there is no need of making any reply to him at all unless he is willing to change his manner. I am enclosing a communication sent in by Daiches to which you might want to make explicit reference by a footnote or otherwise. Mr. Daiches has apparently changed his tune since he faced you in New York.

By the way, I finally found out just a few days ago why Hook went off the deep end as he did. A friend of mine in Chicago sent me a copy of the special issue of the Chicago student paper—an issue dated sometime in November—in which a long speech by Adler[1] was printed. Hook's violent reply to it was also printed there as were replies and commentaries by a number of people on the Chicago faculty. After that tussle, Hook's eyes must have popped out of his head when he opened the Southern Review Autumn number and saw your article. At any rate, his perfervid indignation was already at the boiling point and your essay must have seemed to him to resemble Adler's sufficiently to cause him to feel that there was a dire plot or that at least the enemy were popping up all around him. Incidentally, I don't know whether you've ever read a word of Adler. Your essay and his do resemble each other at some points.

Red and I hate to forgo the use of the MLA program which would include your other essay, but we are anxious to get the essay on literature as knowledge—not because we think Hook either formidable or graceful, and not because it matters a damn in itself whether he has a reply or not, but merely because his brand of positivism has so thoroughly rotted out the whole superstructure of our education that we think not one answer but many answers to it must be made, and made perhaps for some time to come.

The situation on the campus is still a complete muddle. The Board of Supervisors has nominated six candidates, including Hebert but also including a broken down county superintendent of schools and a major

1. The philosopher and author Mortimer Adler (b. 1902) served as chairman of the board of the Encyclopaedia Britannica company and helped develop its Great Books program. For many years, he was on the faculty of the University of Chicago and was a close associate of Robert Hutchins, the president of that school.

general. I can't say that the outlook is too bright. But at least the enemy are out in the open now and the Phi Beta Kappa report (which I told you and Caroline about) has been requested by the Board and now has leaked out into the faculty and out into the state. Every breeze brings in the wind of more or less righteous indignation from some dog who feels he has been hit by a paragraph in it.

It's all very exciting, but for a man who likes peace and his own fig tree as much as I do, it's pretty hard on the nerves. I hope that the Board in the next few weeks will go on and elect for better or worse. Certainly the present situation is not conducive to work.

I am looking about for material for the Princeton lecture.[2] Church wrote me some time ago and then Gauss made the formal invitation.[3] I have replied to both and accepted with pleasure. My special thanks to you, for I still feel that you must have had a great deal to do with it. At any rate, I look forward to seeing you and Caroline in May. Please write to us, both of you, and accept our love.

As ever,
Cleanth

If you prefer that I not send a copy of your essay at all, simply let me know when the manuscript comes in.

We are writing Blackmur that the books are on the way to him and that we hope the check will shortly be on its way too. A requisition went in several days ago and since there have been no kicks, we are sure it will clear.

[OH]   *The Southern Review*
Baton Rouge, Louisiana
Jan. 30 [1941]

Dear Allen—

Your note (just arrived) crossed with my letter to you which was mailed a few hours ago.

Your letter to the *V[anderbilt] Alumnus* is excellent. I'm writing one at once and shall send a copy of it to you.

---

2. Brooks was invited by Princeton to deliver the prestigious Mesures Lecture that spring on literature. The lectures were intended to present the finest in contemporary critical thought to the university community. His lecture was the well-known "The Language of Paradox."

3. Henry Church, a philanthropist and art patron, had funded the Mesures Lecture series. He was a friend of Tate's and a major financial backer of the *Sewanee Review* during Tate's tenure there. Christian Gauss (1878–1951) was a dean of the college at Princeton University.

I saw [I. A.] Richards a couple of weeks ago when he was here to speak. He has come a long way in our direction. He is rewriting *Science and Poetry* and frankly refers to the earlier editions as "dated." I can't predict what he will say in that revision on the basis of his speech—but the speech—particularly the sections on Science gives to poetry about all one would need to claim for it. Incidentally, he gives high praise to Plato now.

I could wish that he would open up this vein further in his lecture for your [Mesures] series.

I shall try to send in my title in a few days. If you have suggestions— you suggested the best paper I ever gave, Xmas before last—please let me have them.

All my best,
Cleanth

[Princeton]
February 8 1941

Dear Cleanth:

Here's the essay—but don't faint when you l[ea]f it. You have full permission to cut it, rearrange it, and in general to do anything you want to with it. It is long largely because I wanted to dissociate in detail the early from the later Richards, and to nail down the defects of the more recent and more rigorous brand of positivism known as Semiotic. I don't think I've said anything new, except perhaps the making of the historical connection between neo-classicism and the doctrine of relevance.

As to Hook. I am in favor of not sending my article to him. Does etiquette demand it? I should think not. Moreover, he would think up some new quibbles that might have to be cleared up. The last two pages of the essay cover him as much as I feel like doing it.

As to Daiches. The insolence of his tone matches the insolence of a letter he wrote to the N[ew] R[epublic], and both insolences contrast strongly with a private letter I've just got from him, in which he insists that there is no difference between us. Public insult and private apology.

I'd rather see it the other way around. In his notes to you, he employs the smear technique—Mortimer Adler. Think of the preposterous claim that Shakespeare was a positivist!

Your lecture here. Why not do a piece of comparative criticism? Two poems, one modern and one 17th or even early 19th century?

I enclose a copy of the address by Adler that set them all by the ears. The sheet also contains Hook's smear article. I don't go all the way with Adler, but the whole negative portion of his attack is undeniable.

We look forward to seeing you. You'd better plan a whole week, and bring Tinkum.

Yrs ever,
Allen

[OH]
The Southern Review
Baton Rouge, Louisiana
Feb. 13 [1941]

Dear Allen,

I'm glad that you sent me Beatty's[1] letter (which I am returning). It's a most remarkable production. Worse than anything actually said in the letter is the general aroma that the letter exudes. His real test will be this: will he edit the memorial volume for Mims? If he does, then I think that one will be justified in ascribing any motives to him one likes. I'm sorry to say this. I like Beatty mildly; I have thought most of his books too glib and rushed out for the sake of publication. But I had not thought of him as an academic politician.

I have had no word from Beatty or Don [Davidson] about my letter, nor about a contribution to the Mims volume. Maybe, I'll have one in the afternoon mail.

Don's part in the matter is very strange: surely Don can't feel that Mims can be divorced from the general change of atmosphere on the Vanderbilt campus. Surely he can't think it trivial that Vanderbilt approximates more and more to the Municipal University of Nashville. How can he see your letter as just an attack on Dr. Mims, personal or devoid of other issues (my warrant for this is the passage quoted from him by Beatty)? Or, how, thinking this, can he feel that a lecture in Wesley Hall and a solicitation of Joel Cheek alters matters in any important particular? It looks bad. And to my mind, Beatty's statement "your implication that only a forlorn remnant is left here now, that our modest efforts are futile, and that the whole institution is damned" is gratuitous.

The obvious answer is that very few departments can show as many as two people of the stature of Don (and Beatty, too, if he demands his crumb). Your point, I took it, was not that Vanderbilt was appreciably

1. Richmond Croom Beatty (1905–1961) was a professor of English at Vanderbilt University and a close friend of Donald Davidson's. Most likely, Tate is referring to *A Vanderbilt Miscellany, 1919–1944*, edited by Beatty (Nashville: Vanderbilt University Press, 1944), an anthology of writings by Vanderbilt alumni that includes works by both Tate and Brooks. The anthology is not presented as a Festschrift for Mims, although Beatty's introduction opens with praise for Edwin Mims for having made places for Davidson and John Crowe Ransom within the Vanderbilt English department.

worse off than other departments—but that it was once miles ahead of the others, and threw away the lead.

But Beatty's statement, I'm afraid, shows what rankles in Beatty and Don.

It's my considered opinion, Allen, that in academic matters one ought never use the rapier when the meat-axe will do. That's not to claim that I wield it with nonchalance or special grace. But no other weapon will work on the academic politician. We've got lots of Mimses here, Pipkin, for instance. Unless they are mowed off even with the ground in two days, they are again flourishing like the green baytree. Unless our Vanderbilt friends are careful, Mims will be completely rehabilitated— a sort of combination of Maecenas and Socrates, the patron, guide, philosopher and friend of the Greater Fugitives. And what is worse, what he represents at Vanderbilt will be strengthened and even more completely dominant.

We look forward to the article on literature as knowledge.

As ever,
Cleanth

By the way, we have asked Crane Brinton to review Mims's *Life of K.*[2] What about starting on the companion piece?—the history of university education in the South since the last war—or since 1875? I know you are overworked, but the Beatty letter makes the time propitious.

[OH]   Feb. 14.

Your ms has come in and it is splendid! It *is* long but we're going to fit it in as it stands. I think it's all necessary. I found particularly fine the comments on Arnold and Coleridge; and the handling of Richards. Hook has had the roof fall in on himself. I'm not sending the piece to him. We'll simply print his communication along with that of Daiches.

I expect that your essay is going to be a landmark. It centers the fight right at the crucial point—I'm convinced more and more that positivism is the real enemy and that the only sound strategy is to attack there. The social sciences [are] even filled with it, naturally. But even on this campus I am made more and more aware that the people who deal with the arts and even the religionists, are infected, often unconsciously, too.

By the way, I'm glad that you reviewed Richards' career. It's due him, as well as furnishing a strategic opportunity. As Red said a few weeks ago: to have started where he did and to have come as far as he has come

2. Edwin Mims, *Chancellor Kirkland of Vanderbilt* (1940).

is a real miracle, for he has certainly arrived at his present position by the hard way.

I wish that you all could get him to give as his [Mesures] series paper an elaboration of his position on Plato. It would fit the series all right, and it was by far the most exciting thing in his speech here, though it was touched on very lightly. Too, it might keep him off the war. I happen to sympathize with him there, but his emphasis on it here was bad strategy from his own standpoint—and took the emphasis off the points which we wanted him to elaborate. All this is in confidence, of course. I suppose that the general topic, "The Language of Poetry" and his sense of the kind of audience he will have, will probably take care of his speech for you. Here he undoubtedly was attempting a more general and less technical paper.

As for my own paper, I'm not sure of a precise title. I've thought of "The Language of Paradox" and if a title must be in at once, perhaps we can make this do. I have an idea in mind which, I believe, would give me a fresh approach, but I'm not sure. At any rate, I shall certainly take your suggestion to found the paper—whatever the topic—on a rather restrained analysis of a couple of poems—17th or 19th century and modern.

Congratulations again on your essay!

Love to Caroline and Nancy from
Tinkum and me. Cleanth

[OH]
The Southern Review
Baton Rouge, Louisiana
Mar. 10 [1941]

Dear Allen:

We've asked Davidson to do an article on Cash's *Mind of the South*—asked him about [a] month ago.[1] But there's no reason for you not to refer [to] the book and comment on it as much as you like. Do you have a copy? If not, we'll try to get you one.

---

1. Brooks and Warren asked Donald Davidson to write a review-essay on W. J. Cash's landmark *Mind of the South*, a seminal book antithetical to the Southern Agrarian viewpoint. Davidson's piece ended with a joke concerning the "lynching" of Cash for his controversial statements about the South, with Davidson's lynch mob in the end inviting Cash to enjoy a jug of whiskey with them. Although the review had been meant in fun, Davidson and the *Southern Review* editors were horrified when they learned that Cash had committed suicide by hanging himself in Mexico. Unfortunately, it was too late to stop its publication.

In the meantime I'll get the Mims and other books to you. I've been stopped in my tracks for a week with academic politics. The Board is expected this morning to name a permanent president and are almost certain to name Major General Hodges.[2] I fear that that kind of appointment will finish us off. I don't know him, but I fear the worst—not in personal retaliations. But I'm afraid that the chances for imaginative reform are over.

As ever,
Cleanth

[OH]   [Princeton]
                                                                   4/21/41
Dear Cleanth:
Please let me know when you expect to arrive, and how long you can stay—which we hope will be as long as possible. We are hoping to have Tinkum too.
Richards was a great success—but very slippery; but of that, later.
And now for a fine reunion!

Yrs,
Allen

                                                                 [Princeton]
                                                                 May 22, 1941
Dear Cleanth:
I've been wanting for some time to tell you about your great success here. By general acclamation your lecture was judged the best. This is the literal truth; so accept it.
Now about the manuscript. When can we have it? We need it definitely by June 14th, when we expect to send the book to the printer. Can you make it?[1]
No more for the nonce.

Yrs.
Allen

2. Following his retirement from the U.S. Army, General Campbell Hodges (1881–1944) served as president of LSU from 1941 until his death. It was during his administration that publication of the *Southern Review* was suspended.

1. Brooks's Mesures lecture, "The Language of Paradox," was published in *The Language of Poetry*, edited by Tate (Princeton: Princeton University Press, 1942). The other contributors were Phillip Wheelwright, Wallace Stevens, and I. A. Richards.

[OH]   16 Linden Lane
                                                 Princeton, New Jersey
                                                       October 4, 1941

Dear Cleanth:

Please send me at once (corrected or not) the proof of your *Mesures* lecture.

A note recently from Red "reminded" me of my essay for the Yeats issue.[1] I didn't know I had been invited to contribute. But I expect to have the piece ready on time.

I was mighty sorry to miss you last month. We got back after the Institute had begun.

I hear you have plans with Ted Greene.[2] All I will say now is: Beware— until I go into it more thoroughly.

                                                            In haste,
                                                               Allen

                                                 The Southern Review
                                               Baton Rouge, Louisiana
                                             Monday [October 1941]

Dear Allen,

Your note came in this afternoon, and I have bestirred myself with the proof. I've checked it and it goes off to you airmail in the morning. I'm sorry about the delay: it's the usual story—a session which looked pleasant and quiet and has turned out thus far to be any thing but that. I've checked the quotations carefully. I've tried to mend the grammar in a few places; but it's still shaky. I hate to put more work on you, but I take it that time is at a premium; so if any question is put to you by the press, or any questionable matter hits your eye, please make whatever change you like. Don't take more time by trying to consult me.

The paper was written to be a lecture. I am acutely conscious of the fact, on rereading it, that it probably speaks better than it reads. But it's too late to alter that.

I could have sworn that you had been asked to do a piece for the Yeats number. I know that Red was absolutely sure that you had been asked. (You've been announced for it some weeks ago.) I don't know which

---

1. Tate's contribution to the special issue on Yeats was "Yeats's Romanticism: Notes and Suggestions," *Southern Review* 7 (winter 1941): 591–600.

2. Theodore Greene (1897–1969) was a professor of philosophy at Yale who specialized in art criticism and aesthetics. For details on Brooks's "plans" with Greene, see the following letter.

one of us fumbled the ball. Perhaps we let it drop between us. Anyway, I'm awfully glad that you're going to pull the thing out of the fire for us by going ahead with it. (Apparently, an identical thing happened with another "contributor" who answered his "reminder" note in the same way that you did. We're rechecking the whole list.)

By the way, our new Managing Editor is just on the point of being drafted.[1] We have a new secretary. (Jean Lowell and Robert are now, as you may know, in New York.) One more blow and the efficiency of the S.R.—what vestiges that are left of it—will go completely by the board. The worst of it is that the new president, the General [Campbell Hodges], knows absolutely nothing about the nature or the needs of the magazine. He is a gentleman; he has the kindest of intentions toward the S.R.; he is even impressed with it. But so far I have been occupied chiefly with explaining to him that prestige won't take the place of cash payments to our contributors—that we don't have *that* kind of prestige, anyway. I am not especially depressed with the situation, perhaps not as much as I should be. I'm even optimist enough to think that we can, in time, explain satisfactorily all sorts of such details to him. But you do get tired of trying to educate deans and presidents over and over again.

I didn't expect to see you at the English Institute though I thought that you might get to the Congress on Religion, Science, and Philosophy since our name was on the program. I called by their desk several times to see whether you had registered. Later I heard (I believe from Willard Thorp) that you and Caroline were expected back at Princeton, and I tried to send you word. (I should have written or phoned.) I thought that we might drive by Princeton and stop for an hour or two on our way back. But on Friday night Tinkum either sprained her back or caught cold in it; she could hardly move, and I seriously doubted whether she could drive or even ride comfortably. School had started here; we simply had to get back. The upshot was that we left earlier than we had planned—Saturday noon to get as much start as we could hoping to limp as far as we could on what remained of the day. With this decision, we gave up whatever hope we had entertained of an hour or so in Princeton. As a matter of fact, Tinkum's back slowly improved and we made excellent time on the last two days of the trip. The trip up, however, had been disappointingly long. We had had to push awfully hard to keep anywhere near our planned schedule, and arrived dog tired.

The Institute went very well. As far as the Criticism section was concerned, the fighting that went on last year bore good fruit. The Old

---

1. John Palmer, who had served as the managing editor for the *Southern Review,* entered naval service. He later edited both the *Sewanee Review* and the *Yale Review.*

Guard didn't want any more fighting. They were respectful and even interested. The irony is that we were actually in far weaker position than last year: Zabel was sick and couldn't come; Horace Gregory's paper was a pleasant essay but not one to trouble the historical scholars; Trilling's[2] effort was good but was essentially an historical paper too; Pottle was picked by Norman Pearson[3] (I am convinced) to be the big gun of the historical approach. That meant that my paper was the only one that got delivered which actually tried to deal with the poem throughout as a poem. Of course, there were so many people there like Arthur Mizener, Wellek,[4] and Willard Thorp to keep matters in hand. But as I have said, matters never really got out of hand: the historians didn't care to fight. (Pottle is a very able man—he could have rallied them for a fight, had he cared to, and had Pearson not assigned him to the last day.)

At any rate, here is where Greene entered the picture. He gave the general paper on the fourth evening. His topic was the relation of philosophy to criticism, or rather, it took the form of the question: is anything to be gained by a collaboration of philosophy and criticism? First he totaled up the case against it; then, the case for collaboration. He then put the question to the group. After some discussion, I suggested that our best critics were precisely the ones who were interested in philosophy— whatever a professional philosopher might have to say about them—and asked whether he did not agree that it was the prevailing historicism and relativism among the English professors that constituted the real bar to any collaboration or cooperation. He agreed, and then proceeded to improve on the theme, carving up in the course of his subsequent talk, two or three of the historians who tried to answer him. His talk was certainly the most explicit, and as far as the rank and file of the Institute were concerned, the most *effective* thing said on what may be called *our* side.

The result was that after his paper, before I knew what had happened, several people had suggested that Greene and I get up a program for the next Institute which would explore the question further. I had lunch with him next day to see what we could suggest for such a program. He told me about conducting a double seminar with John R[ansom] at Bread Loaf this summer. We talked of you and your work, he with high approval.

2. The New York literary critic Lionel Trilling (1905–1975) had a long association with the *Partisan Review*. His major work is *The Liberal Imagination*.

3. Yale professor of English Norman Holmes Pearson (1909–1975) was best known for his work in American studies.

4. René Wellek (1903–1995) was a Czech-born critic, literary historian, and influential scholar of comparative literature.

What we agreed on tentatively was this: that we would have one or two critics and one or two philosophers on the program—number to be determined by the way things worked out: the idea being to get some difference of approach between the critics but not too much. The critics would do independent analyses of some brief poem. Then the first philosopher would do a commentary on the analyses (or perhaps the composite analysis), probably isolating some problem of imagery involved in the analyses. Presumably, he would make a critique of the terminology used by the critics, pointing out possible contradictions, further implications, asking further questions. The critics would then be given a shot at this commentary to ask some questions themselves, to point out what, if anything, was helpful in the commentary, and what was not. Then the second philosopher would give his commentary on the whole procedure. Our intention would be to present the various stages to the audience so that they could see how the critical problems emerged from a discussion of the concrete poem, and on the last day, take part in the discussion themselves. This is all very tentative. I haven't written to or heard from Greene since I returned, and I may have forgotten some of the details of our conversation.

I've given all this in some detail because I'm very anxious to have you go into the Princeton end of the matter and tell me what you think about it. The whole program may be a waste of time—may have the most negative results. I can see little danger, however, that it might be anything worse than just dull. The plan sketched would allow the critics to indicate that they thought there was nothing to be gained by collaboration with the philosophers—at least with those philosophers—and why, if that should turn out to be the case. But please give me your opinion. And tell me about Greene.

He makes a very good impression. He was eminently fair and reasonable. One of my philosopher friends in New York who apparently doesn't like Greene worth a damn as a person indicated that he thought he could give the kind of critique he proposed very well. Any way, I'd like to hear more about him.

There's no news and I've used up too much paper anyhow. The Warrens are getting settled. All goes pleasantly as a wedding bell—well, almost as pleasantly as that. One doesn't ask too much of some situations. But Miss Emma looks well from her trip in Mexico, and Red seems in fine shape from it. Tinkum asks to be remembered to Caroline and Nancy and joins me in love to all of you.

As ever,
Cleanth

[Princeton]
December 15, 1941

Dear Cleanth:

I've been getting to this letter for weeks. At last the decks are clear enough for me to write a letter.

First, let me apologize for the delay of my article and even more for its quality. I have been through the most difficult autumn of my life: I have done a dozen things badly. For one thing I have a stiff shoulder which may stay with me; and I've had trouble with my eyes. But you know all about that sort of trouble.

I shouldn't have said what I did say about Greene without going into it then and there. Apart from Greene personally my point more generally was that I shuddered to see you and John Ransom being absorbed into academic aesthetics. Greene is a nice fellow, even an able one, particularly as an undergraduate teacher; but his mind is thoroughly conventional and wholly lacking in any kind of distinction. He is that typical Yankee professor who imagines that all problems are solved by programs and committees. His value is the great variety of his interests; his limitation, his naïveté and, beyond a certain point his stupidity. I see no harm in participating with him in a symposium on philosophy and criticism.

There is another matter of much greater importance which I want to bring to the attention of you and Red. I happen to get every week some inside information on the doings of MacLeish;[1] when I add to it what I hear about Van Wyck Brooks' influence and the workings of the Donovan committee,[2] I am convinced that something like a conspiracy is under way to suppress critical thought in the United States. Brooks' doctrine is the official program of the movement. Mark the repudiation of rational intelligence in criticism, the dishonest use of the idea of "primary literature" which comes out of the "life-drive" and "biological patterns"; the spurious regionalism, which is only a dodge which allows him to use a good slogan for a base purpose. It all adds up to Dr. Goebbels. Behind this movement are frustrated men like Van Wyck Brooks and MacLeish, who have an account to settle with modern literature. The Donovan committee is undertaking a high-powered campaign to discredit all the good writing of the past twenty years.

1. The poet Archibald MacLeish (1892–1982) was serving as librarian of Congress.

2. The Donovan Committee was a counterintelligence committee chaired by William Joseph Donovan (1883–1959). In July 1941, Donovan had been appointed by President Roosevelt to be the coordinator of information for the federal government. He went on to become director of the OSS, the precursor of the CIA.

THE SOUTHERN REVIEW OUGHT TO ORGANIZE A SYMPOSIUM ATTACKING THIS MOVEMENT. Say six or eight essays. The situation is far more serious than it was in the last war. I can supply you with material for the attack.

I don't think the attack could defeat this group. It is too powerful. For one thing, the academic profession will be its stooges, because the campaign will play upon the professors' hatred of all literature. But a symposium would stand on the record: it would be there as testimony that we didn't take it lying down.

Of course, H. M. Jones[3] is a part of it, and your editorial was fine. But we must have a more concerted attack. You could get Burke, Blackmur, Wilson, Zabel, and Ransom. I would like to take a shot at Van Wyck Brooks.

Please consider this seriously. It ought to be done without delay. I don't want to sound ominous, but you must consider even the probability that the S.R. may be suppressed. It sounds fantastic.

If the MLA meeting, which I hear is cancelled, comes off, we can talk this over at length; but if the meeting is not held, I hope you and Red will give me your opinion of my proposal RIGHT AWAY. There is no time to lose.

Aff. yrs.
Allen

The Southern Review
Baton Rouge, Louisiana
December 20, 1941

Dear Allen:

I was delighted to have your letter. The Yeats piece is fine—really, very good; and we are mighty glad that it's in and in type. I had heard that you were terribly busy; it was good of you to make an extra effort to get it written. The number will be in the mails in another week.

This Spring number will be our last: we are announcing in the Winter number our probable suspension with Vol. VII, no. 4. I should have written you about this earlier except for two reasons: (1) the end came rather suddenly. There had been rumors for several weeks, but we have faced such rumors off and on for years. The final decision came only today. (2) Since favorable comment on the Southern Review has

---

3. The literary scholar and social critic Howard Mumford Jones (1892–1980) taught at Harvard. Some of his critiques of technological society were sympathetic to Southern Agrarian ideas. As an autodidact, he shared Tate's disdain for professorialism. However, as a literary critic, he was solidly opposed to the approach to literature taken by the New Critics.

been attributed to Red and me—"inspired by us"—we have wanted to lean over backwards in keeping completely quiet about our shaky situation. Particularly is this true in view of the comments which may appear: L.S.U. is apparently considered licensed game for the ironic commentator, anyway. What they *could* make of the war may divert attention completely—or maybe there would have been no comments anyway. But at any rate, Red and I want to be in the position of having done nothing to solicit protests or comment of any kind.

If some such sarcastic comment should appear, I want to be able to say quite honestly that I have had absolutely nothing to do with "inspiring" it. Hence our complete silence to you and to all our other friends. But we talked over the matter with the president, General Hodges, today, and have decided to make a formal announcement at once: it will appear in the Yeats number.

By the way, it is only fair to say the General has been very fair and very sympathetic. I think that he honestly regrets the loss of the Southern Review. Of that both of us are thoroughly convinced; but he has been in the University only six months and you can scarcely blame him if he feels that he has to take the advice of his committee. He has dealt very fairly and straight-forwardly with Red and me, and this has constituted another reason for our saying nothing about the suspension until we had talked over the matter of the announcement with him.

In a way, the loss of the magazine will be a relief. Red and I ought to get some books finished now.

Love to Caroline and Nancy from both of us.

As ever,
Cleanth

I wish I could get to Indianapolis but I can't, nor can Red. I'll send your copy of the Yeats number to Indianapolis.

[Princeton]
December 26, 1941

Dear Cleanth:

I am glad your letter didn't come yesterday. It would have made a sad Christmas. Now I feel like the little boy who has just been told there is no Santa Claus. I can hardly believe it.

For the sake of you and Red it is as you say a blessing. You will get your work done as you never have before. But there ought to be a Southern Review, and there isn't one, nor any prospect of any. John has gone off after positivism and aesthetics: the Kenyon is only a branch of philosophy or rapidly becoming that. The Partisan was never very good; it too will probably fold up, or be suppressed. With the passing of the SR the kind of literary criticism that we have all been interested in is liquidated. And there will be nothing to counteract the vicious trend that I described in my last letter. It is a calamity of the first order.

Had you thought of trying to get somebody else to subsidize the magazine? Of course, that would mean that you and Red would continue to sacrifice yourselves. Would it be worth it? If you would like to try it, let me know: I have a card up my sleeve—not a very high card, it is true, but yet a card; and I would like to play it.

I am not sure that there will be any comment from the press at large. Perhaps Time will say something. In fact I am going to prime Tom Matthews with the news.

I believe that you and Red are being far too noble in the stand you have taken. It is perfectly legitimate for you to tell people and to get expressions of opinion. There's a great deal more than a local situation involved.

I had counted on seeing at least you, and perhaps Red, at Indianapolis. Frankly I am sorry I let myself in for the trip. I had expected to see a good many friends.—I would like to know the reasons for the suspension when you get around to it. Economy, I suppose, was the overt reason.

Our love to you all,
Yrs.
Allen

The Southern Review
Baton Rouge, Louisiana
Dec. 31, 1941

Dear Allen:

Your letter was very heartening. There was no doubt in either of our minds about what your reaction would be. But it is mighty good to have your emphatic statement before me.

Perhaps we are playing the whole business too cagily. But we have been and are trying to save the magazine—that matter is first: and we've been developing our whole strategy toward that end. In so far as we can tell here, there is one hope and only one hope: that is the General. I believe that we have impressed him tremendously with the worth of the magazine. I believe he has real confidence in us. The hope is slight, but it's all that we have. There is little or no hope in the Board or the other higher academic officers. (Exception for the new Dean of the C. of Arts & Sciences, who is fine, but who has already done all he can, and can hardly do more until he is supplied with fresh ammunition.)

If there is enough out-cry, if enough comment comes in, it is just possible that the General will flop over and decide that he wants to keep the magazine after all. The other hope is that we might (mirabile dictu) scare up an angel. But to make either plan work, we had to die dramatically, with as much publicity as possible. Hence our announcement in the Yeats issue. The one thing that would utterly destroy all hope would be to go out in a snuff very quietly.

As far as the general is concerned, we have had to lean over backward in avoiding any impression that the comment and protest from outside were being stirred up by ourselves, for the poison has already been spread: namely, that we could and would wrangle a few complimentary notices.

The reason for cutting us off is, of course, economy. And I suppose that, granted the academic mind of L.S.U., that is a valid reason: to most of our people—those in administration—the S.R. must seem a grievous waste of money. But if there were not this reason, there are many in authority, I am sure, who have other reasons to rejoice at our demise.

We have written to the Rockefeller Foundation, the Carnegie, and the Rosenwald to explore the possibilities of help. We got a polite no from each of them. But if we can find the money anywhere else, we'll go ahead: Red and I want to continue the Review. There's only one matter that we'll insist on, should the question of continuing arise: that is, that the University will promise us a reasonable continuance—3 to 6 years. It's demoralizing to try to continue on a hand-to-mouth basis. One can't plan ahead. Worst of all, an immense amount of time is wasted in trying to argue people into continuing the Review. To run it right, would require more time than we've been able to give it: to try to run it *and* at the same time argue the case that it should be run, [would] take more time than is reasonable.

About the announcement: we had to get an announcement that the General would approve. The first draft was a little too ironical, and the General suggested some little changes. But we have felt that our friends would appreciate the irony anyway. A friend here commented that the announcement gave up too much, but then added that it read like a statement made by us with a gun pointed at our heads. That's all right too. No gun was pointed. But such an interpretation would not assume that the editors were complacent about what had happened.

I hope that we shall have better news to send you.

Merry Xmas to all of you from all of us here.

As ever,
Cleanth

[Handwritten] P.S. I'm sorry that I couldn't go to Indianapolis. As it turned out, however, it's just as well that I was away. If you saw Mizener and Heilman[1] you got all the dope that Red or I could have given.

[Princeton]
January 5, 1942

Dear Red and Cleanth:

You've probably heard from Arthur [Mizener]; but in case you haven't, here's the latest news. About 250 names went on a "plea" to your President at the MLA meeting. Ted Greene, who knows Hodges personally, is writing an individual letter. We're asking Ted Spencer to get one up at Harvard. Zabel will send one from Chicago. Mark [Van Doren] and Jacques Barzun[1] are sending one from Columbia. I have just primed Tom Matthews with some inside dope, and urged upon him an even friendlier than usual comment in TIME.

On Wednesday Dick Blackmur and I will see Moe[2] to ask his advice. I will get in touch with Henry Church this week (former editor of MESURES, and very rich), and point a gun at his head.

I think you all did well to stay away from Indianapolis: your absence made it possible for us to come out in the open. Heilman reported your views. You will probably notice that my name does not appear on any of the protests. I wrote the one from the MLA and started it around; but knowing that I occupy a high place in the demonology of your enemies, I thought it would be better for me not to appear.

It's fine you're doing the symposium. Did I suggest Wilson for an essay? I think he is indispensable. He has a minute knowledge of Van Wyck Brooks, and sees him as we do. I saw Edmund the other day, and I am sure he will write an essay if asked.

---

1. Robert Bechtold Heilman (b. 1906) was a friend and colleague of Brooks's in the LSU English department. In 1948 he moved to Seattle to accept a position as chairman of the English department at the University of Washington, where he remained until his retirement.

1. Jacques Barzun (b. 1907), a French-born author, historian, and literary consultant, began teaching at Columbia University in 1928 and became provost there in 1958.

2. Henry Allen Moe (1894–1975) was president of the John Guggenheim Memorial Foundation.

Is there anything else we can do up here? Willard Thorp is getting up the Princeton protest, and will work with great zeal.

Yrs.
Allen

The irony towards the end of the official announcement went over the heads of a good many people.

[OH]   [Princeton]
1/27/42

Zabel gave me this today in N.Y.: It will appear as an editorial, unsigned. If it doesn't accomplish something, nothing will.

Allen

The Southern Review
Baton Rouge, Louisiana
April 15 [1942]

Dear Allen:

This is a hasty note to give you a bit of information which I think you should have. We have heard from Georgia, as doubtless you have, that their deal is off. Perhaps your plans for next year are already made. I do want to let you know however that an effort is being made on the part of some of the people in the Department here to try to get you.

There are difficulties of two kinds: (1) the same administrative officers who have let Red get away to Minnesota (he takes a professorship there this fall) by failing to meet the Minnesota offer completely might try to head off our getting anybody of your caliber; and (2) there may be difficulty in persuading our people in the department who are predominantly "solid scholars" that they wanted a critic and poet. The second objection does not seem so formidable, however, now as a week ago: hence this letter.

Bob Heilman, whom you met in Indianapolis, broached the matter to me as soon as we knew that Red would probably accept the Minnesota offer.

Since both of us felt that I would probably give the kiss of death to you if I talked about the matter, Bob has been the one to talk to various department members about it, including the department head. He has got a very hopeful response. Perhaps this note is premature. But I write it so that, if you should be at all interested, you may take the possibility into account. I hope that the department head will make his decision and write you in the next weeks. Should he do this, you will of course treat the matter as your first knowledge of it.

If the offer is made, I can't believe that it would be less than three thousand; of course it ought to be more. This is a real hell hole—a real sty. Yet I could hope from purely selfish motives that you and Caroline would be able to accept and would accept. It would certainly be nice for Tinkum and me. At any rate, I rush off this note to you. I shall let you know promptly of any developments.

Cordially,
In haste,
Cleanth

[Handwritten] I've talked this over with nobody except Heilman; I haven't mentioned it yet to Red.

[Princeton]
April 18, 1942

Dear Cleanth:

As you may surmise, I am astonished to get the news that I am even thought of for Red's job. There might be some things on my side standing in the way of my taking it; but I should like very much to have a shot at it anyhow.

My final rejection by the Navy was today. I couldn't get the bad muscle in my shoulder fixed up in time.

If I am not offered the job down there, how about putting Walter Watkins' name up?[1] This is his last year here, and he is almost in a state of collapse about it. He has tried both the Army and the Navy, and they won't take him. You know all about him, and what a good man he is. He would jump at it.

There are doubtless other nice people there, but at this distance you and Tinkum would be the only social and intellectual inducement for us to come.

I think what happened in Georgia was that they naively supposed that enthusiasm was all that's needed to start a magazine. When they got around to the problem of money, it turned out to be tough.[2]

---

1. At the time, W. B. C. Watkins (1907–1957), a literary scholar who specialized in sixteenth- and seventeenth-century English literature, was an instructor at Princeton.
2. The University of Georgia had been negotiating to continue the *Southern Review* under its auspices. The talks broke down when the university was unable to make a financial commitment to the review. Several years later, the *Georgia Review* was founded under the editorship of John Donald Wade.

We're looking forward to seeing Red, and wish we could see you all too. Whatever happens, we are going to Monteagle right after June 6th. Why don't you all come up to see us then?

Yrs.
Allen

[OH]
[Princeton]
[Late April 1942]

Cleanth:

I was astonished to get Kirby's letter.

Here's [a copy of] my reply. I want very much to accept. It is simply a practical question of the salary. Keep me posted, please, so that I will know how to answer his reply to this.

[Allen]

[OH]
[Baton Rouge]
Thursday [April 30 (?), 1942]

Dear Allen—

I hasten to reply to your letter of the 28th. Kirby indicated to me this morning that he had not heard from you yet. I ventured to say that he would probably hear soon—that you were probably thinking matters over. I want to note his anxiety.

What he can do, I do not know. He has already surprised me by having the wit and enterprise to go this far: I feel very much encouraged about him. I am convinced that he is terribly sincere in his determination to get you here if he can. I am the more convinced by realizing what a difficult road ahead he has. *Not* from the department. He has talked over the matter quietly with the key men in the department and has them behind him. And not from the Dean of the Arts College, who is a good man and will, I am sure, go along with the proposal very happily. The difficulty will be with the Dean of the University and with other top officials. Apparently, Kirby thinks he can handle them. I hope that he can. If he can get an offer through I do not know what it will be. It will probably not be as much as it ought to be. I hope that it will be of sufficient size to warrant your coming.

Tinkum suggests that I jot down the following information which might bear on the situation. (She'll write further if matters seem to be working toward a conclusion.) Costs are probably lower in Baton Rouge than in Princeton. Rents are higher than they should be; yet, even so, they are probably lower than Princeton rents. Moreover, many people are leaving the University neighborhood for the Army or Government posts. We know of one very nice new house, for instance, well located which will be vacant for next year with the owner, a u. professor, away on leave. There would be a real differential in your favor on this score. Fuel and heating bills, of course, are low here. Utilities are high, but perhaps lower than Princeton's. Our top gas and electric bill for a month this last winter—we heat with gas—was under $14. Water should not be over $1.50 per month.

Information on these matters may be premature. On the other hand, should Kirby name a figure in the near future, you might find it of some value to have it.

Tinkum and I are, of course, very anxious that matters may go through. From a purely selfish view, we could certainly wish that you and Caroline would come.

I send this off by air mail. Meantime, I shall write at once as soon as I have further word.

As ever,
Cleanth

[OH]   *The Southern Review*
                                        Baton Rouge, Louisiana
                                        May 16 [1942]

Dear Allen—

Kirby tells me that he has offered you a full time teaching place at 3600. I certainly hope—I am selfish here, I know—that you and Caroline can see fit to take it. I wish it were a better offer, but the University is in the grip of war-time economies. I suppose this is as much as could be expected.

It does occur to me, however, that the 12 hrs teaching might take up more of your time than you feel you can reasonably give. If so, I am morally certain that the Department would be glad to try to make arrangements for part-time teaching. What could be done precisely, I don't know, but I am certain that they would be glad to discuss such arrangements.

In any case, I know that already Kirby and the rest of us are at work on plans to arrange courses for you which would involve only small numbers of students and, in so far as possible, choice students.

Actually, if matters go on next year as they have this, we are going to be rather short on students in general—which has only this compensation: that classes are small, paper work is light, and student conferences are not oppressive. At least it gives one time for other things.

I should not say any more to urge you: to do that would be to let my personal desire to have you and Caroline here outweigh, perhaps, other considerations. Yet I do think that a year here under the conditions I envisage might allow more time than one might think to get some writing done. (Red says you are thinking of putting in next year on a novel.) The winter climate is not bad, classes will be small, and there is a group of rather pleasant people to see. Anyway, not only Tinkum and I but many others hope that you all may come.

Love from both of us,
Cleanth

Don't hesitate to write or wire for further information if there are questions that Tinkum and I might answer.

Creative Arts Program
Princeton University
Princeton, New Jersey
May 18, 1942

Dear Cleanth:

I have an extra carbon of my reply to Kirby, so I enclose it.

I confess that, considering the parlous times, it took more nerve than I thought I had to turn down this job, which by any applicable standards is a very good one.

If the offer had been for $4000, with not more than 9 hours of teaching, I might have taken it. Here's the reasoning I followed in saying no. The combined publishers' advances of Caroline and myself will amount to $3800 for the year beginning August 1st. The move to Baton Rouge on a salary of $3600 would mean, deducting moving expenses, an actual salary of not more than $3300. The 12 hour schedule would have made it very difficult for me to do any concentrated writing. So there you are. With $4000 and 9 hours I might have taken the job for an added year of security, and postponed concentrated work on my novel for another year—which I should have been loathe to do.

No decision like this can make me angry, and I have certain regrets; but I saw nothing else to do. I am particularly sorry to have put you and others in the department to the trouble of going out for me. Please give my thanks to Bob Heilman. By the way, I am sure that I should have got on well with Kirby; I liked extremely the tone of his letters.

Now how about Walter Watkins? If there's any chance for him, won't you wire me, so that I can get some pressure from Princeton? Red told me you will probably ask Arthur Mizener. There's not much choice in ability; yet it remains that Arthur has not published a book and he has a good job next year at Rochester.

I don't need to tell you that Red did a brilliant job here. I am particularly proud that you and Red, of the eight Mesures lecturers so far, made the greatest hit. Randall [Jarrell] alas came out a bad eighth.

We leave for Monteagle on June 6th. How about coming up?

Yrs.
Allen

Monteagle, Tennessee
August 4, 1942

Dear Cleanth:

Andrew [Lytle] went over to Sewanee yesterday to talk to Guerry[1] and learned that you have been offered the Review. This was fine news, and we hope you can take it; but we are doubtful, for two reasons: they can't pay you enough, and the Review can't pay contributors. And Guerry can't get it into his head that the contributors must be paid.

If you don't take the job, God knows who will get it, and there will be another lost opportunity. Andrew has drilled into him the fact that he (Guerry) is in a position to make history, but he doesn't know what it means, although he seems to use the phrase.

I write this letter for a specific purpose but only in case you turn the job down. I hope you will, in that case, give Guerry as your chief reason for refusing, the fact that the Review doesn't pay.

My connection with this situation is as follows. Up to about ten days ago I headed his list of candidates as being the most available—that is, without a job, etc. But he had not been able to put me over with his Board, five amiable old gentlemen who shook with terror every time my name was mentioned. Andrew says that Guerry's tactic was to work them around to me gradually. I saw no reason for this, since I could not take a quarterly that doesn't pay; so I wrote him a letter saying that although he had not talked to me, it was well-known that I was being considered, that I could not take the job if it was offered, and that it was not worthwhile to publish a review for professors who give their work away for professional advancement.

In short, I hoped to use the situation to force upon him as dramatically as possible the necessity for paying his contributors. It seems that all he got out of the letter was that I didn't want to be considered any longer.

1. Vice Chancellor Alexander Guerry (1890–1948) of the University of the South was one of the most distinguished leaders in that school's history.

As a matter of fact, I am definitely in a position to raise some money for the Review, but I have never been able to tell him this, since he would not openly discuss the matter with me.

To be quite frank, I've had this money in prospect for about six months. It is not enough to make up the whole subsidy of a review, but it would supplement an existing small budget, such as the Sewanee Review has. I deliberately kept it away from The Kenyon Review (I'm not sure I could have got it for John anyhow) because I knew all along that John would raise his fund, as he has, and I wanted it for the Sewanee Review. For it seems to me absolutely necessary to have another review in addition to the Kenyon, which has become more and more specialized in its scope.

The situation has got so tangled because there's so much secrecy that I have despaired of doing anything with it. I wanted you to know what has been happening. Guerry is a really fine man whose great virtue is his absolute honesty and whose defect is literal-mindedness. His experience has been such that he cannot possibly know what to do with a critical review. I think it is evidence of the success of Andrew's efforts to educate him that he has offered you the place. Two years ago you would have been wholly beyond his imagination. It is rumored that some of the Review's Board wanted to invite Alfred Noyes[2] (this is a perfect Sewanee gesture), but Guerry said flatly no. That is greatly in his favor, for not one out of ten college presidents could have made the distinction.

Please let me know what you expect to do. If you can possibly take the job, I hope you will do so. One trouble with this prospective money is that it would come from connections of mine whose interest is almost entirely personal; but that might be changed. I just don't know.

I gather that you are in Chicago, since Andrew says that Guerry saw you there. It would probably be unwise to let Guerry know that I know you have been offered the place. He told Andrew in confidence.

Why don't you all come by here on the way South? We'd love to see you. The Lowells are with us and will remain all winter. Manson [Radford] came by for a few days recently on his way from New Orleans back to New York. We are all working hard, Caroline, Jean, and I on our novels; Cal on Jonathan Edwards.

Aff. yours.
Allen

---

2. Alfred Noyes (1880–1959) was an English poet of strongly antimodernist views. The *Sewanee Review* had long been a bastion of the southern genteel tradition in letters. Tate was to change that in a few years when he briefly became its editor.

[OH]   Sunday
                                                    1321 Forest Court
                                                    Ann Arbor, Mich.
                                              (University of Michigan)
                                                       [August 1942]

Dear Allen—

It was good to hear from you yesterday. I have just sent a letter to
Guerry declining the invitation to come to Sewanee. We did meet in
Chicago merely because that was a convenient intermediate point.

Guerry called me up by telephone two weeks ago, and said that he
was looking for an editor. I indicated in my conversation over the phone
that I probably could not come, particularly since I was getting a good
deal more than Sewanee's top, and that, if I were willing to take less,
my obligations to dependents were heavy, and that in fairness to them,
I couldn't cut down at this time. Before we got to that point in the
conversation, I had promised, however, to meet Guerry in Chicago if
he liked.

Thinking that the latter part of the conversation pretty clearly ruled
out the need for any further conference, I was surprised when Guerry
wired a few days later, setting the appointment. We had a long talk last
Saturday, and I promised to think matters over and send him word.

I was very favorably impressed with him as a man, and he shows so
much more sense than most college presidents that you get a shock from
the contrast. Andrew (or whoever is responsible) certainly deserves to
be complimented. Unfortunately, I didn't know when I talked to him
last week what was up. Had I known, I would have made the point of
payments to contributors much more strongly. I'll try, however, to give
you some account of what was said on the matter, so that you will know
how the land lies.

Though I indicated to him that payment to contributors would not be
a decisive point with me, I did indicate most emphatically that the fact
that the *Sewanee* didn't pay would create special problems. I pointed out,
for instance, that if I took it, it would be with the full knowledge that
I would have to make of it a very different kind of magazine than the
Kenyon or the *S.R.*—that I should have, for my own part, to gamble on
being able to make of it something new, and something which I couldn't
guarantee would be a success.

I went over the state of affairs when L.S.U. had part in the *Southwest
Review* and the limitations set by the fact that it couldn't pay. I went
into the case of mss. lost to the *S.R.* because it couldn't pay on receipt of
ms. I went into the problems of developing young authors and losing
them to magazines that could pay, pointing out a number of instances

where the *S.R.*, though paying, had lost stuff to the *Atlantic*, etc., etc. I made the point that the editor was often put in the position of having to tell an author who could get better pay elsewhere to go on and take it, since to take any other position would be unethical and would be to take advantage of friendship.

I am extremely glad, in view of your letter, that so much of our conversation was devoted to these matters. For, though I couldn't, without making a condition of all that I had said, make the non-payment of contributors the decisive factor in my letter of refusal, I have indicated the importance of the matter as definitely as I could. Anyway, I've gone as far as I could go with the matter. I hope for the best.

In the course of the conversation, I asked whether he had thought of you as a possible editor—that I thought the *VA.Qu.* people had been damn fools not to get you or some such person—that I asked the question merely because I knew that you were, or were to be, at Monteagle, near at hand.

Guerry then replied that you had written to say that you had heard that your name was being considered and that you couldn't take a magazine that didn't pay. I indicated at once that I had asked merely out of curiosity—that I had not heard from you for some time—and that his phone call had been the only word I had had on the subject.

I did go on, however, to indicate why I thought that you felt as you did—the difficulties of doing a good job without payment, the ethical position in which such an editor found himself, with the magazine's interests cutting one way and his obligations to a young writer or a friend cutting the other, etc.

I wish to God you get the place on your own terms. With the rise of MacLeish–V. W. Brooks and Co., we need a fighting magazine in particular at this time. Do let me hear how it all comes out. I hope that I have not queered the possibility of your going in. I don't think I have. I rather think that I may have helped. But I was working quite in the dark.

It's been cool here. But I have been working very hard, and the tempo is increasing. The students are extremely good, and keep on the jump. I've been doing papers or writing all this weekend. (This may account for the jumbled incoherence of this letter.) I'll try to write a decent screech a little later. Regards to Caroline, Jean, Andrew, Edna [Lytle], and Cal from both of us. By the way, I hope that Caroline will be pleased with our account of "Old Red" in the fiction book.[1] The ms. goes to Crofts next week. Little news from Red who's gone on to Minnesota.

---

1. Gordon's story "Old Red" was included in Brooks and Warren's *Understanding Fiction* (New York: Appleton-Crofts, 1943).

By the way, be prepared for a renewal of the offer to L.S.U. for next fall. I think that Kirby means to renew it. I hope you and Caroline will accept.

As ever,
Cleanth

I don't need to say that the stuff about my conversation with Guerry is in confidence. I'm afraid I may have given him the impression that I regarded his offer a little casually, which isn't my feeling about it or him. But I have wanted to give you a complete picture.

I wish we could drop by Monteagle on the way back. I'm afraid we can't. Our tickets are already purchased and we'll be broke by that time.

[OH]   September 10 [1942]
                                                  1707 Cloverdale
                                                  Baton Rouge

Dear Allen:

Whatever happened about the *Sewanee Review*? After I wrote to you, I had a further letter from Guerry in which he very kindly asked me to reconsider. I wrote him I had made up my mind definitely. Naturally, I've had no means of knowing what further has occurred, or whether anything has occurred. Do let me know. Certainly, I hope that Guerry has put the matter up to you. If Andrew is on the scene, perhaps he could steer it. Anyway, I hope that matter works out.

Michigan was very nice, but very exhausting. I got a great deal done, but I got little time for seeing the country or writing letters or reading. Now, Tinkum and I have been home three weeks, and I am still far behind in those matters though Tinkum has cleared up her yard and garden and thus has something to show for her time. The climate does make a difference.

The university here is gradually disintegrating: most of our good men are now in the army or in government jobs; the General seems completely under the sway of the corrupt deans. There is little to do about the whole situation except to hope that matters will get bad enough—and get bad dramatically enough—to force some sort of change. Meantime, I hope to dig in and get a good deal more writing done this winter. I have a couple of books on which I've made a good start. I may call on you to look over them later in the year. (Did you see, by the way, Krutch's stupid article in *The Nation* last month?[1] V. W. Brooks, Krutch, Mary Colum[2] and the rest of

1. Joseph Wood Krutch, "Open Letter on Critics and Criticism," *Nation* 155 (November 28, 1942): 95–96.
2. The Irish American writer Mary Colum (d. 1957) was a frequent contributor to such major journals as the *Dial*, *New Republic*, *Yale Review*, and *Saturday Review*.

that group have apparently just discovered some of the books on modern criticism. They rally very manfully to defend their vested interests.)

I had hoped to go to New York for the English Institute this year, and expected to come back by way of Monteagle, taking advantage of the invitation that we stop off on our way back from Ann Arbor. But travel funds have been done away with by the university. The action was taken just a few weeks ago, and I decided, after looking over my bank statement, to let the trip go. But I do wish we could have some talk, and it would have been good to see all of you there. Are the Lowells still at Monteagle? And are the Lytles there too? Please give them our best regards. Tinkum asks to be remembered to Caroline and yourself.

As ever,
Cleanth

How are the novels coming? And is yours underway? Nobody can predict events here, but I am morally certain that the offer made you a few months ago will be made again for next year. Certainly, it will be made if I am able to tell Kirby that you are likely to consider it favorably. My motives and Tinkum's are thoroughly selfish in the matter, but we do hope that you and Caroline will be willing, and free, to come.

I've had a number of notes from Red, but most of the space has been taken up with details of the fiction book. I've had little news of him except that he and C[linina] are in Minneapolis now and preparing to settle down for the school year.

[OH]   Monteagle
                                                     September 19, 1942

Dear Cleanth:

Yours of Sept. 10th has had to wait until we were moved to our winter quarters, a house with a furnace next to Andrew's place. We are now installed, and we look forward to a good winter—with the army always in the distance.

It seems that Guerry asked nearly everybody in the South (including John Wade) to take the Review; nobody would have it. At last he asked Andrew to act as Managing Editor, with Tudor Long[1] as nominal Editor. Andrew accepted: he gets $600.00 extra and a six-hour teaching schedule in history. But he doesn't like it. He knows he is not fitted for it. As a non-academic writer, he knows few of the good professors who would give him articles; and having been lost in De Soto since 1936,[2] he has no literary "contacts." He simply doesn't know who is doing what.

---

1. Seymour Tudor Long was a popular English professor at Sewanee for many years.
2. Lytle's biographical novel about Hernando de Soto, *At the Moon's Inn,* had been published in 1941.

Don't you think the Fugitive-Agrarians ought to rally and give him at least one article or story or poem? It would be a great help. I suggest this with bad grace because I have nothing to give, unless a little later a section of my novel turns out to be suitable. What about a part of your new book?

Andrew says that at least Alex Guerry realizes that the Review editorship is not a high honor that people are eager to get. Perhaps he will see the necessity of paying his contributors. But at any rate, Andrew is right in taking it over. He can't do much with it at present, but it is potentially an organ for our group, if later on money can be found.

It was a little stupid of Guerry not to make Andrew the editor. Mr. Long is a fine man, but is unknown, and he will not attract money. The money I mentioned to you in my last letter might be available if Andrew's tenure were permanent. It is only for one year.

Is Katherine Anne in Baton Rouge?[3] She wrote me in July that she had accepted the job that I turned down, but that she might not go at the last minute. I wrote her a letter in care of the English Dept., L.S.U. and I hope it will be forwarded if she is not there.

You may say to Kirby whenever it seems discreet that I will accept an offer for next year at any time he cares to make it. I wrote him that I would, and I am still of that mind.

The Krutches and the Colums will make hay during the war. They control the N.Y. reviews, which will endure; but ours will not.

We were mighty sorry that you and Tinkum couldn't come by to see us; and so were the Lowells. Cal goes to the army in November,[4] but Jean expects to stay with us until she finishes her novel.

I am having a hell of a time with my novel: every sentence must compete with the war.

Aff. yrs.
Allen

[OH] Monteagle
October 9, 1942

Dear Cleanth:

It is now Guggenheim season, as I am reminded by requests for recommendations. Are you going to apply? I heard nothing from you after I passed Moe's hint on to you last winter, and I'm wondering

3. Katherine Anne Porter had accepted a teaching offer from LSU but then declined it because she had simultaneously accepted a position at another school.
4. Robert Lowell went on to declare his conscientious objector's status and was imprisoned for his resistance to the wartime draft.

whether you ever got it. Moe told me that you *ought to apply.* I believe the applications must be in by November 15.

What's the news?

> Yrs. in haste,
> Allen

[OH]   Monteagle
                                                 10/19/42

Dear Cleanth:

It's fine news you are coming. We are all hoping that Tinkum will come too, and that the Lytles won't have room for you both, so that you will have to stay with us.

Anyhow, we are expecting to see a great deal of you—one or both.

> Yrs.
> Allen

[OH]   Monteagle, Tennessee
                                        January 10, 1943

Dear Cleanth:

You may now expect to have us in Baton Rouge next year. I have heard from Kirby and have accepted, since I assume that back of the renewal is the same offer he made last year.

What's your news? We are thriving here: all work goes well.

Love to you both.

> Yrs.
> Allen

[OH]   Louisiana State University
                                     Baton Rouge, Louisiana
                                     Jan. 14 [1943]

Dear Allen—

I hasten to answer your note which came in yesterday. It was mighty fine to hear that you will accept an offer, and I hope that satisfactory terms can be worked out. I feel sure that they can be. I mention the matter of terms, only because everything here is so uncertain as to students and classes.

We have now so few advanced students (and may in the future, of course have even less) that Kirby is fearful that the kind of classes in which you are interested may not materialize. I have told him that I thought, if the worst came to the worst, you might not be unwilling to teach students in our introduction to poetry, drama, and fiction. In the poetry section we are going to use *Understanding Poetry* and the same general method is to be used with the fiction and drama. Of course, the classes in creative writing, etc. may materialize after all. This is a big school—we may have enough advanced students after all.

Anyway, Kirby will write you (or perhaps, has written already) about such matters. He is anxious to be honest about the situation, and not seem to get you here by false representations. I think that the best part of the matter is that he is eager to get you here whatever the conditions are. That speaks well for his sense and imagination. It will be a pure delight for Tinkum and me to have you and Caroline in town. We are counting on it.

My draft status remains thus far unchanged. But I have no idea what the next day will bring—not [the] best atmosphere in which to work—but it's all one can do.

Did you see my review of Kazin?[1] I never could get it right—not in tone. But it is a horrible book, and the more dangerous, because it sounds (or will sound to so many people) so plausible.

Tinkum sends love to Caroline and Nancy and you.

As ever,
Cleanth

[OH]   Monteagle, Tennessee
                                              January 16, 1943

Dear Cleanth:

Just a note.

When I replied to Kirby I said that I assumed that the terms would be the same as offered last year, but I referred only to hours and salary. Everybody knows that people have got to teach what they can under the circumstances. I am not only prepared but eager to cooperate in every respect. You might tell him this. In many respects I prefer under-classmen to advanced students.—I am sure that it can all be worked out. Kirby seems to want me. I want to come. That is enough for reasonable people to work on.

Caroline is writing to Tinkum. I suppose we shall send Nancy to Sophie Newcomb—if she doesn't flunk here in June.

In haste,
Allen

1. "Mr. Kazin's America," review of *On Native Grounds,* by Alfred Kazin, *Sewanee Review* 51 (1943): 52–61.

Monteagle, Tennessee
February 3, 1943

Dear Cleanth:

After I wrote to Mr. Kirby that I was accepting his offer, I meant to write you a note too, thanking you for all your good offices; but I have been so completely sunk in a lot of new poems that I have neglected my manners. Here, then, are my best thanks, and a great deal of pleasure in the prospect of being with you next year.

Mr. Kirby's offer wasn't as good as last year's but I felt that he was doing the very best he could under war conditions, and that it was up to me to meet him half way. I was glad to do it. I like his letters and I am sure that I will like him.

Andrew has got together a very creditable issue, the leading items being your magnificent review of Kazin and a very fine poem by [Wallace] Stevens which I got for him. This poem is one of Stevens' best, in the class with Sunday Morning.

I should have written you sooner for another reason: to tell you not to take seriously the sonnets I sent you. They have been completely rewritten, and may receive further revisions. If they do, I will send them on; meanwhile please discard the old version. They were the first poetry I had written in a very long time, and that version was a mere warming up. As soon as some of the others are finished I will send them and ask for your comment.[1]

We are all well. Jean has finished her novel. Cal has written about twenty poems, very fine—the first things he has done which really convince.[2] I have just about persuaded Oscar Williams to publish some of them in his new anthology.[3] Our love to Tinkum.

Aff.
Allen

Monteagle, Tennessee
May 4, 1943

Dear Cleanth:

I am on the spot.

MacLeish has fired Auslander[1] from the Consultantship in American Poetry, and is creating a new Chair (as he called it) which will

---

1. "More Sonnets at Christmas," *Kenyon Review* 5 (spring 1943): 186–88.
2. Jean Stafford's first novel, *Boston Adventure,* and Robert Lowell's first collection of poems, *Land of Unlikeness,* were both published in 1944.
3. The poet Oscar Williams (1895–1959) was a prolific anthologist of poetry.

1. The poet Joseph Auslander (1897–1965) was the first consultant in poetry to the Library of Congress. MacLeish fired him in his capacity as the librarian of Congress.

comprehend Auslander's work and a lot more: Consultant in American Letters. I have been asked to be the first incumbent of this job.[2] T. S. Eliot has tentatively agreed to be second.

I have written to Mr. Kirby about my dilemma, for I feel that I can accept MacLeish's offer only with Mr. Kirby's consent.

I have proposed a "leave of absence" from LSU, since there seems to be a precedent for being on leave before actually taking on the job, i.e., Ted Spencer as visiting professor from Cambridge at Harvard before ever going to Cambridge. There are other less conspicuous examples.

You will see that for a free lance like myself the job at the Library of Congress is made to order, and that having held it I would have certain advantages later on.

What is your view of this? Please write me frankly. Doubtless Mr. Kirby will consult you.

We haven't heard from you all in ages. I think Jean [Stafford] heard from Tinkum some time ago that your father was very ill. I hope he is better now.

In haste,
Allen

Isn't Andrew doing a fine job? If he can only keep it up.

Louisiana State University
Baton Rouge, Louisiana
Nov. 17 1943

Dear Allen:

This is a belated acknowledgment of your fine translation of the "Pervigilium Veneris" which Tinkum and I have thoroughly enjoyed.[1] It is handsomely printed and makes a very beautiful book. My Latin

2. Tate arrived in Washington in September 1943 to assume the post of consultant in poetry at the Library of Congress, a precursor to today's post of poet laureate. Tate's specific responsibilities were not heavy. During his tenure, he occupied himself with expanding the library's series of recordings of poets reading from their own works. With the assistance of his old Tennessee friend Frances ("Fanny") Cheney, he compiled *Sixty American Poets, 1896–1944, a Checklist* (Washington, D.C.: Library of Congress, 1945), which is notable for the brief critical remarks by Tate on his contemporaries. During Tate's tenure as consultant in poetry, the position grew in stature to become what it is today, a genuine bully pulpit for poetry and letters. "It was Tate who gave the consultantship credibility with his peers, made the telling recommendations for appointments, and drew other poets to the Library's cause by the force of his reputation and stature. And it was Tate to whom the Fellows [of the Library of Congress] turned as a leader and a spokesman" (William McGuire, *Poetry's Catbird Seat: The Consultantship in Poetry at the Library of Congress, 1937–1987* [Washington, D.C.: Library of Congress, 1988]).

1. *The Vigil of Venus: Pervigilium Veneris* (Cummington, Mass.: Cummington Press, 1943).

is very rusty now, but it was pretty solidly acquired, and comes back without too much loss when the occasion appears. Tinkum is still a very good Latinist; so together we have enjoyed seeing what you have done. It is a pure pleasure to see the way you have handled stanza XIX, for example—reflecting on what most translators would do with it. And the last stanzas are impressively beautiful. Incidentally, your "Introductory Note" is in itself excellent.

How do you like your work? And does it give you much leisure? I stay on a treadmill here—not a very unpleasant one, but the time slips by at a terrific rate. I am teaching three army sections still—bright enough boys, drawn from all over the country, but who are victims of one of the worst educational systems that any country ever had. Tinkum stays hard at work in her father's plant. It's a very healthful life, but on the dull side. I look forward to getting away for some talk, and some visiting. May it be soon.

Meantime I am trying to finish up the critical book. I've talked to you about it before. The Princeton lecture is to be the first chapter. I enclose in this letter an offprint (from the *Sewanee*) of an essay on Pope which is to be another chapter.[2] I've just finished a short one on Shakespeare which is to be my second chapter, and one which I should like you to look over if you can spare the time.

Have you thought further on the book about the South which we talked of at Monteagle last fall? I still can't see the form of it, though I can sense some of the comments which it ought to contain, and I persist in feeling that it ought to be done in the near future. I have even tinkered with the idea that it might be composed of a group of separate essays modeled somewhat on a cross between Swift's Drapier's Letters and Pascal's Provincial Letters. But perhaps that wouldn't work.

Anyway, it ought to be thoroughly clear—ought to make its points even patiently clear—ought to name names (or at least come as close to that as the law will allow) and ought *not* to be evangelical in tone. In one sense it ought to be even more detached in tone than were the essays in *Who Owns America* or *I'll Take My Stand*. I still think that Southern education, Southern literature (and the Southern end of the New York book racket) ought to bear the brunt of the attack.

Perhaps these last two paragraphs are worth nothing more than evidence that I want, and need, some talk with you. Our best to Caroline and Nancy. We are still hoping that all of you will be down here next year.

As ever,
Cleanth

2. "The Case of Miss Arabella Fermor: A Re-examination." *Sewanee Review* 51 (1943): 505–24. Brooks was at work on *The Well Wrought Urn*.

The Library of Congress
Washington, D.C.
November 22, 1943

Dear Cleanth:

I am delighted to get yours of the 17th. I had begun to think that you had slipped into a bayou and Tinkum didn't have time to notify your friends because she was still looking for you. I had already read with admiration your piece on Miss Arabella, but I'm glad to have this copy. The book ought to be very fine. What else besides this and the Mesures lecture will be in it?

Here's some news for you. Alex Guerry has done two things, one private and the other public, respectively: (1) he has decided that I don't wear horns or bite; and (2) he has raised money to pay contributors and offered me the Sewanee Review. I have accepted, as of July 1, 1944—after my job here is over. Archie [MacLeish] had a big plan to keep me here indefinitely, and I thanked God I had committed myself for only a year. The money raised is $1,000 per annum; I have added $800.00 a year for three years, from sources I mentioned to you a year ago. I can increase it next year. The donors had already given too much away this year to give more and keep their gifts under the 15 per cent exempted by the income tax.

So here is a chance for us to get back on the beam again. Now what is this trip you are planning? Is it eastward? I want very much to talk the whole thing over with you. You are the only present Advisory Editor I want to keep, and I hope you will consent. And I want to talk about the Southern book. We might write it serially for the Review.[1]

I just haven't been able to write Red about his novel, I was so disappointed in it.[2]

I may go to Sewanee for Christmas. Why couldn't you meet me there, if you can't come up here? Let's consider this possibility.

Love to Tinkum.

Aff.

Allen

[Handwritten] Guerry hasn't announced the news yet, but will shortly, as soon as I tell him to. Meanwhile, please keep it to yourself.

1. This project was never realized.
2. Robert Penn Warren's *At Heaven's Gate* (New York: Harcourt, Brace and Co., 1943).

Louisiana State University
Baton Rouge, Louisiana
April 24, 1944

Dear Allen:

I am heartily ashamed of myself for having been so laggard in writing. But I have had little to say, and I have been plagued with dozens of little things which have taken up most of my time and left me too tired out at the end of the day to feel like writing a letter.

But I have something to show for my trouble—Heilman and I are far along with our *Understanding Drama*,[1] my critical book is nearly finished, and the first volume of my brass-bound, valve-in-head research project, the Percy Letters, is about ready to be published.[2] I have finished too, as part of the critical book, an essay on the imagery of *Macbeth* which I am anxious for you and Caroline to see. Red has seen it, and apparently likes it. It is to be published soon in *The American Bookman* (do you know anything about this magazine, by the way?) and I shall send you a copy as soon as it appears.[3]

When do you and Caroline go to Sewanee?[4] Can you plan to come here for a visit during the fall? Tinkum and I would like nothing better than to come up to Sewanee for some talk; but her father's plant still has war orders and its problematical whether she can get off.

Besides, it's your time to come to see us and I think that both of you might enjoy being in New Orleans again. That can still be managed in spite of transportation difficulties. Anyway, one way or the other, we are anxious to see you all and have some talk. Let's all try to manage it without too much delay once you get as near as Sewanee.

By the bye, having mentioned Sewanee, there is a matter which I've intended writing you about for some time. We have here at the University an Austrian scholar who seems to me one of the most able men that I have met in a long time. He has all the German thoroughness plus imagination and ideas. He and his wife are both charming—pleasant

1. Brooks and Robert Heilman collaborated on *Understanding Drama* (New York: Henry Holt and Co., 1945).
2. Brooks and David Nichol Smith, one of his tutors at Oxford, edited over an extended period the correspondence of Bishop Thomas Percy (1729–1811), an Anglican cleric and antiquarian. *The Percy Letters*, ed. David Nichol Smith and Cleanth Brooks, vol. 1, *The Correspondence of Thomas Percy and Edmond Malone*, ed. Arthur Tillotson, was published in 1944 by LSU Press.
3. The essay was not published by *American Bookman*. After being given as the Bergen lecture at Yale in December 1944, it was published as "Shakespeare as a Symbolist Poet," *Yale Review* 34 (autumn 1944–summer 1945): 642–65. It became chapter 2 of *The Well Wrought Urn*.
4. The Tates arrived in Sewanee in early summer.

people to be with, and his knowledge of philosophy, history, and politics is astonishing. *The Southern Review* never could find a person of quite this caliber for its philosophical essays. I think that Eric Voegelin is the answer for the *Sewanee*.[5]

He is something of a Spenglerian—I say "something" because I don't know his position thoroughly. But I do know that he thinks our civilization is in a pretty bad way and that a religious revival—something comparable to the coming of Christ—is necessary to save it. But though he takes this position, he is not, I believe, a Roman Catholic, burdened as so many of their gentry are with the need to do constant apologetics for Mother Church.

He sharpened his wits and his claws by debating with the Marxist dialecticians (at the Communist works school) at the University of Vienna; but was [a] good enough prognosticator of events in our world and time to leave Austria three days after *Anschluss*.[6] He is at present half-way through a two volume work on Nietzsche which simply overturns the present misconceptions. Here, again, I simply am not familiar enough with his MS. to do more than suggest his thesis, but I can say that he rearranges the whole picture around the thesis that Nietzsche was the first—or nearly the first—to detect, and refer to its proper significance, the dissolution of Christian values under the impact of a bourgeois civilization.

Best of all, Voegelin can write damned good English—at least the sections of his work that I have seen are good, lively prose. I have suggested that he send you some stuff, though I have naturally not committed you or the *Review* in any way. Perhaps I am over-sanguine about him, but he looks to me very good indeed.

A note from Ransom indicates that Red is probably not going to Washington—though he said no more than this on the subject, and I take it that at the time he saw him Red was still undecided. But—did Red actually come to Washington without Miss Emma? It seems hard to believe.

I have not heard from Red in some time. I must write him in the next few days. Caroline's letter indicated that you all must have had a full

5. Eric Voegelin (1901–1985), the German-born political philosopher, was a close friend of Brooks's at LSU and later taught at Stanford. His multivolume *Order and History* is one of the major philosophical works of this century. Brooks regarded Voegelin as his "mentor" and once said that Voegelin "could have taught in eight different academic departments at LSU," such was his prodigious learning.

6. Brooks is referring to the March 1938 invasion of Austria by Hitler's forces, which achieved the incorporation of that country into the Nazi empire.

and a trying winter. We are so far in arrears with our letters to everybody, that Caroline's letter constitutes at the moment our "sole link with the outside world." How is Katherine Anne and where is she? What news, if any, did Red have? Is Cinina still in bed or not? (This last question at least won't be in any letter we have from Minneapolis.)⁷ But Caroline's letter, nice as it was, didn't give your Washington home address. Please let us have that.

All our best to you and Caroline and Nancy.

Cleanth

P.S. Heilman asks to be remembered. By the way, he and I are tinkering with the idea of doing a modern "Battle of the Moderns" on the Swift model, with the Ancients and the Moderns in battle array. John Dewey is the obvious generalissimo of the forces of the moderns, and Barzun, Howard Mumford Jones, and Kazin are obvious leaders. But the difficulty is to decide who must be left out on the Moderns' side—there are more candidates than places. Do not be surprised to find yourself among the Ancients. We hope that we can provide you with appropriate company.

[OH]   Library of Congress
                                              Washington, D.C.
                                              April 27, 1944

Dear Cleanth:

I am so harassed that I can do little more than tell you what pleasure it gave me. By all means ask Voegelin to send me something. I can't promise to do anything about pure philosophy; the arts and the intellectual climate must be our main approach.

Now. How about *you* doing me a review of De Voto's *The Literary Fallacy*? I'd like to see him deflated, but you may like him if you want to! Anyhow, please write it. Is there anything else you are interested in?¹

Love to Tinkum.

Yrs.
Allen

Red was more like himself here a month ago than I've seen him in ten years.

7. Cinina Warren was a notorious hypochondriac; the Warrens were still living in Minneapolis at this time.

1. Brooks never reviewed the book by Bernard De Voto (1897–1955), an American literary scholar and journalist whose ideas were antithetical to those of the New Critics.

The Sewanee Review
Sewanee, Tennessee
July 31, 1944

Dear Cleanth:

I am writing this letter to put the Indian sign on you, or, as Don [Davidson] would phrase it, the poet's curse. You haven't answered any of my letters in months, and I don't expect an answer to this one. I have thought it advisable to reorganize the whole staff of the *Review,* and following John's precedent with the *Kenyon* I believe it a good idea to fire all the associate editors and start over again. There is a very specific reason for this, and I am sure that you will understand and approve it. It is simply that most of our crowd have been on most of the magazines for the past ten or fifteen years, virtually taking in one another's washing, and I think it advisable to make our influence more effective by concealing it.

I didn't get a single line from you about the review of De Voto's awful book, so I had to turn it over to Arthur Mizener. When are you going to write something for me? Have you anything on hand now that I could use for the winter issue?

It was agony getting settled here, but we are now settled and enjoying ourselves tremendously. We have an enormous old 1890 house. How about you and Tinkum coming to stay awhile?

Ever yours,
Allen

The Sewanee Review
Sewanee, Tennessee
August 10, 1944

Dear Cleanth:

Caroline liked your letter very much, and I am very much pleased to have yours of August 3rd and 5th. The poem is very remarkable, and I hope that you will let me cool it a little before I attempt a considered judgment of it. I haven't read Poe's story for many years, but every detail of it is fresh in my mind.[1]

I like the piece you wrote on Lundberg.[2] I read Lundberg's preposterous essay at the time. Why don't you take a fresh start and write me an essay on the South, any phase of it which happens to roil you

---

1. Brooks's poem "The Maelstrom" was based on Poe's story "Into the Maelstrom." For the text of the poem, see the Appendix.
2. Apparently, this essay was not published. George Andrew Lundberg was a social scientist who wrote frequently for the popular reviews of the day.

most. In fact, there are numerous essays that you ought to write for me, but meanwhile, I hope you will send me either the Milton or the Yeats chapter, or both, from your book *[The Well Wrought Urn].*

I wish you had accepted the Chicago offer.[3] I have an essay for the October issue by a Chicago follower named Trowbridge;[4] it is very poor; but my hired assassin is John, who, I am sure, will demolish him. John's essay is not yet in.

Katherine Anne's address is 3106 P Street, N.W., Washington, D.C. She has been ill recently, apparently an infection of the lung.

Affectionate regards to you and Tinkum,

Ever yours,

Allen

The Sewanee Review

Sewanee, Tennessee

August 18, 1944

Dear Cleanth:

I sent your poem anonymously to a mutual friend of ours, who shall also remain anonymous, and got back from him the enclosed commentary, which I thought you might want to see.[1] I want to think about the poem a little longer if you don't mind, and I thought that you might want to consider it again in the light of this criticism.

Yours in haste,

Allen

I am trying not to guess who wrote it (I am succeeding, too) so that I shall have an unprejudiced view of it. I should think it a rather extreme form of academic poem (the kind I'm likely to produce) by a person who has practiced the Empson kind of criticism a good deal.[2] It is so

3. Robert Hutchins, president of the University of Chicago, had recruited Brooks for a professorship at the university; however, the strong dominance of the Aristotelians in the English department under the leadership of R. S. Crane, a severe critic of Brooks's work, made the generous offer unappealing.

4. Hoyt Trowbridge, "Aristotle and the 'New Criticism,'" *Sewanee Review* 52 (October–December 1944): 537–55. Trowbridge, a professor at the University of Oregon, specialized in the study of eighteenth-century English poetry.

1. The anonymous commentary was actually penned by Tate.

2. The English literary critic and poet William Empson (1906–1984) is perhaps best known for his *Seven Types of Ambiguity,* originally prepared as an essay for his Cambridge tutor, I. A. Richards. This work helped Richards develop his own thought and influenced Brooks's critical development. Brooks preferred Empson's early work to his later. Empson's posthumous *Using Biography* in fact attacks the New Critics for their neglect of biography in literary criticism.

self-conscious about the machinery of wit that it fails frequently to get any intension along with its extension. Furthermore, it is so incapable of resisting an opportunity for a play on words that it is likely to make one even when it contributes nothing to the meaning and even when it runs counter to the meaning. Finally, it is written by someone who is sensitive to rhythm but has not had much practice at it, cannot always bring it off, and is capable of leaving very bad lines in the poem (st.3 1.2, sta.10 1.5). In sum: The poem is (1) Not of a piece figuratively; (2) Not of a piece in "feeling"; (3) Not of a piece rhythmically.

This adds up to harshness and I don't mean it to. It is a very intelligent poem and none of these flaws stick out, to my eye any way, except the overworking of the wit.[3] There you feel that this is done on the mistaken assumption that because Empson's method makes for good analysis, it ought to work the other way and make for good synthesis. With the result that most of the poem has nothing really to do with its actual subject. Examples: 1.4 "scudding circles" an inaccurate epithet—anyway, it is not the spray which clutches. Sta 2 1.2. In order to get the play on "he who runs may read" we say "the fool that runs"; but he doesn't run; he's in a boat. Sta. 2 1.4. In order to get the play on *hands,* we say he is "the second hand"; but in terms of an image of a watch he is most like (though not very like any of its hands) the minute hand: but of course this won't fit the word-play. "At first hand reads" is supererogatory, except for the word-play. St. 3, the moonlight is part of the data but plays hob with the figure of speech, etc.

If I understand it this means to be a poem about living through the moment of complete terror and, at the end, coming out the other side. But the wit runs away with the poem into all sorts of side alleys and only the general framework carries this meaning, in the end rather vaguely. Again, I do not mean this to sound harsh. This is a hell of an intelligent guy who, through lack of habituation, has allowed himself to be carried away by the first realization that he, too, can do this subtle-figurative-language trick; with the result that he goes hog-wild with it and the real poem gets lost in the shuffle.

The Sewanee Review
Sewanee, Tennessee
September 8, 1944

Dear Cleanth:

I should have written you several days ago that we are going to publish your poem. I am not slighting its other merits when I say that it will be a

3. One of Brooks's favorite literary devices in studying seventeenth-century English poetry was, indeed, wit.

very considerable novelty to have this poem in the *Review*. Am I right in supposing that you have not published any poetry at all since you have made your reputation as a critic?[1] To many people this will be your first poem. I will try to use it in January, but I hope you won't mind if I have to put it off until March.[2] Love to Tinkum.

Ever yours,
Allen

[OH]   Louisiana State University
                                                          Baton Rouge, Louisiana
                                                                Sept. 13 [1944]

Dear Allen—

I am flattered, naturally, that you think the poem worth publishing; but I am asking you to hold it for the spring number—not the winter— and it is possible that I shall, by winter, decide to ask you to let me withdraw it.

I think enough of your candor to believe that you wouldn't publish it merely out of kindness—that you would think it publishable if you accepted it at all. But I would like to have a little more perspective on it myself—and I would like to see how the other pieces I have in mind come along. It would be silly to publish one poem if there were good reasons to think that it would be the last one.

At any rate, don't try to get it into the winter number; and I'll write about it later.

The drama book is taking longer than we had thought. But I hope to be at work on some essays by next month. If either of two that I have in mind look likely, I'll send them on to you to let you see whether they are what you want.

I've secured a part-time secretary and I hope that this will speed up matters by helping me move off some of my routine work a little more rapidly. It's an experiment—but if it works, I'll be able to get to several matters in which I am interested. The truth of the matter is that, for months, I have been bogged down in class work and routine work that has taken all my energy. The summer here has been devilishly hot, and that hasn't helped.

Has Bob Heilman written you that he and I are thinking of doing a "Battle of the Books"? The war between the ancients and moderns seems to have come to a definite head. If one could get the right tone, such an essay might be amusing.

---

1. Brooks began his literary career intending to be a poet and published several poems in the 1920s.
2. "The Maelstrom" was published in *Sewanee Review* 54 (1946): 116–18.

Are you going to review *Strange Fruit*?[1] Will there be a notice of John Dewey's article in *Fortune*? There should be, if one could find the right person to do it. I can think of nothing more damning than for Dewey, who, certainly, is as much responsible as any one man for ruining American education, to look blandly over the scene and say his work is good. All this means that I am eager to see your first *Sewanee*. Please hand the enclosed check to your business manager and ask him to start my subscription with the current number (summer).

Best regards to Caroline from both of us.

Cleanth

[OH]   The Sewanee Review
                                                Sewanee, Tennessee
                                                September 17, 1944

Dear Cleanth:

I will bow to your final wishes about the poem, but even if you never wrote another one I should still be in favor of publishing it. It would be the Phoenix of modern poetry.

I am glad you have a secretary. Perhaps she will get some of the essays typed so that you can send them to me.

Ever yours,
Allen

                                                1707 Cloverdale Avenue
                                                Baton Rouge, Louisiana
                                                Nov. 5 [1944]

Dear Allen:

This is a very belated acknowledgment of your fine first number. It's worthy of its new editor—thoroughly so. I was a little disappointed in the Entretiens de Pontigny, and in John's piece,[1] and in [Horace] Gregory— but probably because in each case my expectations were unreasonably high. Even so, they make it a good first number, for surely a first number ought to serve notice, among other things, of the kind of fare that is going to be served up.

I need not tell you that I was delighted with your own comment. I'm glad that it's to be made a regular feature.

1. This was the controversial novel by the writer and social activist Lillian Smith.

1. John Crowe Ransom, "The Bases of Criticism," *Sewanee Review* 52 (1944): 556–71.

Have you seen, by the way, De Voto's preposterous piece in the current *Harper's*?[2] It ought to be answered, I suppose, though I doubt that *Harper's* would publish an answer. In a way one feels that De Voto has been so thoroughly discredited lately—what a beating his last book has taken!— that no reply is necessary. On the other hand, the kind of thing that he pulls here is just the kind of thing that otherwise intelligent people have a weakness for. I suppose that it is really a shrewd move of his to recoup his fortunes a little by making an attack on the South—the kind of attack that most people in their bones feel is correct.

What do you think of the business? Will John be likely to answer? The reference to the "bridgehead north of the Ohio" is particularly nasty, it seems to me. But what would John's attitude be?

I have accepted an invitation to give a Bergen Lecture at Yale early in December. Any suggestions or tips from you would be welcome and appreciated. I think now that I shall give them a paper on the symbolism in Macbeth. Would the *Sewanee* be interested in it? I mention this because at the moment it looks as if this will be the first thing which I could possibly have ready to offer.

The University of Chicago was kind enough to repeat their offer promptly, so that I am to be there for two, and perhaps three, quarters of 1945–46. It will be interesting for me, and probably good for me. What effect on my fortunes here it will have, I don't know; but the new Dean seems to be very friendly, and the new president is at least a great improvement over our general who, I suppose, was literally the worst possible.[3]

I still long for some real talk with you. T. keeps very hard at work, but it would seem that her career as a merchant of death is beginning to play out.[4] Perhaps she will ease up soon. All our best to you and Caroline.

In haste,
As ever,
Cleanth

2. Bernard De Voto wrote a monthly column in *Harper's Magazine* called "The Easy Chair." In the offending column (November 1944, pp. 554–57), De Voto responded to irate responses to his comments on Lillian Smith's *Strange Fruit* in the May issue of *Harper's*. De Voto wrote: "I want an explanation of this defensive arrogance, this sense of inadequacy, this inferiority complex that makes a southern intellectual see red—see that banner being furled sadly—when a Northerner disagrees with him."

3. Hodges's replacement as president of LSU was William Bass Hatcher, who served until 1947.

4. Tinkum Brooks was working at her father's plant in Baton Rouge, which had been transformed by the U.S. government into a munitions factory.

Louisiana State University
Baton Rouge, Louisiana
Feb. 8 [1945]

Dear Allen:

I was surprised to see the proof—I had not actually come to any decision about the poem. It is flattering to be nudged on toward publication—and I appreciate the token of your taking the poem seriously by going ahead and having it set up. If you think that it ought to be published or is worth publishing, go ahead and use it now or when it is convenient. (I don't intend to pose as the coy author—if I have seemed to, it has not been intentional.) But do use your best judgment: don't take the poem out of friendship. I have two more that I am tinkering with which I hope to show you.

Bob H. and I have been immersed for the last three weeks in proofreading.[1] There's always something: and I've got no further with an article. Do you have a book or small group of books that I might review for you? If you do, let me have them. It will be good for me to have something specific set for me to do.

By the way, have you seen the symposium on Naturalism (Dewey, Hook, et al.) which came out a few months ago? Isn't this a case of the enemy's committing his main fleet? Wouldn't it be a good idea to put a first-rate man on the job—or perhaps two or three. I am thinking that the Austrian emigré here, Eric Voegelin, about whom I wrote you some months ago, might do the job beautifully. Have you planned to review the book? Or do you have someone already lined up?

This note makes no pretense of being a real letter. I shall write again within the next few days, but I musn't hold the proof here longer. The last *Sewanee* was very, very fine.

As ever,
Cleanth

[Handwritten] P.S. Tinkum continues at her 12 hour a day pace, making ammunition boxes. Love from us both to you and Caroline. We hope one of these days to send you all a sample of our bookbinding.[2]

The Sewanee Review
Sewanee, Tennessee
February 15, 1945

Dear Cleanth:

I despair of ever again writing my friends decent letters. My God,

---

1. Heilman and Brooks were working on *Understanding Drama*.
2. A longtime hobby of Brooks's was bookbinding, which he enjoyed practicing on volumes in his vast antiquarian collection as well as on copies of his own books.

what a job this is! I suppose you and Red had a hell of a time too. My retroactive sympathy is very strong.

I am sending you Sedgwick's Melville, hoping you will want to review it. It is the only decent book on hand at the moment.[1] Why don't you suggest something in addition to this?

I missed completely the symposium defending naturalism, is it a book? If so, published by whom? Let me know, and I'll get it and ask your friend Voegelin to work on it.

Your poem will probably not appear in the April issue, but will certainly come out in July. I know you're not being coy. Please answer me this: did you or did you not publish some poetry many years ago? If you didn't, I want to be able to say that this is the one and unique poem by C. Brooks.

John was here for a day before he went to Washington, and we had a fine time. He remarked that you and Tinkum were going up to Gambier this spring for a visit. If you all don't stop here, your name is mud with les Tates from now on. We have a large house and not much society; so we're hoping for a visit from the Brookses.

I've wanted to give my new book, the Winter Sea,[2] to various friends, but it is so damned expensive I just can't, being as hard up as I am. Being a grandfather is even more expensive than being a father.

Our love to you both,
Allen

A long ecstatic letter from Katherine Anne the other day. I have my fingers crossed, but I am inclined to think she may actually return from Hollywood with real money in her pocket. You've probably heard that she begins at $1500 a week, and goes up to $2000 after 13 weeks.

The Sewanee Review
Sewanee, Tennessee
2/23/45

Dear Cleanth:

We are sending you today the new edition of Mary Colum's FROM THESE ROOTS, which I hope you will want to review. It has always seemed to me to be an overrated book, even stupid: but you are the doctor. If

---

1. Brooks never reviewed William Ellery Sedgwick's *Herman Melville: The Tragedy of Mind*.

2. *The Winter Sea: A Book of Poems* (Cummington, Mass: Cummington Press, 1944).

you don't want to do it, please turn it over to R. B. H[eilman] to include in his review.—Dead-line is May 1st.[1]

Yrs.
Allen

Louisiana State University
Baton Rouge, Louisiana
March 1 [1945]

Dear Allen—

Tinkum and I are planning—God and the railroads willing—to pay John and Robb a little visit between our quarters here. I haven't seen John in a long time. That, and the debacle in my plans to be with him this spring quarter at Kenyon, make me want equally to get in a visit at this time.

But we don't want to pass so near you and Caroline without stopping briefly. And so, if we can get reservations, we intend to get into Chattanooga on March 6 and come up via bus to Sewanee for a day. Will this be convenient for you and Caroline? Please be candid. It can't be much of a visit anyway. But, if it is perfectly convenient, we do want to stop for that long.

Actually, Tinkum has got to be such a tycoon that she may not be able to come with me. (They're taking up for new ammunition boxes and there's lots of pressure on them just at the moment to deliver boxes as fast as they can.)

As for the poem: it's not the first, but it's the first in 15 years. I published a poem in *The New Republic* in 1929 and in the old *Midland* in the same year. I printed a couple in one of the evanescent Oxford undergraduate magazines in 1931. This is the first since.

I still haven't been able to locate the naturalists symposium. I shall get Bob to help me look it up. He saw it reviewed in *The Nation* some few months ago. I can't believe that he was just seeing things.

I'm glad to have the Mary Colum book which I shall do a piece on. If I find that I can work in the Melville book, I shall. Otherwise, I shall return the Melville to you. I know so little about Melville that I hesitate to try to treat it.

I hope to bring up with me a copy of *The Mediterranean and Other Poems* bound in a Brooks special "turkey-egg" binding without which soon no collector will feel his collection complete.

---

1. Brooks's review of *From These Roots* by Mary Colum and *Ideas in America* by Howard Mumford Jones was published as "Mrs. Colum and Mr. Jones," *Sewanee Review* 54 (1946): 334–43.

I am anxious to see *The Winter Sea* and am sending off my order card at once.

Love to Caroline,
As ever,
Cleanth

The Sewanee Review
Sewanee, Tennessee
March 21, 1945

Dear Cleanth:

We are getting out a leaflet to send to about three thousand names in the hopeful illusion that some of them will subscribe to *The Sewanee Review*. How about giving us a testimonial, a sentence that we may quote conspicuously? It would help a great deal.

Ever yours,
Allen

The Sewanee Review
Sewanee, Tennessee
March 22, 1945

Dear Cleanth:

I enclose for your *confidential* scrutiny a remarkable letter from A. H. Scouten,[1] with my reply. What in heaven's name do you make of it? Please return.

I have ordered a copy of H. M. Jones' Ideas in America, to which I hope you will do justice in a review.

I was amazed to hear from John the other day that the floods kept you from ever getting to Gambier. You should have stayed here longer!

Love to Tinkum,
Yrs.
Allen

---

1. Arthur H. Scouten (1910–1995) arrived at LSU on a football scholarship and caught the eye of Huey Long, who patronized him. Scouten pursued a graduate degree in English at LSU and later taught Renaissance literature at the University of Texas and the University of Pennsylvania.

Louisiana State University
Baton Rouge, Louisiana
March 26 [1945]

Dear Allen:

I am thoroughly ashamed of myself that I have let time slip. I had a thoroughly delightful time with you and Caroline, and I should have written at once to tell you all so. But I lost so much sleep on the journey back that the difficulties of starting the new term came down on me almost before I got fully awake, and then the Erskines arrived for a few days on their way to New Orleans. This is not only a bread-and-butter letter, therefore, but a testimonial to the *Sewanee* and thumb-sketch of Joe Scouten combined. When I got into Chattanooga that night after leaving Sewanee I went to the ticket-office to get a ticket to Gambier or to the closest station. The clerk was even more lugubrious than he had been the day before. One train was still running into Cincinnati—the one I was to take—one bridge was left, the one I was to go over, but he couldn't tell me more, and wouldn't try to make any guesses. I might be stopped before I got across the river—after crossing I might be kept from getting to Gambier. With that, I tried to get John on the phone, and succeeded in getting him before train-time. But John's own pessimism about the prospects decided me on the spot. I couldn't risk being delayed in getting back to classes here, and if I were delayed much in reaching Gambier, I wouldn't have such of a visit anyway.

I knew that Nancy and her husband were coming in. I knew that you and Caroline would want to see them and that you, and especially Caroline, would have your hands full. So I decided not to go back to Sewanee (as definitely I would have had conditions been quite different). Instead I caught a train leaving for New Orleans at 3 in the morning. That wait and the trip back wasn't too pleasant. But every minute at Sewanee was—the visit there thoroughly justified the trip for me. We must try not [to] have too much time elapse between seeing each other henceforward. Both Tinkum and I look forward to the time when you and Caroline can come down to spend a week with us here.

Now for the circular: what about: "*The Sewanee Review* is absolutely indispensable to anyone who pretends to more than a book-of-the-month-club interest in letters"? That states the fact as I would put it. It may be that the adjective "book-of-the-month-club" is too tendentious to suit the purposes of such a circular. If you think so, alter it to "superficial." And in general, edit the statement to make its best effect. You know what I think about the *Sewanee,* and about your editing. The statement can't be made stronger than I would want it.

I am glad that you sent me a copy of the Scouten letter. It is quite preposterous, but then, Scouten is a preposterous person. Your letter to him covers the situation perfectly. What I shall say is not set down because I think that anything has to be cleared up in your mind, but because I think it may amuse you, and because it throws a little more light on the impact of Agrarianism on academic circles in the South.

Scouten came to L.S.U. originally as an imported foot-ball player from New York State. But he was a little light in weight and he had acquired a bad knee in his high-school (and I believe semi-pro) football activities. He was, however, vaguely literate, and so the athletic department found a place for him on its payroll, tutoring illiterate tackles and half-backs. Somehow he managed to hang on, gradually got through our phony graduate school and finally emerged as a Ph.D., having written his dissertation under our major fraud in English (of whom you have heard Red speak), John E. Uhler.

He got a job in one of the small state colleges of Louisiana and, a year ago, somehow got into the University of Texas. Since he has been there he has become, apparently, an ardent Agrarian. So, at least, his letters to me have indicated. And, in justice to Scouten, so perhaps he has. I do not know that he is insincere. He has come a long way; he has never lacked the willingness to work hard; he has always managed to hang on somehow, and pull himself up eventually into a better place.

What amuses me in his attack on Bob [Heilman] is that Joe (as he is still known around the stadium and the field-house) has given there a perfect portrait of himself. One would have, of course, to substitute "poor" for "proud" and "New Yorker" for "Pennsylvanian" in order to make the picture fit completely. But in essence Scouten is the perfect example of the man who sized up the situation and had the cunning and the grit to climb. I don't think that he sees himself in such terms, of course. And he is so naive that he *couldn't* see himself in such terms—and perhaps couldn't be the conscious fraud. Since Scouten has raised the question, I deliver myself of a word or two on the subject of Bob.

I suppose that perhaps the first big intellectual influence in Bob's life was the impression made upon him at Harvard by Irving Babbitt.[1] Undoubtedly contact with Red and me has had some influence on Bob, but the influence could easily be exaggerated. Though he was no slave to Babbitt's ideas, certainly he was prepared to see the parallel between the Agrarian critique of our own civilization and the Humanist. Bob is not, however, the person to swallow anything whole. He chews a long

---

1. Irving Babbitt (1865–1933), a professor of French at Harvard, was a leading critic of the neo-humanist school. He was an important influence on the young T. S. Eliot, who was his student.

time. Bob and I have spent quite as much time arguing with each other as agreeing. In fact, Bob's characteristic difficulty is that he needs to (like the elephant) test every plank of the bridge before he will venture across it.

The thing however, that makes Scouten's charges most completely absurd is that Bob has never tried to fly the Stars and Bars. He has too much good taste to try to be a jerry-built Southerner. One of the reasons why I have been delighted with your liking his stuff and running it is that I know it has done him a great deal of good emotionally to feel that his work was admired by someone whom he genuinely admires but someone whom he would never presume upon as one "Southerner" to another.

Incidentally, Bob is probably going to get an offer to the University of Oregon, an offer which I think—unless it is especially good and unless the University here shows no desire to keep him—he will turn down (this is confidential, of course). I expect that I and R. M. Weaver[2] (who likes Bob very much) have more to do with that than Heilman himself has had.

Of course, Bob has blown off about the stupidity and poor intellectual morale of the students here—as I have and as has everyone else. But, ironically, Bob is probably the best liked of all the professors as far as the good students are concerned, and takes his teaching duties far more seriously than I do.

The only thing that I can make of poor Scouten's attempt to make Bob out to be a "rice Christian" is this: perhaps something which may have happened to him as a student still rankles with Scouten; or, more likely, Scouten has become interested in Agrarianism without discarding the ideas and attitudes held by people like Uhler to whom Red and I were anathema, and whose usual charge was that Red and I were using *The Southern Review* to exploit for the sake of our own careers.

I was astonished to see Scouten's name in the *Sewanee* last week—then further astonished to see that his essay was far above (whatever its final merits) anything which I thought he could do.

This is all too long. But I got started writing and found it hard to stop. I repeat: your own reply to Scouten is masterly and takes care of the situation completely. I have taken your request to keep this confidential

2. The political philosopher Richard M. Weaver (1910–1963) wrote his dissertation, published as *The Southern Tradition at Bay*, under Cleanth Brooks. He went on to teach at the University of Chicago until his untimely death. Weaver's thought helped shape subsequent generations of southern conservatives, perhaps the most representative of which was M. E. Bradford (1934–1993).

to mean that I was not to show it to Heilman, and I have not—or to anyone else from which it might come back to him.

I shall be delighted to have the H. M. Jones book, and have the knife now singing on the grindstone by way of anticipation. I shall throw the review of it together with the review of the Colum book in one article and I shall return the Melville—which is probably quite good but which calls for much more background than I possess.

I have started binding the books for you and Caroline, but work stopped while the Erskines were here for the last few days. They went on to New Orleans yesterday.

The visit was very pleasant for us. Albert seems to have changed very little; his wife is quite charming as you know. Albert, by the way, confirmed your diagnosis of Don [Davidson].

Tinkum sends cordial regards.

As ever,
Cleanth

[Handwritten] P.S. Please remember me to Guerry. The breakfast meeting with him was most enjoyable.

P.SS. I remind you of the Naturalism symposium by Krekorian (Columbia University Press) though you have doubtless written for it. The last *S. Review* is excellent as the [John Peale] Bishop piece is the best thing of his that I have ever seen. The [Theodore] Spencer review is extraordinarily good—better than one would expect from that quarter.

The Sewanee Review
Sewanee, Tennessee
4/24/45

Dear Cleanth:

[Howard Mumford] Jones' Ideas in America just came in this morning. If it will rush you too much to get the review done for the Summer issue, do it for the Fall—dead-line August 1st. Our dead-line for Summer is really May 1st, and I doubt that you could make it. Is there anything else you'd like to do along with the Jones?

I'm demoralized. Mildred[1] had to leave to nurse a sick uncle; don't know when she'll be back.

A.T.

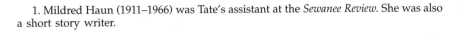

1. Mildred Haun (1911–1966) was Tate's assistant at the *Sewanee Review*. She was also a short story writer.

1707 Cloverdale Avenue
Baton Rouge, Louisiana
June 27 [1945]

Dear Allen:

I have just finished a review of *The Winter Sea* for *Poetry*.[1] It is a fine book. I hope that I have done it justice. I used the limit of space that I thought I could get by with, but even so, I felt that I could do little more than hint and suggest. At any rate, I should like to know what you think of it when it appears. (If you should happen on a copy of the Yale Review Summer number), I would like for you to look at my Shakespeare piece. I don't have an extra copy of the Yale, but I shall try to get one, and if I do, I'll send it on to you.

I enclose a poem by Edward Hardy[2] which I brought up to Sewanee this spring, and which I thought that I had left with you. I was much chagrined to come upon it last night among my papers. The fault is *mine*, but I should appreciate it if you could look it over the more promptly since it has been delayed so long. I think Hardy is developing right along, and that this is one of his better pieces. (You may write to him direct or through me. He is here in B.R. for the summer, and though I do not have his street address at the moment, he would get a letter sent c/o the University.)

This does not pretend to be a letter. But do remember us to Caroline. We hope that all goes well in your household. I know from experience what it is to have a long lingering illness to watch over.

Love to you both,
Cleanth

P.S. I have read the H. M. Jones and the Mary Colum and propose to get a joint piece on them written and off to you within the next two weeks. PSS. Marshall McLuhan[3] has written of seeing you and the pleasant time that he had at Sewanee. We were delighted with him here.

1. The review was published in *Poetry* 66 (April–September 1945): 324–29.
2. John Edward Hardy had been a student of Brooks's at LSU; Brooks and Hardy would later coedit an edition of Milton's poems.
3. Marshall McLuhan (1911–1980), the Canadian communications theorist and cultural thinker, was a longtime friend of Brooks's.

Louisiana State University
Baton Rouge, Louisiana
August 1 1945

Dear Allen,

I enclose my review of Mary Colum and H. M. Jones. I hope that you do not find it too bitter. I am satisfied in my own mind that it is just, but it may overreach itself in attempting to slash them.

Still, you are tempted to use a bullwhip on a bull. Will you supply the title? I can't think of an appropriate one at the moment.

My review of your *Winter Sea* ought to be in the next copy of *Poetry*. I don't feel that I have done that fine book justice, but you will see the space-problem that I had to struggle with, and there was the additional problem of time—for the Editors had to hurry me.

It's been as hot as blazes here, but there have been lots of rains. T. is not working very hard while they "reconvert."[1] We are beginning to make plans for Chicago, and I am going to try to finish the last chapter of my critical book before I go. Reynal and Hitchcock is to publish it, but I don't know, and probably they don't know, when.[2]

Give our best to Caroline. We hope that matters go well with all of you, and realize that with serious illness in the house, the summer may well not be an easy one. But let us hear from you all when you can.

As ever,
Cleanth

I have been reading Urban's *Language and Reality*[3]—devilishly hard reading, but, it appears to me, eminently sound. I think that he really answers the logical positivists, and reestablishes the necessity of [handwritten] metaphysics. His view of poetry is really very close to ours. It is a pity that the book is so unattractive as well as difficult in its style.

The Sewanee Review
Sewanee, Tennessee
August 7, 1945

Dear Cleanth:

Many thanks for your fine review. I think you are extremely good on Jones and Mrs. Colum. Do you mind if I hold it over to the Winter issue?

1. With the war practically over, Tinkum's family factory was being converted back to commercial production.

2. *The Well Wrought Urn: Studies in the Structure of Poetry* was published by Reynal and Hitchcock in 1947.

3. Wilbur Marshall Urban, *Language and Reality: The Philosophy of Language and the Principles of Symbolism* (New York: Macmillan, 1939).

We have several things which we must get out in October because they are appearing in books this fall.

I look forward to your review of *The Winter Sea* because I am confident that you will know more about it than anybody else. I suspect that Marguerite Young had some inkling of it, but she couldn't reduce it to language.

Your handsome bindings of our books are a daily pleasure. Why don't you all plan to stop off here on the way back from Chicago?[1] It would be very fine for us.

Love to you both.

Ever yours,
Allen

[OH]

The Sewanee Review
Sewanee, Tennessee
October 20, 1945

Dear Cleanth:

I've made so many trips and been so generally harassed that I've never found the time to thank you properly for this fine review in *Poetry*. As usual you hit the nail on the head: violence, inner and outer, is the theme; and your extremely sensitive statement of my approach to it gives me very great pleasure.

How long will you be in Chicago? Can't you stop by on the way home? There is a lot I want to talk to you about.

Aff. yrs.
Allen

The Sewanee Review
Sewanee, Tennessee
November 2, 1945

Dear Cleanth:

This letter is absolutely confidential.

I may have to leave Sewanee. If I do, I want to see that the Review gets into the right hands. Would you be interested? The salary now is only $4,100, but I think it could be boosted to $5,000—that is, I am sure I could talk Alex [Guerry] into it on the ground that the Review is a 12 months job, and his other salaries are scaled to nine. There would be not more than three hours of teaching unless you wanted to do more. Mildred

---

1. The Brookses were going to spend the fall term at the University of Chicago.

Haun is the perfect Assistant, and now has the title of Managing Editor; she deserves it.

I can't yet tell you in a letter what this is all about. I hope you will answer me as soon as possible.

Aff. yrs.
Allen

The Sewanee Review
Sewanee, Tennessee
December 16, 1945

Dear Cleanth:

Not long ago I wrote you that it might be necessary for me to leave Sewanee. That isn't certain at all now, but I must tell you what was behind it. Caroline is getting a divorce from me on January 8th, and will leave at once for New York.[1]

She would like to get a teaching job if possible, and I am wondering if the one that was offered to K.A.P. at LSU has ever been filled? I don't need to say more about her qualifications than that at Greensboro she was a great success.[2]

I don't like to be so abrupt about this, but I am sure you will understand why I am abrupt.

Affectionately,
Allen

The University of Chicago
Chicago, Illinois
Jan. 6 [1946]

Dear Allen,

Tinkum and I are much distressed at the news which you give in your last letter. Since we know nothing about it, all we can say is that we earnestly wish the best for both of you. We are glad to know, however, that you may decide to stay at Sewanee and continue the Review. It would be a great shame if now, after its brilliant resurrection, it had to be abandoned, or fall into less capable hands.

---

1. Tate and Gordon were divorced on January 8, 1946; however, they remarried in the Princeton home of their friend Willard Thorp on April 8 of the same year. Tate resigned from the *Sewanee Review* and took a position as an editor with the Henry Holt publishing firm in New York.

2. Mark Van Doren helped Gordon obtain a job teaching creative writing at Columbia University. She augmented her small income by teaching at New York University and by reading manuscripts for Macmillan.

I broached the matter of a creative writing place at L.S.U. to Kirby when I was home for a brief Xmas visit. He has so many men coming back from the service and so much general budget trouble at present that he did not rise to the suggestion and I did not think it wise to press the suggestion then. But I shall recur to it again. Meantime, did you know that North Carolina College for Women was looking for someone to handle creative writing? Will you get that word to Caroline or give me her address. Last Xmas (1945), Elmira College at Elmira, N.Y., was looking for such a person. They may have secured someone by now. It might, however, be worth the inquiry. This place needs such a person. I have no notion of prospects here, but I'll sound [R. S.] Crane out.

I go to Iowa to give a lecture this week. Later in the month I am going to New Haven to have a further talk with the Yale people. Their offer is very attractive, and they have been surprisingly and flatteringly persistent. I think—since they have expressed willingness to adjust matters to my convenience at all sorts of points—that we may get together. But I ask you to keep this quite quiet. There are a number of reasons—among them the fact that I do not want to burn my bridges with Baton Rouge until I am sure that I want to go permanently.

We wish that you could come up next month for a visit. I want to talk to you about all sorts of things. The visit I think would be good for you. Since we are in a small apartment, you would have to bunk in our dining room–kitchen, but if you didn't mind, we certainly shouldn't. We would both really like to have you very much. I hope that you can decide to come.

Tinkum joins me in cordial regards,
Cleanth

Since I didn't stay here for the MLA meeting I did not see Red, but John Ransom was through here in the middle of December and we had some very pleasant talk.·

[OH]
Louisiana State University
Baton Rouge, Louisiana
May 8 [1946]

Dear Allen—

I am to lecture at Vassar on the 15th of this month and of course shall pass through New York City on my way there. I am assuming that you are now in N.Y. and wonder whether we might have some time together on the 16th or 17th. I shall expect to get into New York in the late afternoon or evening of the 16th and to leave for Louisiana in the early afternoon of the 17th. I certainly want to see you if it is possible and shall want to see Albert Erskine, who, by the bye, is publishing my next [book] next month.

I hope all goes well with you.

Cordial regards,
Cleanth

Henry Holt and Company
257 Fourth Avenue
New York
May 10, 1946

Dear Cleanth:

I am mighty glad to get your letter of the eighth and to know that you will be in New York soon. It just happens that we have a single bed, not too uncomfortable, waiting for you. There is no telephone at the apartment but you can wire or telephone me here the exact hour of your arrival.

There is a matter I hope you will be thinking about between now and then. Delmore Schwartz has just written in proposing an anthology of modern criticism which would be along the lines of your "Understanding Poetry." Charlie Madison[1] tells me that you spoke to him about such a project several years ago and, of course, this is your monopoly if you still want it. I believe this book should be done fairly soon so that it could ride on the wave of previous books. I mentioned to Charlie Madison that Reynal and Hitchcock is publishing your next book. He seemed surprised. It was his impression that you were to bring it here.

There are a lot of personal matters I want to talk over with you so please save a good slice of time for me.

Love to Tinkum.

Ever yours,
Allen

[OH]

[Baton Rouge]
Aug. 11, 1946

Dear Allen—

This is a letter long overdue, but it's been a hard summer in which I have been teaching all morning and worrying with half a dozen papers, essays, and books in the afternoons. But the summer session at the

---

1. Charles Madison was an editor with Henry Holt.

University is just over, and I must begin looking forward to the English Institute meeting which comes early next month.

When I saw you and Caroline this spring, you suggested that we try to get reservations at the Brevoort as a place which would be near you, and said that you would be glad to try to make the reservations for me. We would want a room September 7–14—anything with a bath. Could you call them for me?

As our plans are now, we would get into New York on the 7th and perhaps go on to New Haven that day or the next. But in any case I must be back in New York from 9–13, for the meetings themselves go on through those days. Since we may be at New Haven only for a day and night—or may even just make a couple of day-time visits, I think that it would be simplest and safest to get our New York hotel room for the entire period—7 to 14.

There is little in the way of news here. I have got a moderate amount of work accomplished—though mostly on the textbooks. I've read Red's *All the King's Men*[1] and find it very fine indeed. Because of the [Huey] Long material I expect it to make a big stir here locally. I'm anxious to talk to you about it—particularly the ending.

I've also read recently Wilson's *Memoirs of Hecate C.*[2] with mild astonishment. Am I seeing things, or is the situation as bad as *that* with the New York literary crowd? I have reference, of course, not to the *Memoirs* as an actual sociological document—about which I can only guess—but with the attitude, evaluations, control of tone, etc. of Wilson himself. Unless I am missing much, the book strikes me as strangely *naive*.—But this is merely by way of saying that I have lots of such matters to talk with you about. Indeed, both of us are looking forward to seeing you all.

Give our best to Caroline, and both of us insist that neither of you let us make nuisances of ourselves by taking up too much of you all's time. But it will be good to see you all.

In haste,
Cleanth

Guerry has just offered the editorship of the *Sewanee* to John Palmer whom you may remember having met. He's a good boy, and I think will do a good job. He will certainly try. I was a little surprised at Guerry's action—it is a better one than I thought he would make. Evidently he found that my prediction in getting a seasoned man was correct and therefore jumped to one of my suggestions.

---

1. *All the King's Men* was published by Harcourt, Brace in 1946.
2. Edmund Wilson's *Memoirs of Hecate County* (New York: Doubleday, 1946) was considered somewhat bold in its treatment of sexual matters when it first came out.

Henry Holt and Company
257 Fourth Avenue
New York
August 16, 1946

Dear Cleanth,

It was mighty fine to get your letter of August 11th. I have already made your reservation at the Brevoort, a double room with bath from September 7th to 14th. We are looking forward with much pleasure to your visit and we will expect you to save a lot of time for us. John Ransom was here the early part of the week and we enjoyed it very much.

Love to Tinkum.

Ever yours,
Allen

Henry Holt and Company
257 Fourth Avenue
New York
October 31, 1946

Dear Cleanth:

John Palmer has asked me to suggest reviews and reviewers, and with great zeal I have suggested you as the reviewer of the Gregory-Zaturenska HISTORY OF AMERICAN POETRY.[1] This seems to me to be an appalling book, but it will have great influence especially in academic circles simply because there is no other in the field. There is no doubt that there is a certain ability in the book which lends it plausibility, but anybody who, like myself, has been close to the literary scene for twenty years, can detect on every page dealing with living poets the malice, misrepresentation, and the bid for approval from people like Bill Benét and Louis Untermeyer.[2] As an example of the kind of detraction I have in mind I cite the section on Leonie Adams. It happens that the two poems of Leonie's which are supposedly influenced by John's ANTIQUE HARVESTERS were written before John's poem. I cannot bring myself to think that John was influenced by Leonie. If you review the book, I will be glad to supply you with copious notes of this sort.

---

1. Brooks's review of *A History of American Poetry, 1900–1940* by Horace Gregory and Marya Zaturenska was published as "Poets as Historians," *Sewanee Review* 55 (1947): 470–77.
2. The poet and critic William Rose Benét (1886–1950) was a founder of the *Saturday Review of Literature*. The poet Louis Untermeyer (1885–1977) was best known for his anthologies of American verse.

We are thinking of going to Sewanee for Christmas. Will you be going to the MLA meeting in Washington? Maybe our paths can cross. Love to Tinkum.

Ever yours,
Allen

[OH]   Henry Holt and Company
257 Fourth Avenue
New York
11/1/46

Dear Cleanth:

Have you an extra copy of your review of *The Winter Sea* in the Sept. 1945 issue of *Poetry*? I need it to send to London. I'll return it after I get it copied.

Allen

[OH]   [Baton Rouge, Louisiana]
Nov. 7, 1946

Dear Allen—

I enclose a copy of my review of *The Winter Sea*. My regret is that space limitations kept me from exploring further that fine book. You will notice that I have made a few corrections which were to be made in proof but which did not reach the office of *Poetry* in time to get in. This is my only copy and so I should be glad to have it returned; but, of course, there is no hurry.

I ought not to undertake the Gregory-Zaturenska history but if Palmer asks me (I have checked with your letter and see that it is Palmer) I shall. I'm still so far behind with all sorts of commitments that it is foolish to undertake any more. But this is a special case. I shall, however, if I do the review, depend upon you for the notes you promised. They could be invaluable for setting matters straight. You might type them out; or, if this proves a cozier method, scribble them in a copy of the book which I would undertake to return to you.

Yale has announced my appointment, and the news is out here.[1] My friends here regret it, but I have seen nothing here that makes me regret the action and much that confirms me in the belief that I have done the right thing.

1. Brooks accepted Yale's offer of a tenured appointment to commence in the fall of 1947.

We probably won't go to Washington but we might get as far as Sewanee. Let us know when you are able to be there and how long. Love to Caroline from us both.

Cleanth

[OH]

Henry Holt and Company
257 Fourth Avenue
New York
November 12, 1946

Dear Cleanth:

Many thanks for your letter and for the copy of your review. I've had my secretary copy the latter; so I return it at once. Reading it again, a year later, makes me feel more keenly than ever, grateful for your intelligence and insight.

John Palmer will certainly ask you to do the review. Please do it. I will be glad to annotate the book.

We expect to arrive in Sewanee around Dec. 22 and to stay until about Jan. 5. Couldn't you all come up for a few days? I am glad the Yale announcement is out. I have hesitated to speak of it because I wasn't sure you wanted it talked about generally.

Our love to you both,
Allen

Henry Holt and Company
257 Fourth Avenue
New York
November 15, 1946

Dear Cleanth:

I am writing you about a plan that I have had in mind some time. It seems to me that a new series of small well-edited volumes of the English poets is very much needed. So far as I know no such series exists without very important gaps. For example, although Oxford and Cambridge have pretty good editions of what twenty-five years ago were called the standard English poets, the new perspective on English poetry, as I need not tell you, has made editions of people like Raleigh, Fulke Greville, Wyatt, etc. very necessary. What I would like you to consider is the possibility of a joint editorship of such a series by you and me. It would be very useful here in the office, for the purpose of presenting the plan, if you could write me a very full letter, outlining your conception of such a series, its general scope, and even a list of the poets to be included. I think a great point would be that the series would include poets not available elsewhere in convenient editions. And then, of course, we could include, in order to round the series out, the "standard" names. Of course, it would take several years to complete the project. My idea would be to get out five or six volumes a year. Perhaps in size the books should be somewhere between the volumes in The World Classics and the Oxford editions of the poets.[1]

I will write you about some personal matters in a few days. I hope you are going to do the Gregory review.

Ever yours,
Allen

Louisiana State University
Baton Rouge, Louisiana
November 21, 1946

Dear Allen:

Needless to say, I think that your idea for the series of English texts is excellent, and I am flattered by the suggestion that I join you in the enterprise. My first impulse is to give a hearty yes. But two matters come up which I think I ought to mention. The first is the fact that I am so behind with commitments to various publishers that I simply do not think that I could pull much weight in the enterprise for a year or two. The second point is this: that I have had in mind such a series for some years, but a series so special in method that I am not sure that a publisher would find it expedient. I am not sure myself that it is practical. To be very brief with a description of it: the edition in question was to make use of analyses, each poem to be analyzed, though some of the analyses might of course be brief in so far as no special problems or difficulties arose in connection with it. At the end of the book was to appear a ten thousand word essay in which the editor, having displayed for the reader the concrete judgments on which his generalizations were to be based, could proceed to generalize with a good deal more daring and power than he could otherwise. The attractiveness of the scheme to me is this: that such an edition might be useful, not only to the intelligent layman, but to the student since the editor would be indicating to him precisely how particular poems "worked." Moreover on the basis of such a wealth of concrete material, a high level of real critical generalization could be obtained. (I know that we should both agree that the specifically critical matter in most editions of the English poets is relatively worthless.)

1. This project was never realized.

Yet, I can understand some of the difficulties the scheme presents. It may make the poets seem too difficult. It would be denounced as high-flown "Alexandrianism." And indeed it might be using a cannon to kill a sparrow.

I have done about half the rough drafts for such an edition of Donne's *Songs and Sonnets*. I can see that on the basis of my work I shall be able to make some generalization about Donne in the critical epilogue—and can make them stand up—which I should not dare to do in another kind of edition. One of my former students, Edward Hardy, now teaching at Yale, and I are pretty far advanced with an edition of Milton's minor poems. We have done most of the analyses though we have made only a start on the critical epilogue. Perhaps in a few months I should be able to show you what the work will look like.[1]

I say all of this, not to try to switch your idea into something else, and perhaps pervert it in the process. If my idea has any merit, such a set of editions might run parallel to what you have in mind, or some of the texts of the edition which you have in mind might take the experimental form which I have suggested. But I have wanted to start the matter in some length before I gave you an answer to the invitation which you make.

There is no question that [editions] of men like Raleigh, Greville, Wyatt and others are needed—though if some of them are to be really well done—I am thinking of the present state of Wyatt's text—there is a hell of a lot of work for somebody to do.

I hope that this all-too-long letter indicates my interest in the matter. I hurry it off to you. Let me have an answer soon so that I can write you a letter to be shown around the office—though I have no objections to your showing this one if you care to.

My Yale appointment has been announced, as I may already have written you. I doubt that we shall be able to get up to Sewanee this Christmas but I shall write you later about that. Tinkum joins me in cordial regards to you and Caroline.

As ever,
Cleanth

P. S. I have talked about my special plan for [the] series of editions with Albert Erskine, but the fact that Reynal and Hitchcock have no text books probably puts it out of the question for Reynal and Hitchcock—even if I had made a definite commitment to Albert.

[Handwritten] My new secretary has made so many mistakes that I am afraid this letter in places is reduced to nonsense.

---

1. Brooks and John Edward Hardy's edition of Milton's poems, *Poems of Mr. John Milton: The 1645 Edition with Essays in Analysis*, was published in 1951 by Harcourt, Brace.

Henry Holt and Company
257 Fourth Avenue
New York
December 12, 1946

Dear Cleanth:

I am going to answer your long and interesting letter in a few days, but meanwhile I need some information which I myself ought to be able to supply but cannot. In our ad for UNDERSTANDING POETRY last summer in the SRL I stated that there were three books competing with UNDERSTANDING POETRY. Two of them are the Thomas and Brown book and a book in which John Holmes was a collaborator. I am sure you will know what it is. A man has requested this information and I am embarrassed not to be able to give it to him.

Love to Tinkum.

Ever yours,
Allen

[OH]   Louisiana State University
Baton Rouge, Louisiana
Dec. 14, 1946

Dear Allen—

I think the book you mean must be a book by Earl Daniels of Colgate—*The Art of Reading Poetry*?[1]—I am not sure of the title—but it is published by Farrar and Rinehart. Of the last point, I am sure.

In haste,
Cleanth

Henry Holt and Company
257 Fourth Avenue
New York
March 5, 1947

Dear Cleanth,

We have had a letter from Bob McMurphy about Hodding Carter. Bob says that he talked to you about Hodding's publishing plans and that you told him that Hodding may be about to make a ch[ange].[1] I am sure

1. Earl Richardson Knapp Daniels, *The Art of Reading Poetry* (New York: Farrar and Rhinehart, 1942).

1. Hodding Carter (1907–1972), the Pulitzer Prize–winning newspaper editor and author, had been Brooks's roommate at Tulane. At the time Carter was publishing with Farrar and Rinehart.

you understand that we could not approach Hodding [di]rectly at this stage, since officially he is supposed to be [a]nother publisher's author. I need not say that we would be [delight]ed to have him on the Holt list. Can you tell me a little [more] about this situation? Are you willing to go into the matter [with] Hodding? Of course, propriety in the matter would require th[at] [he] approach us first, so that the record will be cleared.

When are you coming East again? There is a lot I want to [talk to] you about. Love to Tinkum.

Ever yours,
Allen

[OH]   Louisiana State University
                                                        Baton Rouge, Louisiana
                                                             Mar. 8 1947

Dear Allen—

A hasty note to remind you that you promised to give me some notes on the Horace Gregory *cum* Zaturenska book. I am trying to get the review written and I now need the material. I expect the best way would be to make marginal notes in a copy and send it on to me. I have an extra copy which I could send to you to replace it, or could return your annotated copy if you preferred.

Life is still very busy and very grim here. But I hope by summer to have got my commitments disentangled. I want to be able to begin *The New Republic Mind* one of these days. Any more word on your edition of the poets?

Tinkum joins me in kind regards to you and Caroline. Apparently you all are having a snowy winter.

As ever,
Cleanth

[OH]   Louisiana State University
                                                        Baton Rouge, Louisiana
                                                            May 26 [1947]

Dear Allen—

What about a word from you? (Actually, I expect that it is I who owe a letter to you.) But I am anxious to hear from you.

Have you thought any more about the series of English classics? My collaborator on the Milton edition is pushing me along. Our edition of the minor poems—a critical edition with elaborate analyses—is nearer completion than I had thought. Do you think Holt would be interested? Should inquiry about this question wait upon further canvassing of a possibility of launching the series?

A letter from a friend at Chicago this morning states that you are said to be seriously interested in an offer to come to Chicago to teach Humanities in the College. This may be the wildest of rumors, but if there is a morsel of truth in it, I should like to discuss the matter with you before you decide. There is much to be said for the matter—and much, in view of the present state of the College, to be said against it.

I see that you are to be at writers conferences in Missouri and Utah this summer. I wish you might be near enough to pass by and pay us a visit. We shall be here, it looks now, until late summer. If you are not *too* far from here on your travels, do come by and stop with us for a while.

When you see the new *Sewanee* you will see my handling of the Gregory-Zaturenska opus. I am not proud of it. I had to be general where I should have liked to be specific. Worst of all, the writing had to be sweated out under the lash because of the press of duties here which had swallowed up the time that should have gone to it. The review will certainly anger the Gregories: I hope it will do more than that.

Do let us hear from you. T. joins in regards,

As ever,
Cleanth

Henry Holt and Company
257 Fourth Avenue
New York
May 28, 1947

Dear Cleanth,

No, I am the bad correspondent. I not only owe you a letter; I owe you many thanks for the inscribed copy of THE WELL-WROUGHT URN. I have been so harassed recently that I have not had time to formulate my views of the book, but you will know, of course, that I admire it. My one regret is that the piece on the Cromwellian Ode was not written in time to appear in the book.[1] I want to talk to you at great length about your kind of criticism, which it seems to me that you have developed to its fullest possibilities.

---

1. "Criticism and Literary History: Marvell's 'Horatian Ode,'" *Sewanee Review* 55 (1947): 199–222.

We have made very little progress as yet with the series of English poets, but I think it will be plenty of time to discuss this at the end of the summer when you come East. I am sure that we would be definitely interested in your edition of Milton's minor poems, and I hope you will put us down first on your list.

The Chicago matter is hanging fire and I don't know what I shall do about it. It might be difficult for me to get away that long, and as you say, I might not care for certain people in the college, but I will let you know when I hear something further from them. I have decided to cut out of the Missouri Writers' Conference simply because I could not stand some of the company I would be in. I allude to your own dear friend Mr. Hudson Strode.[2] But I expect to go to Utah.

I am sorry I never got around to giving you the gossipy notes on the Gregory-Zaturenska book. However, I imagine your review will be all the better without them. We look forward to seeing you at 108 Perry Street.

Love to Tinkum.

Yours ever,
Allen

PS I expect to see Red in Washington tomorrow. I will ask him to give me the king's touch.

The University of Chicago[1]
July 20 1947

Dear Cleanth:

We do not know whether you have pulled up stakes for N Haven yet or not. But we ought to be able to see you there or else in N York at the English Institute.

Chicago has been a real summer resort the last few weeks, with temperatures mostly in the seventies.

Pargellis[2] is trying to persuade me to join him at the Newberry; much as I dislike the administrative routine at the University, I am not convinced that I want to settle down with old Oxford for the rest of my career.

Sincerely yours,
Allen

2. Hudson Strode (1892–1976), a writer and educator, was well known for his travel accounts and for his biography of Jefferson Davis.

1. Tate was teaching the summer term at the University of Chicago.
2. Stanley Pargellis was director of the Newberry Library.

[OH]   Yale University
                                      New Haven, Connecticut
                                              Oct. 24 [1947]

Dear Allen—

   A brief note, long overdue! We've been here nearly six weeks but I
have hardly had a moment to call my own. First the furniture was days
late while we camped around and waited; then Tinkum's sister (whose
husband has been a law student here for the last year or so) came down
with an emergency appendicitis operation—followed a week later by
a Caesarian operation. The result is that T. camped at the hospital, and
since has had Eleanor with us convalescent. Things go fine now, but only
recently have curtains begun to go up, my books get unpacked, etc.

   All this to explain why I have not written and why I have not yet been
in to New York. But we are anxious to see you and Caroline in New York
and out here. Now that things begin to mend with us, let's make plans
to get together.

   I suppose that you saw the *Sat. Rev.* of Oct. 11. I have just seen it, and
my blood pressure has been up points ever since. I can understand H. N.
Smith up to a point—a nice boy, badly fuddled and confused.[1] I find it
harder to understand the people who trained him, and the editors who
took the piece with its factual inaccuracy and its amazing non-sequiturs.
But the review does constitute a sort of highwater mark: to believe in a
religion now evidently proves that one is perhaps a fascist and makes
one suspect slave-holding ancestors.

   I think that I am going to have to do the book I talked to you about
(New Republic Mind) after all.[2] But this and many more matters will have
to wait until we can meet and talk.

   Tinkum joins in love to both of you.

                                              As ever,
                                              Cleanth

[OH]   Yale University
                                      New Haven, Connecticut
                                      [early December 1947]

Dear Allen—
   Would it be possible for Edward Hardy and me to see you Saturday,
the 13th, in the late morning at the Holt office (or elsewhere?) It's about

----

   1. In his unsympathetic review of Allen Tate's *A Southern Vanguard* (*Saturday Review*,
October 11, 1947, pp. 19–20), Henry Nash Smith, a professor of English at the University
of Minnesota, said that Tate had developed "a portentous philosophy of reaction."
   2. This project was never realized.

the little Milton book that I've written you about in the past. The book is rounding out pretty rapidly now, and Hardy is most anxious to begin sounding out publishers.

I go to Syracuse, N.Y., for a lecture Thursday, and since we go back to Louisiana on [the] 18th for the holidays, Saturday, though a bad day on some counts, is the only one available.

On the other hand, there is no reason why the whole matter cannot be put off until January, if this Saturday is inconvenient. Don't hesitate to say so, therefore.

In any case, please send your reply to the Dwight St. address (176 Dwight) or phone collect. Our number is 762–630.

Tinkum joins in regards to you both,

Cleanth

[OH]
Yale University
New Haven, Connecticut
Friday [December 12, 1947]

Dear Allen—

It's quite all right about tomorrow. We'll make a date early in January. I want to see you on a number of accounts—most of all simply to have some talk with you.

Tinkum joins me in love to you and Caroline. Have a good Xmas. We'll hope to see you soon after our return from Louisiana in the new year.

As ever,
Cleanth

108 Perry Street
New York, N.Y.
February 12, 1948

Dear Cleanth:

I am sending you a letter I've just received from Ward Dorrance about a student of his.[1] I think you know who Ward is, and I can put in my word that his recommendations are always good. Won't you write to Ward direct, if you think anything can be done? His address is Dept. of Modern Languages, Univ. of Missouri, Columbia.

About two weeks ago I heard you were in town, and was aggrieved that you didn't come to see us. I am now out of the Holt office completely,

1. Ward Dorrance (b. 1904), a French literature scholar and a friend of Gordon's who spent his career teaching at the University of Missouri, had written Tate on behalf of a student, Andrew Susac, who wished to study English with Brooks at Yale.

and it has added I am sure ten years to my life. Now, please plan to come down for any weekend except Feb. 28th. We'll be right here, and want to see you and Tinkum very much.

I've just returned from Louisville where I participated in a ridiculous ceremony: I was made D. Litt. by the Univ. of Louisville—along with John Mason Brown—as "Kentucky writers." Don't hold it agin me.

Yrs
Allen

[OH]   Yale University
New Haven, Connecticut
Feb. 18 [1948]

Dear Dr. Allen—

We were distressed to hear, when Tinkum 'phoned last night, of Caroline's bout with the flu. We had hoped you all might come up this weekend. We must plan a meeting soon, either here or in New York. I have much to talk with you about, but most of all I simply want us to have a visit together.

My trip into New York the other day was much too brief to try to see you, if I missed you at Holt's. Actually, things are beginning to fall into place for me—I have more time for myself—and hope to get into New York several times in the coming weeks.

I am glad to get Dorrance's recommendation of Susac. He sounds very promising, and I have no doubt that arrangement can be made at this end of the line. I shall consult the powers-that-be within the week on the matter.

My congratulations on the Doctor of Letters. It is richly deserved, and even if it is the university that is primarily honored by the gesture rather than the poet, still I am glad that it was done. The new president of U. of Louisville was at L.S.U. for some years. I should like to think that he demonstrates that he learned something there about modern literature.

I hope that the spring weather we are enjoying today will help Caroline to throw off her influenza.

Tinkum joins me in love to you both.

Cleanth

[OH]   108 Perry Street
                                                                    New York, N.Y.
                                                                    February 19, 1948

Dear Cleanth:

It's good to get yours of yesterday. I've got the germ now, but I hope in a mild form. Caroline will stagger up to her class this afternoon—she's better; but it would have been risky to attempt a weekend trip. Next weekend (28th) we go to Princeton, but all is clear after that. Let's plan a weekend soon as possible, here or N.H.

It is fine that we shall have six weeks together at Gambier.[1] I will be on shaky ground teaching *The* novel, but I never again want to teach a course in modern poetry, largely for personal reasons. I can't believe Matthiessen is the man for the course: the piece I ran in the Sewanee, covering the period, was not good at all. You should be teaching it.

I am looking forward to your paper on John for the special issue of the S.R. It looks now as though we weren't going to fill the issue, and I am baffled and a little irritated. There's no trouble at all in getting up for a special [Wallace] Stevens or [William Carlos] Williams issue of a magazine; but for my money, John is far out in front of both of them.

                                                                    Love to Tinkum,
                                                                    Yrs,
                                                                    Allen

[OH]   108 Perry Street
                                                                    New York, N.Y.
                                                                    October 5, 1948

                            ? (Chink)

Dear Cleanth:

Lyle and Chick Lanier[1] and I are coming to the Vanderbilt-Yale game, and we wonder if you could conveniently get us three tickets. I don't know the price, but we'll reimburse you at sight. Caroline refuses to see another football game, having been to her last fifteen years ago. We shall arrive by train at 12:15 and lunch at a hotel or some convenient joint, and we hope that you and Tinkum will join us and, if you have no other plans, arrange to go to the game with us.

1. Tate and Brooks were set to teach summer sessions at Kenyon College's School of Letters, founded by John Crowe Ransom.

1. Lyle Lanier (1903–1990), a psychologist and university administrator, was one of the original Agrarians. After teaching at Vassar and New York University, he became chancellor of the University of Minnesota.

I will have decided about Chicago by that time.

Love to you both,
Allen

[OH]

108 Perry Street
New York, N.Y.
October 7, 1948

Dear Cleanth:

Princeton Univ. Press has sent me, as editor of *The Language of Poetry*, a cheque for $25.00, the fee for permission to a person unnamed for a quotation from your essay. Should not the quotation come as from *The Well Wrought Urn*, and Reynal and Hitchcock been approached? The copyright must have been transferred. Please advise me: should I send the $25 to you, or return it to Princeton?

Yours in haste,
Allen

[OH]

New York, N.Y.
10/13/48

Dear Cleanth:

Many thanks for taking the trouble about the tickets. It's really *too* much for us to descend on Tinkum for lunch, but the prospect is so inviting that I'll not say no; and I'm sure the Laniers will be delighted. Maybe I can hypnotize Caroline at the last minute. While the good weather holds she begrudges every minute taken from her gardening at Pawling.

Yrs,
Allen

It's very gratifying that you're doing me up in the Hudson.[1]

[OH]

108 Perry Street
New York
October 14, 1948

Dear Cleanth:

A note from Lyle this morning says that they have to go to see their son at Taft and can't come to the game. Is it too late to cancel the

1. Brooks's review of Tate's *On the Limits of Poetry: Selected Essays, 1928–1948* (New York: Swallow Press, 1948) was published as "The Limits of Poetry," *Hudson Review* 2 (spring 1949–winter 1950): 127–33.

order for their tickets? If it is they insist on paying for them. I will be there.

Yrs. in haste,
Allen

[OH]   108 Perry Street
New York
November 16, 1948

Dear Cleanth:

We're having our party for J. C. R[ansom] and T. S. E[liot] on Monday the 22nd. We hope you all can come. Try to arrive at about 6:30. After dinner some other people are coming in. Don't fail us.

Yrs.
Allen

[OH]   108 Perry Street
New York
December 5, 1948

Dear Cleanth:

You will remember the matter of a permission fee from the Princeton Press. I believe you decided that they lacked the authority to grant permission. They sent me a cheque for $25.00 which lay around for days until Caroline deposited it, not knowing what it was, along with some others. So I'm sending you my cheque for $25.00, since I was instructed to pass it on to you: and you can take up the question with the Princeton Press.

We greatly enjoyed you all, and were glad to be able to bring you and John and T.S.E. together. When will you be down again? Are you going to the M.L.A.?

Yrs.
Allen

New York University
Washington Square
New York
December, 1948

Dear Cleanth:

I am a little uncertain about your Christmas plans, whether you intend to be at the M.L.A. or not. For many reasons I hope you will be, and I have a particular reason for wanting you to be here for lunch on Thursday,

December 30, to join Dick Blackmur, Austin Warren[1] and myself, along with Paul McGhee and Ralph Ross, of New York University, for a discussion of a project about which we are considerably excited.

We feel that a special school of literary studies modeled on the Kenyon School of English would go very well as a winter program here. What titles should be given to the staff, we don't know, but we should definitely want you to join us in a capacity equivalent to that of Senior Fellow at the Kenyon School of English. We don't feel that a winter school of this sort would at all compete with John [Ransom]'s project, but would in fact reinforce it.

If you can't be here would you please let me know what you think of the plan, and whether you would be willing to cooperate with us in presenting a case to the Rockefeller Foundation?

Ever yours,
Allen

[New York]
January 3, 1949

Dear Cleanth:

The bank informs me that I gave you a rubber cheque. Please accept my apology, and this new cheque which I assure you *is* good.

The M.L.A. had need of thee when Mr. Bush[1] read his attack. I was shown a carbon copy and asked to appear with him on a radio program to defend myself. I declined, assuming that Mr. Bush was entitled to his opinion of me, which in any case I saw little hope of changing. Those attacked were you, Empson, John, and I. John got the roughest treatment, I believe.

My paper seemed to go well; at least a very large crowd appeared, no doubt led by curiosity. One of your colleagues said to Sam Monk: "Why have I heard all these writings about Tate? Why, his paper was not only good criticism, it was *historically* sound." (Italics mine.) I never expected that compliment from Yale of the ante-Brooks regime.

I go to Chicago Thursday for two days, and two days a week for three weeks. Shall we see you all before we go finally on the 27th?

Yrs.
Allen

1. Austin Warren (1899–1986), the literary critic and educator, is best known for his collaboration with René Wellek on *The Theory of Literature*. Brooks considered that work the best theoretical exposition of his own critical method.

1. Douglas Bush (1896–1983), a professor of English at Harvard for many years, was a respected literary historian and perpetual adversary of the New Critics.

[New Haven]
Jan. 8, 1949

Dear Allen,

Forget about the check—it caused no inconvenience, and as a matter of fact, the good one came in before I learned that the other had bounced.

I'm sorry that I wasn't at the MLA, particularly with such interesting things going on as that about which you and Blackmur and Austin Warren were talking. We must get together for a talk before you leave. Am I right in understanding that you will be away every weekend until you leave for good? A week day must do, then. Now why don't you and Caroline come up for that visit, any time at all between now and the 27th. (With these exceptions: I'll be away on the 22nd, and all Wednesdays are bad for me.) We hope you all will do this now, but if it is completely impossible, we shall certainly try to come to New York to see you. Will you all, then, pick a date and let us know whether the traffic is to move west-east or east-west?

By the way, I've heard good things about your MLA paper, including a very hearty tribute from Fred Pottle, who, I assume, is the colleague whose reaction Sam Monk mentioned to you. I am preparing a load of buckshot for Douglas Bush—one that I was intending to fire merely on general principles.[1] News of his paper at the MLA makes my trigger-finger itch. I must try to get a copy.

As ever,
Cleanth

1315 Davenport College
Yale University
New Haven, Conn.
March 5, 1949

Dear Allen,

I am to be in Madison, Wisconsin, for a centennial doings March 14–16 (double billing with Howard M. Jones, as I believe I told you). Is there a chance that you might come up there? It's four hours from Chicago.

Otherwise, would you and Caroline be free the evening of March 16 in Chicago? I will be back in Chicago about 6 p.m. and my train leaves about 11. If this suits, let me know how to get in touch with you by phone, and we'll plan for you all to have dinner with me.

As ever,
Cleanth

1. See Brooks's response to Bush's attack on his reading of Marvell's "Horatian Ode" in "A Note on the Limits of 'History' and the Limits of 'Criticism,'" *Sewanee Review* 61 (1953): 129–35.

[OH]

The University of Chicago
Chicago 37, Illinois
March 7, 1949

Dear Cleanth:

It's good news you are coming. I'm afraid Madison is out of the question, but we are counting on you for the evening of the 16th. Let me know the exact time you will arrive, and I'll meet you in the new Dodge.

Love to Tinkum,
Yrs,
Allen

[OH]

The University of Chicago
Chicago 37, Illinois
April 9, 1949

Dear Cleanth:

I only hope that I deserve one-tenth of your praise in the Hudson. I know you are not capable of doing this simply out of friendship, because you have other friends for whom you don't do it. So I gratefully read your words, with the reflection that I had better do as well in the future as you think I have already done.

We greatly enjoyed your day here. Two days later we went to Memphis and had a fine visit. But, alas, when we got back we found Cal, who after five days cracked up completely. We let him go to Bloomington to see Peter Taylor where he repeated his violence on a larger scale. Peter got his mother and Merrill Moore to take him to Boston, where he is now in a hospital.[1] It was a shock, but not unpredictable. It is delusional paranoia, far advanced religious mania (Christ, etc.) mixed up with sexual delusions. Now please don't mention this unless to counter false rumors which you've doubtless heard. The enemy will use it. *All* non-positivists are crazy, etc.

Love to Tinkum,
Allen

1. Robert Lowell endured a severe mental breakdown during his visit to the Tates. Tate was deeply concerned and sent Lowell to their mutual friend Peter Taylor. Taylor (1917–1994) had studied with Ransom at Kenyon and with Brooks at LSU and was the only friend of Lowell's who could be counted on to know how to handle the poet during his bouts with madness. Former Fugitive poet Merrill Moore (1903–1957) was both Lowell's therapist and a trusted family friend. It was Moore who had first introduced the young Lowell to the Southern Agrarians.

1315 Davenport College
Yale University
New Haven, Conn.
April 30, 1949

Dear Allen,

First let me say how much pleasure your good word about my Hudson Review piece gave me. I hoped that you would like it, but, as you are well aware, I did not shape the piece in any way to make it attractive to you. I meant, and mean, just what I said, though I suspect that some of my vehemence sprang from my sense of the blindness of so many people to the full significance and power of your achievement. At any rate I was very happy to get it off my chest, and if you feel that it makes sense, that's very fine indeed.

By the bye, we had just got the news about Cal on one of our infrequent expeditions to N.Y. a day or so before your note came in. It is all very sad, and we hope that it will not prove to be as bad as it sounds. But the breakdown at this time certainly accounts for a number of things: Cal's state of euphoria when we saw him with you and Caroline last fall; and the telephone calls to Chicago; and, I suppose, the violence of his attack on Miss Ames, who may well be a vinegary old maid, but I dare say is not an agent of the Kremlin.[1]

If you and Caroline have further word on Cal, we shall be glad to have it. We have heard nothing further, and have made no effort to find out from Albert [Erskine] or from Jean [Stafford] anything further.

There is no news to report from us. I have looked through Richard Chase's recent book *Quest for Myth* and should be glad to hear what you think of it. Chase is a pleasant enough person, as we found at Kenyon, but I must say that his new book seems to me disappointing. To argue that myth is simply art, and that it answers to our "needs," seems to me to say entirely too much or entirely too little. The general position reminds me very much of the early Richards. It looks to me like the old reductionism at work again, but perhaps I am too hard on the book, and at any rate I should like your opinion.

The little visit with you and Caroline in Chicago was most pleasant.

---

1. Brooks is referring to allegations made by Robert Lowell, Katherine Anne Porter, and several other writers in residence at the Yaddo Writers Colony that Elizabeth Ames, the proprietress, was in league with Communists. The allegations were never proved but raised quite a stir. Ames was a close friend of the writer Agnes Smedley, who specialized in Far Eastern affairs. On February 11, 1949, the *New York Times* purported that a report by Gen. Douglas MacArthur identified Smedley as a Red Chinese agent. The U.S. Army later distanced itself from this accusation.

Tinkum and I hope we shall have an early meeting with you, though, this fall. She joins me in cordial regards.

Cleanth

[OH]

5521 Kimbark Ave.
Chicago 75, Ill.
May 4, 1949

Dear Cleanth:

I'm mighty glad to get yours of the 30th—As to Cal, we've had two letters from Merrill Moore, who paints a very rosy picture of Cal's progress, which is somewhat qualified by a report from Robert Fitzgerald.[1] Robert went to Baldpate (the hospital) and talked to Dr. Watson, who has charge of the case, and it seems that Cal must stay there at least all summer. That, coupled with the fact that Robert was not allowed to see him, looks gloomy.

There is no doubt of his *insanity,* in every ordinary sense of the term. Those were the most terrific five days we've ever been through; and Peter Taylor writes the same of his experience with him. But for public consumption Cal's friends ought probably to stick to the story of a "severe breakdown," even though people generally know better.

I haven't seen Richard Chase's book, but I saw parts of it as articles. I'm inclined to agree with you about it. He's somewhere on the fringe of criticism.

We're buying a small house in Princeton, just to get out of N.Y., but, we shall keep a toehold at Perry Street, since we'll both commute once a week for teaching.[2] Speaking of teaching, I tell you in confidence that I've had another of those useless, handsome offers: the lure of Texas this time, at $9,000. This didn't give me as much pause as Iowa; I wrote back my *no* at once. We simply couldn't face living at either place. When I had more youthful bounce I might have been able to take it.

We'll be back in the East around August 10th, but we don't take possession of the Princeton house until September 1st. We shall go up to Pawling for those three weeks. Couldn't you all drive over to see us? Love to Tinkum.

Ever yrs,
Allen

---

1. Robert Fitzgerald (1911–1985), a poet and distinguished translator of Homer and Vergil, taught poetry for many years at Harvard.

2. Tate had left Henry Holt in 1948 to become a lecturer at New York University and then in 1949 took a position as a visiting professor of humanities at the University of Chicago.

[OH]   1315 Davenport College
                                        Yale University
                                        New Haven, Conn.
                                        Monday [May 1949]

Dear Allen—

I was very happy to see your reply in the *Partisan* this month.[1] It was well said, though one requires no imagination to guess the response it would evoke in that particular dove-cote. By the way, Barrett might have noticed (had he cared to) that though *he* disclaims having insinuated that the judges were anti-semitic, Robert Gorham Davis in the current number implies as much. And Barrett seems to approve of Davis's statement.

Barrett's original statement (April no.) makes the old vicious, disabling distinction between form and content that one had hoped had been disposed of. Of course, it hadn't been (cf. the discussion at Kenyon this last summer). If one pushes the discussion, however, people look pained: *this* point has been "made"; let's have something new now, louder and funnier. (The critic ought to be an entertainer.) But at the first opportunity to blur the distinction, blurred it becomes. "Technique" is something like a metrical pattern: it can be peeled off the "content."

I was put up at Harvard last week. Mattie [F. O. Matthiessen] reported that Trilling had pulled out of the Kenyon session at the last minute—Mattie seemed to feel that Trilling had treated John rather badly in the matter, having no real and pressing excuse. I see from the morning's mail that the Kenyon schedule has had to be adjusted.

I'm glad to hear that you and Caroline have bought the Princeton house. It sounds very nice, and, selfishly speaking, it's good for Tinkum and me to know that you all are to be no farther away.

Our plans for the summer are still quite vague. But it would be nice if we could have a visit after the summer session is over. At any rate, will write later on when we know where we shall be.

Tinkum joins in love to you and Caroline.

                                                            Cleanth

T. has begun bookbinding and brought in a fine assortment of tools the other day from an old binder who is going out of the business:

---

1. In 1949, the Fellows of the Library of the Congress (Robert Lowell, Conrad Aiken, Louise Bogan, T. S. Eliot, Karl Shapiro, W. H. Auden, and Robert Penn Warren) awarded Ezra Pound (then an inmate of St. Elizabeths Hospital for the insane in Washington, D.C.) the Bollingen Prize in Poetry. Although the award was given on artistic merit alone, it provoked a storm of controversy over Pound's radio talks on behalf of Italy during World War II. Tate's comment on one of those responses, William Barrett's "A Prize for Ezra Pound," was published as "The Question of the Pound Award," *Partisan Review* 16 (May 1949): 520. Tate's "Further Remarks on the Pound Award" appeared in *Partisan Review* 16 (June 1949): 666–68.

brass tamping tools, sets of type and ornaments, morocco and sealskins, marbled papers, gold leaf, etc., etc.

[OH]   1315 Davenport College
                                                              Yale University
                                                          New Haven, Conn.
                                                              July 11 [1949]
Dear Allen—

I enclose a letter which is self-explanatory. Since I have just returned from Louisiana and the forwarding of my mail has been mixed up, it may well be that a letter has gone astray. At any rate, if you can recommend Darden, and wish to, you may write me or the Dean of the Graduate School here.

I hope that the Kenyon School is having a good session. I've had an amusing note from Mrs. Parker whose judgments are always sensible and sometimes acute. Is Winters behaving?[1] If you find time, I should enjoy an account from you. (In rereading, I see that I have implied that Mrs. Parker has glanced, in her letter, at Winters. This is not so. Her account is general.) By the bye, Wyndham Lewis[2] would like to get a temporary place teaching or lecturing at some university in this country. I have told him I would listen out, and you might sound out any sympathetic people at Kenyon on the subject. I do not admire his last book *(Cosmic Man)* at which I have just glanced. But on the record, he certainly deserves a place and many a department could brighten its offering if it had him lecturing on literature or painting.

Tinkum remains in New Orleans but will join me here at the end of the summer or earlier. Our love to Caroline. Speak my regards, please, to the Ransoms, the Coffins,[3] and other friends.

                                                                 As ever,
                                                                 Cleanth

                                                              Gambier [Ohio]
                                                               July 17, 1949
Dear Cleanth:

I was mighty glad to hear from you. The session here is just half over, and it has gone quickly. I suppose it isn't as good as last summer. The

---

1. The poet and critic Yvor Winters (1900–1968) was known for his controversial views.

2. Wyndham Lewis (1882–1957), an English novelist and painter famed for his biting satires and as a leader of the art movement known as Vorticism, had been an early contributor to the *Southern Review.*

3. Charles Coffin (d. 1956) was chairman of the English department at Kenyon.

students are a little younger and less mature, and the staff, while we get along beautifully, lacks the high spirits which we seemed at times to feel last year. Winters declines to argue. He is (as of this date anyhow) almost irritatingly amiable. He even refused to argue with Herbert Read[1] when Herbert praised spontaneity in his lecture. The Welleks live next door (we're in the same house as last year) and we find them extremely pleasant. Here is a scholar for us all to like and respect. They gave a farewell party yesterday for Herbert; it was very pleasant.

The session has been somewhat overcast by the Hillyer outburst in the SRL.[2] Its repercussions here have been very marked. There is not one person on this campus, winter or summer, who has a shred of respect for Hillyer. Everybody thinks that Chalmers[3] has behaved like a fool, or worse, in bringing him here over the head of every member of the Department. There is even some talk of a signed faculty protest. Hillyer's egomania and bad taste have offended the entire community. He has even gone so far as to say that he intends to supplant JCR. All this has come about because Chalmers has a foolish wife who writes bad poetry, admires Robert Frost, and hates the Kenyon Review. I will tell you more at the end of the summer, but meanwhile please say nothing of this.

It is impossible to take Hillyer's articles seriously, in themselves; but we should be very foolhardy if we failed to see them as a straw in the wind. Every mediocrity in the country has come like a rag out of his hole to bite his superiors. The Bollingen Award to Pound may set poetry back a generation. One would have thought that Eliot was beyond the reach of these jackals. But no. This has been their chance to rebel. But I do not see how we could have awarded the Prize otherwise than we did.

Caroline had made good progress with her new novel in Chicago, but has had to put it aside in the midst of the noise of the two grandsons, who are very cute and very loud. Nancy is here with them for the session (she is taking Winters' course!), and we are having a real family reunion for the first time in several years. Percy[4] was here for ten days.

We'll expect to see you and Tinkum early in September. We're buying the house in Princeton but can't get possession until the first week in September. We go up to Pawling for two weeks. You and Tinkum must drive over to see us. We'll send you a card at that time.

1. Herbert Read (1893–1968), an English poet, art scholar, and literary critic, was a friend of Tate's.

2. Robert Hillyer, "Poetry's New Priesthood," *Saturday Review of Literature*, June 18, 1949, pp. 7–9, 38. Hillyer (1895–1961), an educator and poet who spent his academic career at Kenyon College and Brown University, was a leader of the forces opposed to the awarding of the Bollingen Prize to Pound.

3. Gordon Keith Chalmers was president of Kenyon College; his wife was Roberta Teale Schwartz.

4. Tate's son-in-law, Dr. Percy Wood.

About Wyndham Lewis. My feeling about him is a little ignoble. I feel that other people have greater claim to the very little influence that I may have in getting jobs. He is a malignant megalomaniac; and although I admire much of his work I am getting too old (or life is getting too short) to feel much patience with persons who insist upon insulting people for their best efforts. I wish him well, but I can do nothing.

Ever yrs,
Allen

[Handwritten] I've just read your Muller.[5] You handled him very well.— The same old delusion about cooperation of "science" and literature.

[OH]   1315 Davenport College
                                                        Yale University
                                                    New Haven, Conn.
                                                    August 5 [1949]

Dear Allen—

Thanks for your good letter from Kenyon, and my apologies for this tardy answer. Since hearing from you, I have looked up the two Hillyer articles and then went on to read some of the letters to the editor in [the] subsequent issue. It's as dirty a performance as I've seen in a long time.

I hope, therefore, that I don't seem to be an incorrigible optimist when I say that I get a certain satisfaction over the turn matters have taken. "Satisfaction" is scarcely the word; nobody could be *satisfied* at that spectacle, but I am not much depressed, and I do think that it is fortunate that Hillyer took so low a line. It ought, for example, to indicate to the *Partisan* crowd the kind of Babbitry that they must be prepared to associate with if they take the line that they do. (Why should J.C.R. have got Barrett to review Eliot's *Notes*?[1] It's all very well to "represent both sides," etc., but there are certain basic distinctions that must be accepted if we are to talk about literature—or anything else, for that matter— at all.)

To take the long view (about the only one it does us any good to take). I think that maybe it's just as well that Hillyer has vulgarized the whole matter. His vulgarization is not, in my opinion, a distortion. He

5. Brooks and Herbert J. Muller, "The Relative and the Absolute: An Exchange of Views," *Sewanee Review* 57 (1949): 357–77.

1. William Barrett, "Aristocracy and/or Christianity," *Kenyon Review* 11 (summer 1949): 489–96, a review of Eliot's *Notes towards the Definition of Culture* (London: Faber and Faber, 1948).

simply carries out to its final extreme the conception of literature that the Marxists, the fellow travelers, the unregenerate Ph.D.s, and the social-agony boys held, and continue to hold. But Hillyer's vulgarization is going to make that conception a good deal easier to attack.

I can imagine, however, that John is pretty sick over the whole affair. I can't see how Hillyer would have written as he did unless he felt confident of Chalmers' support.

Peter Russell (who has doubtless written to you) has asked me to urge that you contribute to the Pound volume. I shan't urge, and I realize that "practically" it's probably not wise to contribute. But in the terms in which the invitation was made (no encomia—independent critical evaluation, etc.), I felt that it would be cowardly to refuse, and though I know nothing about Peter Russell, the fact that the volume (I am told) has Eliot's blessing made me feel that I ought to accept. You, of course, will have made your own decision whether to contribute or not—and with you, of course, the question of cowardice does not arise—you have already been on the firing line—as I have not.

I quite understand about the W. Lewis matter. I don't know him, but can readily surmise that he might be an unpleasant customer.

I suppose Kenyon has ended its session or has just ended it. At any rate, I write you there, feeling that even if you have left, the letter will be promptly forwarded.

Love to you and Caroline.

Cleanth

Russell writes: "The S.R. 'rumpus' as Auden refers to it in a letter to me, has been a nasty affair . . . I [Russell] think that Eliot has been deeply wounded by it, though he wouldn't admit it." My guess is that Eliot is more hardened than that.

[OH]

Gen. Del.
Sherman, Conn.
8/13/49

Dear Cleanth:

Thanks for your letter. Why not drive up to see us? We will be away 19–23, but any time before or after till Sept. 10th (when we move to Princeton) would be fine for us. Just come to Sherman and ask for Sherman-Patterson (N.Y.) road. It's the second entry on right after you cross [the] N.Y. State line. The sign on the lane reads Jenkins-Brown. Please do come. There is much to talk over. Hope Tinkum is back and will come too.

Allen

465 Nassau Street
Princeton
September 26, 1949

Dear Cleanth:

You will forgive my recent silence when you reflect that it took us three weeks to get this house so that we could sit down in it. The ordeal was trying, but we like the place very much. You and Tinkum must come down very soon, while the weather is still good.

I [would] like very much to go over the Putnam papers if there's no great hurry. I couldn't get to them till after Christmas. Could they be sent down to me? Would there be any objection to printing my little piece about Phelps in a magazine first?

The Hillyer affair still stinks. I wonder what the view at New Haven is? We are getting up a counter-attack to be published as a pamphlet by PO-ETRY [in] October. If you feel inclined to make a statement we should like very much to have it. There are at least 500 Hillyers in this country, but only one journal, the SRL, irresponsible enough to give him [free] rein. They are the real enemy. I think this thing has done more harm than you seem to believe. It is linked up with [Howard Mumford] Jones and [Douglas] Bush, and every third-rate professor in the country is delighted.

Please plan to come down some week-end very soon. I will be away on the 8 of October, but any other time will be fine.

Yrs.
Allen

[OH]

1315 Davenport College
Yale University
New Haven, Conn.
Thursday [September 29, 1949]

Dear Allen—

It's good to hear from you. I hope that you and Caroline are now comfortably settled. Tinkum has been vigorously house-cleaning and getting the apartment ready for the winter. I have been going through the beginning-of-term chores—at the moment overwhelmed, but hoping soon to get clear.

Please inquire about the Putnam papers at once: (1) whether they can be sent to you, (2) whether [your] piece could be done after Xmas rather than immediately, (3) and whether it would matter whether the piece were published first in a magazine.

I am to give a paper to Ushenko's class in Princeton on Oct. 12. My plans are up in the air still—I don't know how I shall come—or when I shall arrive, or how long I can stay. But I do hope to get a glimpse of you and Caroline on the next morning. What I do hope is that Tinkum and I can persuade you and Caroline to come up for a visit *here*—and very soon—one that will give us a chance for some real talk.

I should like to be in on the protest that *Poetry* is to print—if it is not too late. For the life of me, however, I don't see that one can say much more in a *short* statement than that Hillyer is an ignorant and venomous s.o.b. The crowd that listen to Hillyer are beyond argument, and you can't have an engagement in a brief statement anyway. But maybe the protest will bear weight anyway. I'm certainly for it and would like to participate.

The best answer, I think, might be an issue of a pamphlet using the format of the *Sat. Lit.*, and a parody of it, down to their crossword puzzle and their pansies' correspondence column. The leading article, should, of course, review Hillyer's last book, and assign the Bollingen award to him. I may persuade the boys here to do such a rag. If it were witty enough, and cruel enough, it might hurt that crowd where they are sensitive.

Most people here don't read the *Sat. Rev.* (though it is a kind of bastard issue of Yale originally). I have had, however, of late, a steady stream of students and faculty people who have looked up the articles and come in to indicate their surprise and disgust. But I dare say that the articles have done plenty of temporary damage—perhaps permanent damage.

As for the academic wing, preparations are being made to pay them off. Cornell is having this year a series of lectures in which two people speak at each meeting. The series pits Mack (of Yale)[1] against Sherburn of Harvard (he made at the MLA in California, I hear, a vicious attack on the "New Critics," Eliot, etc.) and the next week, me against Douglas Bush. Mack is a tough opponent for anyone. I hope he won't pull punches. Since the series is to be published, I hope we can leave plenty of arrows sticking in the Harvard contingent.

But what we need is a new "Battle of the Books." I remember with admiration a rewriting of the *Modest Proposal* that you did years ago. Why not come on up for a visit and rewrite Swift's *Battle* for the new occasion—by yourself, or in collaboration, as you will? The pattern is made to order.

As ever,
Cleanth

Tinkum joins in love to you both.

1. Maynard Mack (b. 1908), the Sterling Professor of English at Yale, was a Pope scholar and a longtime friend of Brooks's.

465 Nassau Street
Princeton
October 2, 1949

Dear Cleanth:

You must spend the night with us, and bring Tinkum. You all are home folks, and won't mind our going through your room to get to the bathroom. This is a very small house, but we can sleep you pretty well.

The copy for the pamphlet is already in Chicago. The only letters we are using were declined by the SRL. We are using Cowley's article, Carruth's editorial, and an editorial from the coming issue of The Hudson Review. Our point is that *none* of the material was written especially for the pamphlet, but resistance can be made.

I used Mr. Sherburn's The Best of Pope at Kenyon. I found six errors in grammar in the preface which bear the marks of an illiterate mind; to say nothing of the opaque incomprehension of what any of the poems are about.

About the pamphlet again. Here's a useful thing you might do, and there's just time for it. In Hillyer's second article he makes the really libelous statements about the characters and motives of the New Critics— frustrated men with power complexes, men of no personal courage, etc. Couldn't you get off at once to the SRL a letter challenging them and Hillyer to produce an exact list of the names of these vicious persons? This could be demanded as a public responsibility; that is, the public ought to know definitely who these men are, in self-protection; and persons who are not guilty of their crimes will thus, if the list is produced, be freed from suspicion if their names have been elsewhere associated with ours. If the SRL prints your letter, well and good; if they don't, as they surely won't, we can rush it to Chicago to go into the pamphlet.[1] But haste is of the essence.—If the SRL produces the list (their lawyers won't let them), they will have about ten libel suits on their hands.

We'll look for you and Tinkum on the 12th. Our telephone is 3655-R.

Yrs.

Allen

[Handwritten] I suppose your letter to the SRL, if you write it, should be accompanied by a covering note asking for an immediate reply as to whether they did print your letter and when. If they don't answer at all, we can state the fact in a footnote in the pamphlet.

---

1. The letter was published by the *Saturday Review of Literature* as "List of 'Wicked Esthetes' Wanted," October 29, 1949, p. 24. In the letter Brooks criticized Hillyer for his heavy-handed attack on the supporters of the Pound award.

[OH]

1315 Davenport College
Yale University
New Haven, Conn.
Oct. 4 [1949]

Dear Allen—

I enclose carbons of the letters I shall send to the S.R.L. by registered mail the first thing in the morning. I hope that the letter suffices— though it's a hasty job, and shows it. At any rate, I'll let you know what response I get as soon as I get it. (I've decided that it had better be by registered mail: I don't put it past that gang to deny that they ever got the letter.)

Tinkum won't be able to make the Princeton trip. Because of Wednesday classes that I must meet, I shall have to come by train and by the latest train that will get me in time for the dinner that Ushenko says the philosophy department is giving. The paper—still unfinished—is being written more or less to order, and will be pretty special and technical (on the problem of mixed imagery) since, I take it, the audience will be small and special. After the dinner, the paper, and the discussion, I don't know what happens. Ushenko has not indicated further plans or plans for the night. I would like nothing better than coming over to the Tates for the night, but it seems embarrassing to show up at that hour— especially when you and Caroline are still in process of getting settled. I ought to get in to Princeton about five in the afternoon. Suppose I ring you immediately when I get in. Do be candid about the convenience of having me, promise not to let me impose.

One of the many reasons for seeing you all is to arrange for you to come up for a visit here—with long enough stay to have some real talk.

In haste,
as ever,
Cleanth

1315 Davenport College
Yale University
New Haven, Conn.
Oct. 17, 1949

Dear Allen,

I so much enjoyed the visit with you and Caroline—a fine breakfast and satisfying talk. We must plan for a longer meeting—a longer weekend here. Tinkum will be writing soon about this with some definite dates in mind. At the moment, I want to find out what you think of a proposal which will have to be acted upon at once if it is to be used at all.

To my surprise, I learned on my return the other day that the Yale Lit is definitely planning a parody number of the *Sat. Review*. (I had mentioned it several weeks ago as something that ought to be done but had got no intimation that it was being acted upon.) Actually, the group has been hard at work and is already getting in material, with plans well advanced. They will have a double crostic, personals, letters, ads, etc., as well as the articles, editorials, and reviews. It's a bright bunch and I expect them to do something a cut above the usual college skit, for many of them see what the real issues are. But of course we must not expect *too much* from a bunch of undergraduates.

At any rate, what they would like to get would be a group of "retractions and confessions Soviet style" to print as communications. They would like to have you, me, and a dozen or so other people write in such communications to appear over our names—confessions in which we admitted our sins and kissed Canby's[1] rod. (I don't think that there would be much danger of people missing the irony in *this type of parody:* undergraduate high-spirits will see to that.)

But is this a good idea? And will it seem so to others? If you think so, will you let me know, along with the names of some of the people who ought to be asked to send in such confessions? And will you help me enlist their support? I have thought of Red, Cummings, Eliot, Blackmur, etc., but I shall write to no one unless I hear that you think the idea is a good one. I can imagine that some of these retractions could be very funny—but maybe not.

In any case, I hope that you will later help me get the parody number to the attention of *Time* through Fitzgerald or anyone else you know who might help. If the boys could get a little publicity of this sort—always supposing that the parody is wicked enough—the number might reach more than a local audience.

Shapiro's paper is really excellent. I'll return it soon.

In haste,
Cleanth

[Handwritten] P.S. I've heard nothing to date from the *Saturday Review* about my letter: I've had the return card indicating that they received my letter and *three* ads asking to subscribe. Their business department at least is on the job.

---

1. Henry Seidel Canby (1878–1961), a teacher, critic, and biographer, was a cofounder of the *Saturday Review of Literature*.

1315 Davenport College
Yale University
New Haven, Conn.
Tuesday [October 18, 1949]

[OH]

Dear Allen—

I've just heard from the *Sat. Review* that they mean to print my letter—in the issue of Oct. 29. I hurry off this information to you.

Regards to you both,
Cleanth

[Princeton]
10/19/49

Dear Cleanth:

A group of American writers have agreed that a protest should be sent over their names to the editors of the Saturday Review of Literature, setting forth their conviction that the SRL's attack on modern poetry and criticism, growing out of its attack on the Bollingen award, has done great harm to the cause of letters in our time. About 100 writers, including yourself, are being asked to sign the enclosed letter to the editors of the Saturday Review of Literature. If you are willing to support this group statement, will you be so kind as to sign the enclosed copy and send it back in the enclosed envelope by return mail?

[Handwritten] I am sending Bill Wimsatt and Maynard copies of this. Maybe you will want to speak to them about it.

Please sign and return at once.

Allen

465 Nassau Street
Princeton, New Jersey
October 22, 1949

Dear Cleanth:

I've been so busy the past few days getting out (with John Berryman's help) the circular letter that I couldn't until now really consider your suggestion about the mock confessions. I do think it is a good idea, but not for any of the Fellows of the Library. We have followed a policy of individual silence. The pamphlet contains a long *joint* statement sponsored by the whole group; and we have invited others, like you, to contribute letters and articles. We have wanted to avoid anything that looks like self-defense; we think of the pamphlet as a factual statement.

At the same time I look forward to the undergraduate parody which might well turn out to be the most effective way of dealing with the SRL attack. In September Willard Thorp, Bill Meredith, and Louis Coxe, after reading some of Hillyer's verse, wrote a "Hillyer sonnet" which is actually no funnier than many of his, but very funny. I'm sure they would give it to the boys to be run under a parody of Hillyer's name. They could claim it as a feather in their cap, that they have got a special contribution by "Bobert Filthier." In getting hints the boys should not overlook the footrace between Osborne and Curll in the Dunciad.

We hope to see you all very soon, here or there. I feel I can now get back to work. I've done all I can about Hillyer.

Aff.
Allen

P.S. I wired Hayden Carruth about your letter. He will run a note to the effect that it is appearing in the SRL on Oct. 29 and reprinted in the pamphlet with your permission.

[OH]   465 Nassau Street
                                                 Princeton, New Jersey
                                                 November 11, 1949

Dear Cleanth:
    I will arrive at 12:30 and I'm looking forward to a very good time.
                                                 Yours in haste,
                                                 Allen

                                                 465 Nassau Street
                                                 Princeton, New Jersey
                                                 November 30, 1949

Dear Cleanth:
    The Shattering Review arrived just as I was leaving on Saturday. I just got back last night. It is a masterly performance—full of Irony, Wit, Paradox, and Tension.[1] It is hard to single out any one piece, it is all so good. I am beguiled by the photograph of T. S. Eliot.

    Please have the boys send two copies at once to Louise Bogan,[2] 709 West 169th St. Louise is either reviewing or will get reviewed The Case

1. The "Shattering Review" was the parody of the *Saturday Review of Literature* published by the Yale undergraduate magazine, *Yale Literary Magazine*. Tate's reference to "Irony, Wit, Paradox, and Tension" alludes to Brooks's emphases in his poetry criticism.
2. The poet Louise Bogan (1893–1970) was an editor for the *New Yorker*.

Against the Saturday Review of Lit., and The Shattering Review might well be included.

To bring you up to date: John Berryman gave [Harrison] Smith[3] until Monday the 28th to commit himself on the letter. On Monday John received a letter from Smith repeating his demand for the names of those not signing as a condition of publishing the letter—which by the way he calls a "petition." He said that Hillyer had already prepared a reply. John had told him that he could not reveal the names, that it would be improper, etc. (e.g., Kenneth Burke didn't sign because he hadn't read the affair, but said very firmly that this did not indicate that he was on the SRL side. Smith would pretend that all non-signers were against us.) So the Letter is being withdrawn, and will be published in The Nation on December 17, with an explanatory comment by Margaret Marshall.

JCR was here last week-end, and I am up on that front too. A monster celebration of Frost's 75th birthday has been scheduled by Chalmers for the spring—speakers, guests, etc., costing $10,000 given by an alumnus. The speakers will include Mark Van Doren, Ted Morrison, and Senator Taft.[4] I told Mark about it Sunday.

The Senior Fellows of the School of English meet with Chalmers and John Marshall today in NY. I will see Coffin and JCR afterwards, and will let you know what developed. According to John, the renewal will be asked for. The real problem is the appointment of a Resident Fellow for the winter to supervise the M.A. work. John says that Chalmers wants to appoint Hillyer, without taking account of the fact that no students of the school of [the] English brand would turn up. So John will try and I think succeed in establishing the rule that the Resident Fellow must be selected from the present body of Fellows or even from the group that have already taught in the School.

More very soon.

Aff.
Allen

3. Harrison Smith (1888–1971) was at this time an associate editor of the *Saturday Review*.

4. Robert Taft (1889–1953), a powerful and influential U.S. senator from Ohio, was a leader of the conservative wing of the Republican Party.

[OH]   465 Nassau Street
                                              Princeton, New Jersey
                                               December 15, 1949

Dear Cleanth:

   Here are the carbons of the letter which may interest you. I thought
perhaps you might wish to write a letter to [Hiram] Hayden.[1]

                                                          Yrs,
                                                          Allen

1. Hiram Hayden was editor of the *American Scholar.*

1950s

465 Nassau Street
Princeton, New Jersey
January 7, 1950

Dear Cleanth:

I was informed yesterday that the arrangement is really *made,* and that all that remains to be done is to work out the details.[1] I thought you people at Yale might need the names and addresses of the Fellows of the L. of C. in order to avoid unnecessary delay. I leave it to you to explain to your colleagues how you got these addresses. At any rate it should not be known by anybody that you and I have communicated about this matter.

The Foundation will no doubt instruct you people to the effect that the Fellows should be invited not as Fellows, but as individuals. This can't be emphasized too strongly. When the list is published in the papers everybody will know that the Fellows have been retained under the new arrangement, but if they are not so designated it will permit the Librarian of Congress to issue a public statement (he has promised to do so) applauding the continuation of the Prize. This statement is highly desirable from every point of view. The SRL has tried in many ways to divide us; we must maintain solidarity on as many fronts as possible.

I can't tell you how delighted I am by this victory. Willard [Thorp] was saying last night that intelligence and decency in this country still count. They do, for a fact!

Yrs.
Allen

1. Yale University Library entered into a partnership with the Bollingen Foundation to decide the annual recipient of the Bollingen Prize in Poetry. The Library of Congress withdrew its sponsorship of the award due to political pressures following the controversy surrounding the awarding of the 1949 Bollingen Prize to Pound.

[OH]   Department of English
                                                       Yale University
                                              New Haven, Connecticut
                                                       Jan. 9 [1950]

Dear Allen—

It's very fine news that you send. You got it before I did. I tried this
morning to see Jim Babb,[1] the librarian, but missed him. I shall try again
tomorrow. Thanks very much for the addresses of the Fellows. I shall, of
course, say nothing about having heard from you, but I shall try to steer
matters a little: to speed up the announcement before the 20th; to see
that the Fellows are named as individuals (though I am sure this is what
is being planned); and to provide the addresses where needed. (I have
a likely story on this point to account for my having the hard ones—the
easy ones I'll look up or have his secretary look up on the spot.)

I can't help being proud of Babb's having pulled it off. As I told you
over the 'phone, he deserves the credit for having got the idea and for pos-
sessing the imagination and integrity required to be able to see its importance and to carry it through. I think I need not say that those of us whom
he called in to talk it over urged it with all our might. It is a real triumph
for our side and goodness knows there have been few enough of late.

Bill Wimsatt showed me today a copy of the *Mercury*'s Hillyer piece.
I have thus far been unable to buy a copy here, but the stand should be
supplied in a day or so.

At the moment I am working on my counterattack to Bush (on the U. of
Rochester program next month). It's hard to find the best angle of attack.
If you have any ideas, let me have them. (Maynard Mack, I understand
is hard at work on his counter to Sherburn, the work before mine on the
same series.) I shan't magnify the importance of the program, but since
the papers are to be printed, I hope that we can give a good account of
ourselves. After all, it's a chance to catch the *academic wing* of the Army
of the Philistines out of position.

A note from Arthur Mizener says that he saw you and Caroline
recently in Princeton. I should have liked to see Arthur while he was
in the East. I hope for the best in his Fitzgerald book, but the chapters
in the new *Partisan*—just between us, for I wish Arthur well—will do
neither Arthur nor Fitzgerald much good, I fear.[2]

1. James T. Babb was the Yale University librarian under whose leadership Yale took
over responsibility for appointing the board to award the Bollingen Prize.
2. Mizener's biography of F. Scott Fitzgerald was published in 1951 as *The Far Side
of Paradise*.

We must plan to get together soon for a visit and some talk. I was distressed to hear what little you could tell me over the 'phone about the Kenyon matter. I had a good letter from J.C.R. recently, and replied warmly and at length. But he had little to say about the renewal of the Kenyon grant except that the renewal was being applied for. If you've heard any recent news on it, please let me know.

Tinkum joins in love to you and Caroline and wishes for a happy new year.

As ever,
Cleanth

[Telegram] Western Union
New Haven
Jan., 1950

Saw Librarian last night matter definitely settled he hopes to make announcement before Jan. 20th. He will probably phone or write you in next few days. I have made no mention of my conversations with you.

Regards,
Cleanth

[OH]   Department of English
Yale University
New Haven, Connecticut
Wednesday [early February 1950]

Dear Allen—

I hope that you and Caroline had a pleasant drive back. It was good to see you all, and the Brookses had a wonderful time. Let's do it again soon. I enclose the program which we had forgotten to pick up for you, and which you had expressed a desire to have.

Let me ask a favor, which I had meant to ask while you were here. I am in charge of the Cooke prize in poetry this year. I hope that you will be willing to help judge it. I will promise, on my part, to prune the MSS. mercilessly, sending out to the judges only those that seem to have some chance. The MSS. will therefore not be very numerous or very bulky. It's a chore, but I hope that you will say yes.

Love to you and Caroline from us both,
Cleanth

[OH]   465 Nassau Street
                                          Princeton, New Jersey
                                            February 12, 1950

Dear Cleanth:

We're just back from four days at Pawling. One night at home last week!

Yes, I will be glad to act as a judge in the Cooke contest. Just send on the mss. when they are ready.

We had a wonderful but all-too-short time. Come April, you all must drive down, without fail.

                                            Love to Tinkum,
                                                  Allen

Many thanks for the program.

                                              [New Haven]
                                               May 8, 1950

Dear Allen,

You were good enough some months ago to say that you would act as one of the judges of the Cooke Prize, and I am imposing on your good nature by simply sending these MSS on to you without further confirmation. I have cut the list from 22 to these five which I enclose. I am afraid that none is terribly good. For that reason I think that you need not worry about any delicate balancings one against another. Simply rank what you regard as the top three in 1, 2, 3 order.

Tinkum and I have been so busy with trying to get a revision of UP[1] through the press that we have had to let slip our vague idea of coming to see you. It has been mostly proof sheets, and at the moment, doctoral dissertations with me. But there are a couple of items of news that I shall jot down.

Last Saturday the New England CEA met here at Yale with a program featuring an attack and a defense of critical methods. (Last year the CEA in its regional meeting launched some very bitter attacks on criticism.) This time I think the enemy were steam-rollered. I read a paper along with Dorothy Bethurum, but can take little credit. It was Bill Wimsatt, our Telemonian Ajax,[2] who simply got up on his hind legs and thrashed the opposition into stunned silence.

---

1. The revised edition of *Understanding Poetry: An Anthology for College Students* was published by Henry Holt in 1950.
2. Brooks is alluding to the fact that William Wimsatt was not only a titan of literary criticism but also stood six feet ten inches tall.

The other bit of news is that we are buying a 1720 Connecticut farm-house. The complications are numerous and we will not be able to move in until some time next fall, but when we do we shall want you and Caroline to come up and help us christen it.

As ever,
Cleanth

[Handwritten] The prospectus of the fiction book that you and Caroline have done is most interesting.[3] I am anxious to see it—even though I know that *Understanding Fiction* will suffer a sad dint on its account. It will, I know, prove a very fine job.

465 Nassau Street
Princeton, New Jersey
May 15, 1950

Dear Cleanth:

I haven't had much trouble in deciding on the first two, but a third has been more difficult. Anyhow here they are:

Wandering Aengus

U. Ges. Who

C. Dexter Harper

I hope this agrees with your judgment.

We had hoped that you all would be able to come down, but I gather that you've had to give up the plan. Won't you be driving down to Louisiana? We'll be here until June 14. Remember we are on Route 1.

This has been a tough spring. I had flu for about six weeks, and had to cancel my Boston lectures, as well as one at the Frick Collection; but the 1720 house sounds very fine. We want to help in the baptism; so don't forget us when the time comes.

The news from the New England front is heartening. I was in Pittsburgh last week. There's certainly no visible opposition to criticism out there. They were quite docile.

Love from us both to you both,
Allen

1315 Yale Station
June 8 [1950]

Dear Allen,

I am heartily ashamed that I have waited so long to thank you for your

3. *The House of Fiction: An Anthology of the Short Story,* edited by Gordon and Tate, was published by Charles Scribner's Sons in 1950.

kindness in judging the Cooke prize and your promptness in getting the stuff back to me. I think I hardly need to say that our votes coincided almost precisely. The poems were not a very good group on the whole. The fifteen batches or so that I discarded in order to get the five I sent you were quite poor. Your first choice (and mine) was the work of Edgar Bogardus[1] who did a couple of years work at Kenyon College before coming here. John R., I am sure, knows him.

I haven't written because for months I've hardly had time to eat or sleep. The final accumulation of papers and theses for the year coincided with the work on the proof of the revision of *Understanding Poetry.* A big Canadian adoption hung upon Holt's delivering bound books by July 1st. I think now that they are going to make it, but the effort has taken it out of all of us, including Tinkum.

We've seen a little of Red (who's postponed his trip to Europe) though that little was spent huddled over galley proof. We saw a glimpse of Zabel on his way from N.Y. to Wellfleet.

But we are always promising ourselves that next year will be different. I hope it will. *If* all goes well in that matter, but I can see that we will have many a headache before the last clapboard is in place. If we can get settled in a house here, we want you and Caroline up more frequently and for a longer time. And we promise ourselves to get down to Princeton once or twice during the year. As it is, there's no chance of a visit this time: you and Caroline will be soon setting out for the West, and, though we shall be here for ten days or so more, we will after that be in the South—for most of the summer, I suspect.

Now that the last dissertation is read and now that the last of the proof is in—or will soon be in—among the things that I promise myself is to sit down and go through the fine book on fiction that you and Caroline have done. It won't help the sales of *Understanding Fiction*—though I see that you all have pointed your book to a less elementary reader. But I am glad to see it, anyway, and look forward to reading it at my leisure.

I have just got into the first few pages of Red's new novel.[2] It starts very finely, but my reading there too has had to be postponed.

I hope that you and Caroline have a fine summer. Tinkum joins me in all cordial regards.

Cleanth

1. Edgar Bogardus was the author of *Various Jangling Keys* (New Haven: Yale University Press, 1953), for which W. H. Auden wrote the preface.
2. Warren's *World Enough and Time* (New York: Random House, 1950).

[OH]

1315 Yale Station
Yale University
Dec. 15 [1950]

Dear Allen—

I should have written long ago, but I have put it off because our plans for the holidays and the week after have been completely up in the air. They have just settled themselves, and I hasten to write to urge you to bring Caroline with you and to plan to stay with us at Northford.

I had expected to spend the season here except for a brief run into N.Y. for the wretched MLA. Now it turns out that we are both going south. Mine will have to be a very brief visit since I must get back for the MLA—I'm presiding at one of the section meetings. But Tinkum, since she does not have to be back plans to stay longer.

Indeed, she probably won't be back until the middle of January, but she joins me in the hope that *both* of you will come. As you know, there is plenty of room here, plenty of wood cut for winter fire, and everything will be in order for you all. It would actually be a kind of act of charity to me if Caroline would come. And in any case, you Allen, and best of all, both of you, do plan to spend some time here. We do see you from time to time, but never for long, and rarely long enough for any real talk.

Have a very happy Christmas season!

Tinkum joins me in all warm regards.

Cleanth

465 Nassau Street
Princeton, New Jersey
January 20, 1951

Dear Cleanth:

First, I want to congratulate you on your fine Credo in the current Kenyon.[1] From now on it will be hard for the Bushes to make out a case. As to Bush himself, I thought his piece a smug bit of platitude. For a moment I considered writing a letter for the correspondence column of the KR to this effect: "Mr. Bush seems to have no difficulty in seeing himself as the representative of the common reader in all ages. Apart from the presumption of seeing oneself as representing anything, there is the impiety of presuming to represent common humanity in any of its aspects; for the only Man who has succeeded in doing this is Jesus Christ." But I shall not send it.

1. "The Formalist Critics," *Kenyon Review* 13 (1951): 72–81.

Second, I've done what I should have done, and what I don't know why I didn't do, years ago: I have joined the Catholic Church.[2]

Now a problem about a student that we've both had. Miss [Alexandra V.] Krinkin came to see me in October to see if I could suggest a job for her. She came again the other day, for the same purpose. Obviously she is in a very difficult situation. She told me the Dean wouldn't let her return to Yale, but I can't be sure she told me the whole truth; and if I'm going to be able to do anything for her, I must know the facts. Why wasn't she allowed to come back? I will keep anything you tell me confidential, even from her.

Haven't you all neglected us this fall? We'd love to see you. I go to Boston Feb. 10 and 11 to give the Candlemas Lectures at Boston College; and weather permitting we hope to drive up. In that case we shall want to drop in for a moment to see you all in your new mansion.

Love to Tinkum.

yrs.

Allen

Department of English
Yale University
New Haven, Connecticut
Jan. 8 [1951]

[Handwritten] This is when I started my letter. But since then exams and it seems that everything else has intervened.

Dear Allen,

I wish that we might have a meeting—there's so much to talk with you about. Immediately, there is the article in the current *Hudson* by Dick Blackmur.[1] I've just put it down, and though I mean to read it again much more carefully, I can't help setting down some first impressions. One of them is that Blackmur's "complete criticism" amounts to a philosophy and a religion. I know that he repudiates the idea that literature is to be substituted for religion, but I think that that is what he is asking for—unless he is asking for what Richards proposed: that literature be used as a kind of testing ground for responses so that the properly trained man would not need dogma but would be, as it were, automatically, self-adjusting in the face of any conceivable situation.

2. The well-known Catholic converts Jacques and Raissa Maritain were Tate's godparents at his December 1950 confirmation ceremony.

1. R. P. Blackmur, "The Lion and the Honeycomb," *Hudson Review* 3 (winter 1951): 487–507.

Another impression is that Blackmur stands in much too much awe of the "scholars." (You mentioned the point to me once, I believe.) I hope that I have a proper regard for scholarship. I pretend in a modest way to be one myself; even in the old brass-bound sense. And God knows that I have lived, moved, and had my being among droves of them for years. One needs all the facts that he can get—can never get enough facts— yet I can't quite swallow the implications of Blackmur's article. For he intimates that the critic has never had very much of what scholarship could do for him, and that is just demonstrably not true.

A third impression—and here in particular I may be unjust to B.—is that he is just waking up to some of the problems that have exercised a number of people for years. I find this a little hard to believe, and maybe another reading of his essay will correct the impression. Yet what is one to make of a statement like "In Miss Tuve's meaning the specific and demonstrable mode of Christian allegory, both as a device of poetics and as a means of representing Christian thought aesthetically, is brought back into the poem . . ."

January 26

I resume this letter after examinations—I've just finished reading the last paper, and now have a little respite for the next few days. Meantime your letter makes me hope that we will have a meeting very soon. You and Caroline must plan to stop here on your way up. Plan to come early enough to stay the night. We have much to talk about and much to show you all.

Among other things, the old salt-box house has taken a prodigious spurt during the last month. It has a roof now, and is getting clapboards. Inside, the mason is at work on the fireplaces and the old chimney. (Tinkum and I managed to save about three-quarters of the old bricks, and these are going back into the fireplaces and the parts of the chimney that will be exposed.)

Some one told me a few weeks ago that you had entered the Church. Your *general* sympathies have long been on record in your writings and I have, of course, been familiar with it. When I mentioned the matter to Bill Wimsatt the other day, he remarked that this was surely the most distinguished accession that the Church had had in a long time.[2] You will realize the spirit in which Bill said it to me and the spirit in which I pass it on to you—and I think that you deserve to have it passed on to you.

I must leave room for a brief note from Tinkum. Love to you both.

Cleanth

2. Wimsatt was a devout Catholic.

[Handwritten] Not much room to say how much I hope you all will stay with us. Sorry our housing project is not as finished as yours—but we do have lots of room and beds on Dwight St.

Love,
Tinkum

I was forgetting to mention Miss Krinkin. The story is a little complicated, but in no way reflects discredit upon her. She did excellent papers for me, and sound work for most of her other teachers. But I should count on talking with you about it early next month when you and Caroline are here—I am *counting* on your coming here.

465 Nassau Street
Princeton, New Jersey
February 4, 1951

Dear Cleanth:

We greatly enjoyed your nice letter; but alas it will not be possible for us to stop off after all. The Cheneys[1] are here from Nashville, and will remain through next weekend; and Nancy and the children will probably arrive on Saturday. This will keep Caroline here. Moreover, I must be in Washington on the 9th, and thus must take a train from there direct to Boston that night, in order to be there in time for my first lecture the next afternoon. But we will hope to see you all anyhow very soon.

It was nice of Bill Wimsatt to make that remark. I'm afraid the hierarchy will scarcely agree with him. If you saw last Thursday's NY Times and my letter on the attempt to suppress that bad movie The Miracle, you will understand why Cardinal Spellman may wish that I had remained a heretic so that I might join Farinata in Circle VI.

I'm taking the liberty to send you a copy of my Candlemas Lectures for your advice before publication. (My agreement with B.C. is that they may publish them as a brochure.) One more thing, and not a very disinterested thing at that: I am so hard up, as the result of our building project, that I'd like to make as much money out of the lectures as possible. I have the permission of the Candlemas Foundation to repeat them as often as I wish up to the time of publication, which will be late in the Spring. The lectures fit together, but each is complete in itself.

1. Brainerd ("Lon") and Frances ("Fannie") Cheney were old Tennessee friends of both Tate's and Brooks's. When they were young students at Vanderbilt, Fannie and Brooks kept company for a while before deciding just to remain good friends. Brainerd wrote several novels, and Fannie served as Tate's assistant and bibliographer during the time he was poetry consultant to the Library of Congress.

We saw Red last week, and thought him [in] fine shape. Love to Tinkum.

Yrs.
Allen

465 Nassau Street
Princeton, N.J.
June 6, 1951

Dear Cleanth:

A few days after Miss Krinkin saw you she came to see me again, but I could get very little out of her about her present standing with the Graduate School at Yale. She merely said that you had suggested that she apply for readmission. Now my problem in her regard is rather pressing: she says she wants to go to Minnesota or Chicago, but before I can write in her behalf to either place—particularly the former—I've simply got to know what her difficulty with Yale was. If you can tell me, I will keep it absolutely confidential, from her and from the universities, though naturally any letter I may write for her would be influenced by the information.

She is a brilliant student, though I surmise that she has difficulties. Elliott Coleman at Hopkins told me that some years ago she had psychiatric treatment. This is not necessarily against her, in an age in which every second person has had it.

I was surprised to get a letter from the Operations Research Office about your application for a job in psychological warfare. I hope you get it if you want it. At any rate it means that you think we are very close to a big war. I hope you're wrong.

When shall we ever see you? We leave June 20 for Bloomington. And in September for Minneapolis.[1] Our love to Tinkum.

Yrs,
Allen

1. Tate taught at the Indiana School of Letters (formerly the Kenyon School of Letters) during the summer. He had accepted an appointment as professor of English at the University of Minnesota, to begin in the fall of 1951.

465 Nassau Street
Princeton, N.J.
August 12, 1951

Dear Cleanth:

You will hear in a few days from a student I had this summer at Bloomington (I've also had him at NYU), who wants to do his Ph.D. at Yale. Arthur Mizener and I agreed that Yale is not only the best place, but the best place for him. His name is Irwin Primer.

The term paper that Irwin Primer wrote for me this summer is in many respects the ablest I've ever had from a student done in so short a period. He had only three weeks in which to do it. I believe he is sending it to you.

This boy is a terrific worker. He is primarily interested in criticism but is perfectly willing to do all the routine of the graduate school; and he will do it with great thoroughness. He feels completely frustrated at Columbia.

What chance have we of seeing you all before we leave for Minneapolis on Sept 12? The house here is absolutely full—Nancy and Percy and the children are here—and there's not one extra bed; so we could not offer you all much hospitality. Are you likely to be in New York? Or could you come down for a day?

We join in love to you both.

Yrs.
Allen

[OH]   [Memphis]
                                                  August 21 [1951]

Dear Allen—

Your letter of the 12th has just been forwarded to me here. I shall get on the job for Primer at once. (A letter from him has come in since you wrote.) He sounds very good. I have no doubt that admission can be arranged and I shall do my best in the matter of some kind of fellowship for him.

I plan to be back in New Haven on the 26th of this month. We must certainly have a meeting before you and Caroline get away. I wish that you all would come up to New Haven. We have—at long last—lots of space including lots of bedrooms. That is *our* first choice and Tinkum and I shall be writing or telephoning you shortly to *urge* you and Caroline to make the visit. Do plan to do so. If that is quite impossible, [we] will drive down for the day or see you all in New York—but will count on the visit at Northford.

I shall be in touch with you again the next few days. Meantime, all cordial regards to you both.

Cleanth

465 Nassau Street
Princeton
August 27, 1951

Dear Cleanth:

Mighty glad to get yours of the 21st from Memphis.

We hope that you and Tinkum will come down here for lunch next Sunday September 1st. I can well imagine that you might hesitate to take to the highways on Labor Day weekend; and if the prospect is too forbidding, could we meet the next week in New York, say on Wednesday for dinner, or on Thursday for lunch? That would be better than nothing, but not too good, as it would mean that we should have to have our visit in a restaurant. But let us know which plan suits you best.

Yrs affly.
Allen

[OH]

1315 Yale Station
New Haven, Conn.
April 13 [1952]

Dear Allen—

A voice from the tomb—or so it must seem. But it's been a harried year—the worst of all thus far. I have been robbing Peter to pay Paul— pulling the iron out of the fire that was hottest—and then rushing to pull out the next one. Things that could be postponed, but which shouldn't be, have suffered in the process, including writing to my friends.

First for the poem: it is very fine indeed. It is pure Tate, but Tate at the height of his powers, and the sharpness and vitality of the detail don't impede the narrative drive. I think that you've got here the style for a long poem. I hope that the poem has been going ahead—though I know that I have no right to assume that Parts I and II have been finished yet. I am anxious to see more—whenever you have an extra carbon. I suppose that the core incident is one that I have heard you talk about—something that you witnessed in your boyhood.[1]

1. The poem is Tate's "The Swimmers," one of a series of terza rima poems intended as parts of a long poem. Tate never completed the long poem, and in his last published collection these poems were included as individual pieces. In "The Swimmers," he

There's little news. At the Washington meeting of the Fellows, I thought that we had handled Luther Evans properly by alternately holding his feet to the fire and then volunteering to help him with the human problem of handling Mrs. Whittall.[2] That is, we insisted on the principle involved, but pointed out that university libraries handled every day the problem of difficult donors—but they got the donations without giving up the only principle on which it was safe to accept donations—and that as far as shaking down Mrs. Whittall we would help with that.

Later news has indicated that I was perhaps naive in assuming that Evans had got the point. I have written a stiffer letter since, hinting at resignation. I haven't heard from that letter yet. I wish that you could have been on hand to help with strategy. Auden did well enough and Red and Mrs. Chapman did yeoman service, but your talents were needed.

During the last weeks I have been hard at work on a book on criticism that Bill Wimsatt and I are collaborating on.[3] Bill will have to bear the burden—particularly in the chapters on Aristotle, Plato, Aquinas, etc. But I am getting excited about it now and look on it as a fine opportunity to get my own mind cleared on the issues. If we can make the book what it ought to be, it will come at a strategic time—what with the Chicago crowd now out in force in an omnium gatherum book, with Blackmur's roving eye of late turned toward poetry as philosophy, etc., etc.

In reading for the book, I have been going over—among other things— John Ransom's later work. All honor to John as a man and as a friend, but I am really surprised at what the position adds up to: John has agreed himself back, unless I utterly misread him, into the position of Eastman, the earlier Richards, and of Matthew Arnold![4]—positions which he has so ably castigated at our time. I have been reminded forcibly of what you told me as far ago as 1936 of John's basic view of poetry. I am bound to say that you are entirely right.

Our book will take a formalist position, as you would suppose, and will see poetry as cognitive. Nothing new there. But we have got—or

recounts the traumatic childhood memory of witnessing the lynching of a black man in his hometown.

2. Luther Evans was at this time the librarian of Congress. Gertrude Clark Whittall, a prominent Washington socialite and philanthropist, was a major patron of the library.

3. Their work in progress was *Literary Criticism: A Short History* (New York: Alfred A. Knopf, 1957).

4. Ransom's "Why Critics Don't Go Mad," *Kenyon Review* 14 (spring 1952): 331–39, critiques Brooks's critical method.

rather Bill has got—a way of handling matters that I think is going to be awfully effective. The book will be a sort of history—not an exhaustive one, to be sure—but the historical background will provide a great deal of power for the argument, which will become more and more overt in later chapters. One will be able to show where the errors start and these references back to history—plus the exercises—will give us a chance to answer objections while we maintain primarily the exposition of a thesis. If this were not to be two-thirds Bill's book, and if Bill were not the man he is, such a plan would be out of the question. I am no theorist. I want to go on to write about the work of Milton or of Faulkner or of Joyce or about your work or Red's. But I think the opportunity is heaven-sent, and I think that the job has got to be done—however much I may be relieved when it is over.

We've seen a little of Red this spring, but he frequently goes back to New York for the week-end and has certainly been kept busy the time that he is here. All seems to be going well with him, however, and though his big poem has been stopped for the time being, it is very fine, and he is hoping to push it to a conclusion this summer.[5]

I mean to sit down and write Caroline this week about *The Strange Children*.[6] I wolfed it down when it came out and have been rereading it in more leisurely fashion later. It's a very big novel—probably her best, it seems to me, for all my special liking for that very special book, *Aleck Maury.*

I hope that you both have got through the winter handily and as the spring opens, if either one of you turn toward the East, do plan to pay us a visit.

We have only during the past few days got any more work done on the house. Tinkum had to be in Louisiana during much of the fall and early winter, and even since she's been back, the demands on our time have just been too heavy to allow much time for the fun of painting and paint-scraping. But we did paint some this week-end, and when the sun came out ten days ago, I cut brush around our little river.

Do let us see you all when you can.

Love to Caroline,
Cleanth

I am to be out in California teaching part of the summer, but Tinkum will be here right through entertaining little nieces and nephews.

5. Warren's *Brother to Dragons*, a long poem on Thomas Jefferson's nephews and the nature of evil, was published by Random House in 1953.
6. Gordon's novel was published in 1951.

1801 University Avenue S.E.
Minneapolis, 14, Minnesota
April 15, 1952

Dear Cleanth:

I'm answering your letter directly it was read, because if I wait five minutes it will be drawn off into the hole where lie buried all the things I want to do. I thought I'd got through the Minnesota winter without a cold, but the flu hit me ten days ago, and I'm still groggy. I have to write an entire lecture to give at Carleton on April 25, and I must fix it so that it will do as the Phi Beta Kappa speech here the next week; and I must also keep an eye on the possibility of giving it in Paris between May 15 and 30. I've accepted an invitation to "represent" the U.S. at a grandiose festival of the arts sponsored by the Congress of Cultural Freedom. I'm sad because Red recently wrote me that Yale wouldn't let him go. I like the idea of helping to preserve peace in Paris in May.

Yes, the trouble with Luther Evans is that he doesn't *stay* handled; and he never answers difficult letters. In spite of his excellent qualities, he has learned to be a perfect Washington bureaucrat, and I predict that you all will have to resign pretty soon. He is determined to change the character of the group, and not *merely* because he wants Mrs. Whittall's money: if the money were all, we could handle him. He is tired of being bossed by a group of poets who got him in trouble with Pound.

I'm delighted that you like Part III of my poem. Since I sent that version to Red, I've made six or seven changes of the sort that to me at any rate seem to make all the difference. It will be out in the Summer Hudson. Part I will appear in a couple of weeks in Partisan.[1] I have no extra carbon, but I hope you will glance at Partisan and tell me what you think. Part I was very tough going because I had to insert themes to be used later, at the same time that I had to create some action to hold the reader. I've just read TSE's remarks on terza rima in the current Kenyon. I think he's not at all right about terza rima in English, and I don't agree with him that Shelley was a master of it; and I wish when TSE quotes Shelley he wouldn't misquote him.

We like it out here enormously, and except that we miss old friends that can't at our age be replaced, I would be reconciled to staying the rest of my life. We may do just that anyhow, and return to Princeton in the summer.

For the next year Nancy and her family will occupy the house. They now have their third child, little Caroline, born Jan. 31. We haven't seen

---

1. "The Swimmers" was published in the *Hudson Review* 5 (winter 1953): 471–73; part I was published as "The Maimed Man" in *Partisan Review* 19 (May–June 1952): 262–67.

her yet, but I expect to see her the week-end before I take the plane to France.

Red was kind enough to ask me to come up to New Haven that week-end, and I wish I could, and I may be able to in the end if only for a few hours. But I do wish that you and Tinkum and Red would come in to NY for the evening of Sunday May 11, so that we might dine and talk. Otherwise I don't know when I'll see you all again.

The book that you and Bill Wimsatt are doing sounds extremely interesting. I've just done a little essay in critical scepticism which I'm trying to get in shape to print. I fear you may not like it, but I know you'll tell me what you think.—I feel as you do about JCR's recent criticism: if I weren't so fond of him I suppose I'd get mad at him. I never talk criticism with him anymore, but we're still very good friends. The recent job on you I didn't like at all. I haven't yet been able to get at your Milton, though it is by me now. In order to teach my seminar in criticism I've had to restudy everything I've ever read, and it has been back-breaking.

I'm hoping to get a glimpse of you all in May.

Love to you both from both of us,
Allen

1315 Yale Station
New Haven, Conn.
April 22 [1952]

Dear Allen—

Thanks for your good letter of the 15th. I rush off a reply to say that we will definitely count on seeing you in New York on Sunday May 11—though I hope that we may in the meantime persuade you and Caroline to come out to New Haven for a visit—even a very, very brief one.

When I wrote to you last I had not read John's piece in the *Kenyon,* and whereas I wish that John would change his critical direction, I must say that he is here—as always—amiable and handsome. For me (as I know for you) the matter isn't a personal one at all. What it comes down to finally, I suppose, is a concept of poetry which at least allows it to be fitted in with religion and metaphysics or a concept that forces it finally into a positivistic and materialistic scheme of the world. The people who have insisted, instinctively or formally and specifically, on the "limits of poetry" have been protecting poetry from invasion by science and materialist philosophy quite as much as they have been taking it out of competition with "philosophy." It is no accident surely that nearly all these people believe in metaphysics or (as in the case of most) have made their submission to an historical church. It is John's refusal to observe the "limits of poetry" that I suppose ultimately disturbs me. But more of this when we have a chance to talk—which I hope may be soon!

Cordial regards to you both,
[Cleanth]

As you may have heard by this time, John Palmer has had to resign from the *Sewanee*.[1] The Navy has put great pressure on him to take a post in London. He has agreed, reluctantly, and is now worried about a successor. He phoned me the other night. He indicated he was also going to ask you whether you could suggest names. He rightly sees how important it is to get the right man. Can you send some to him direct or to me to be relayed to him just as soon as you can?

[OH]
University of Minnesota
College of Science, Literature, and the Arts
Minneapolis 14
April 23, 1952

Dear Cleanth:

I suppose you know that John Palmer is resigning from the Sewanee. Unless you have a candidate, I hope you will send John a recommendation for Morgan Blum. I'm convinced he would do a fine job. John leaves for England May 27; so there's need of hurry.

Yrs.
Allen

1801 Univ. Ave. SE
MPLS. 5/1/52

Dear Cleanth:

Could you all make it *lunch* on Sunday May 11, instead of dinner? I will have to go back to P'ton late in the afternoon. I didn't send my schedule in time to P'ton, and things have got in motion that I can't well stop. I'm delighted that you could come to dinner; now I only hope lunch won't be impossible. Let's meet at the Princeton Club at 12:30.

Yrs.
Allen

1. Monroe K. Spears (1915–1998) was brought in to replace Palmer and began his editorship with the fall 1952 issue of the *Sewanee Review*. He remained in the position until 1961, when he was succeeded by Lytle, who continued as editor until 1973.

Dept. of English
Univ. of Minnesota
Minneapolis 14
October 21, 1952

Dear Cleanth,

Much water has run under the bridge since that Sunday in NY last May; not only another trip to Europe (Italy) but more recently the enclosed poem. I have just written it. In any case I should want to get your opinion of it, but particularly because I can't believe that I could have written 126 lines that are any good in six days.[1] I have never before written so much in so short a time. I know you are busy as hell, but if you can, look it over. I've got somehow to get this section off my mind before I go on to another. I have three completely "finished," a fourth almost finished, and three yet to do. As you see I am not writing the sections consecutively.—The problem, as you will see at a glance, is to get into the strait-jacket of the terza rima, as great a stretch as possible of tone and style. As I see it, I have got three different styles here—the flat narrative (the scene in Hell), the metaphysical, and the pastoral. I can't tell at present whether they get along together.

Another thing. I want to come East for spring vacation. I used to be invited (when we were still at Princeton) to give a lot of lectures and readings around the decadent East, but now that I'm out here it seems to be assumed that I'm too far, or it would be too expensive, etc. Well, I think it may be a little improper to suggest this sort of thing, but I don't know what else to do. I'd like to make enough money to pay travel expenses, and I could appear in the New York area on either March 19 or 20. I could read some of my new poems, with comment, or give a lecture on the Oedipos Tyrannos which I will have already given here.

Still another thing. I am trying to get started my MLA paper (for Maynard [Mack]'s program), and even if I get it done I shall not be able to come to Boston. Maynard seemed to agree to that plan. Would you do me the honor of reading it for me? That is, if you're going to be there.

Caroline is going to Seattle to teach the spring quarter (Bob Heilman's invitation), and that's one reason why I want to go East—to see the children and friends. Everybody here wants to fly away somewhere just at that time—the ice block that we've been frozen up in is just beginning to soften.

1. Tate had just completed his last major poem, "The Buried Lake."

I'd like Red to see my new poem, but I heard the other day that he's off on a trip, and I thought I'd wait till I could get more definite news of him.

Write me when you can the news of you and Tinkum. How's the book with Bill Wimsatt coming along? He asked us up last summer but I was about to take off for Italy. I'll tell you about that later.

Love to you both,

Affly.

Allen

[Handwritten] This letter was unaccountably held up. I will be giving a reading at Radcliffe on March 18.

[OH]

1315 Yale Station

New Haven, Conn.

Nov. 11 [1952]

Dear Allen—

Your "Buried Lake" is splendid! It's the best thing that you have ever done—or so at least it seems to me now. This is not random enthusiasm—I've had a week for my first impression to cool before I have read it again this morning. I like particularly the effect of the rimes: they give enough arrest—enough wrench and shock—to keep up a real excitement, but they do not wrench the poem apart.

I am anxious to see more of the poem. I should be very happy if you will give me the chance to look at any new sections that you finish. Red is teaching here this fall. I've hardly seen him for the last ten days, but I expect to see him tomorrow, and I am passing my copy of "The Buried Lake" along to him.

Do plan to stop with us on the spring vacation for as long as you can. I shall hope to have some word to report to you about a lecture in the next few days. You are perfectly right to mention that you will be available. Our only difficulty here is that the lecture funds—the larger funds, at least—are out of our hands, and in the hands of a whimsical and somewhat crotchety Secretary of the University[1] who sometimes comes begging for suggestions and quite unaccountably at other times has filled up the dates in his own way. But there are several possibilities which I am canvassing. Needless to say, the students here know your work and would pour out in great number for a chance to hear you. Our problem lies in a different quarter.

1. Carl Albert Lohmann.

I am delighted to know that you are again to give a paper [at] the MLA, but not surprised, seeing that it's Maynard's program. I hadn't heard it from Maynard since he is now in Rome and had left before I returned at the end of the summer. It looks now, however, as if I shall have to miss the MLA this year. I feel an obligation to visit my mother during the Xmas holidays if I can. I would be honored to read your paper if I were to be.

My book with Bill Wimsatt is at a standstill but I am trying to get next year off. I am applying for a Guggenheim and have taken the liberty of giving your name as a reference. But I cannot say that I am sanguine about getting it: the committee looks to me rather loaded with historical scholars. Anyway, I shall be grateful for your letter, and I shall hope for luck with the committee. (Henri Peyre, by the way, in spite of his Hopkins lecture and his book, *Writers and Their Critics,* is sympathetic and I am not at all worried by *his* presence on the Guggenheim Committee.)

Bill Wimsatt, by the way, likes your *Partisan* piece on criticism very much indeed.[2] That is high praise, for Bill's knowledge and insight into theory is really profound. I hardly need add that I like your piece very much too—though I wish you had had space to elaborate some of the sections. But that must wait for another letter. I have to hurry away to a department meeting. (This letter has been interrupted *three times* since I began it—and that is a fair index of my life at the moment: too many talks with students and too few letters to my friends!)

I know that Bob H is delighted with Caroline's acceptance of his invitation for her to come to Seattle. I hope that she will like it.

Tinkum joins me in love to her and to you both,

Cleanth

University of Minnesota
College of Science, Literature, and the Arts
Minneapolis 14
November 18, 1952

Dear Cleanth,

I can't tell you how pleased I am that you like the Buried Lake. I wish I had some other sections to show you. I think you've already seen two others. A fourth is nearly finished, and a fifth begun. It will run to seven or perhaps even nine sections, a total of about 900 or 1,200 lines—a long

2. Tate's "Is Literary Criticism Possible?" *Partisan Review* 19 (September–October 1952): 546–57.

poem for me. If you get any leisure in the next few weeks I wish you'd check the soft spots in it; I know they are there.

Red wrote me that he would help about a lecture. I hope you boys won't go to too much trouble. My chief desire is to finance a visit to friends in the East, chiefly at New Haven.

I am glad too that you and Bill Wimsatt like my PR essay. As usual, it is a patchwork and rather haphazard. Maybe in the next year I will try to develop at length each of the ten "propositions" in the second part. But I am scarcely capable of this. You and Bill ought to do this job, since I'm rather short on theory.

Yrs.
Allen

[OH]   [Minneapolis]
                                                                    12/12/52

Dear Cleanth:

Won't you please help me? I can do this job in about two months. I need the rest of the time to finish my poem—but this is between ourselves.

Allen

I'm a little late getting the application.[1]

[OH]   1315 Yale Station
                                                            New Haven, Conn.
                                                                 Feb. 14, 1953

Dear Allen—

Norman Pearson tells me that he has invited you to speak (or perhaps it is to do a reading) at the Elizabethan Club. By this time you should have heard from Father Lakas who was to issue an invitation to you to speak at the Catholic Graduate Club. I do hope that you can accept. We are anxious to see you and want you to stay with us just as long as you can.

Father Lakas, by the way, is an excellent person with a good head. I gave him honors in my seminar two years ago. He is now at work on his dissertation under Maynard Mack and Bill Wimsatt.

In a way a Bergen lecture would be better, but as I told you, we have no direct control over that and the Secretary of the University

1. Tate was awarded a Fulbright that enabled him to lecture in the American studies program in Oxford during the summer of 1953 and to work at the University of Rome in the fall and winter of 1953–1954.

tends to be capricious. One year he is begging me for nominations; the next year I never hear from him. This happens to be my off year, and besides the Bergen nominations apparently were made and accepted very early.

At any rate, the two groups are the best that we have—our new English graduate Club has no funds—and between them they will include many, if not most, of the people who want to hear you and ought to hear you. I hope that you can accept.

Your "Man of Letters in the Modern World"[1] seems to me one of the very best things that you have ever done. I am grateful to you for sending me an offprint. I was so enthusiastic over it that I was on the point of sending you my Phi Beta Kappa Oration in (1950) that I gave at Harvard to let you see why I was so enthusiastic. But I let the occasion slip and did not write *this letter* several weeks ago as I meant to. Having waited this long, I shall wait until you are here—hoping that you *will* be here—and show it to you then. It has been a brisk year with all of my time gone and very little to show for it. Yale manages to absorb nearly all of the time—or perhaps I have simply not yet learned how to cope with it.

I go down to Sewanee this week for a lecture and to Johns Hopkins the next week. On the Hopkins trip I shall see Spitzer[2] and I want to talk with you about the project that I expect him to bring up. I have many other things to talk with you about, including the Indiana School of Letters, where I shall teach this summer, and the Bill Williams matter[3] about which you have probably already heard something.

Have you completed any more sections of the big poem? I am most anxious to see them if you have. I think it is to date your very best work.

Red and his bride[4] are househunting on the other side of New Haven. They had located—when I saw them last week—a fine old barn that they hoped to buy and remodel. If you come in March, you may just catch them, though I think that they still hope to get away to Europe early next month.

1. "The Man of Letters in the Modern World," *Hudson Review* 5 (autumn 1952): 335–45.
2. Leo Spitzer, an Austrian-born scholar who left Germany following the establishment of the Third Reich, was a professor of Romance languages at Johns Hopkins.
3. William Carlos Williams had been offered the position of consultant in poetry at the Library of Congress. He accepted but then withdrew his acceptance. When the position was offered again, he expressed a desire to take the job, but the appointment ran into political problems. The offer was renewed later, but by that time the poet was too ill to accept.
4. Warren had married the writer Eleanor Clark. He was divorced from Emma Brescia (Cinina) Warren in 1951. Warren's marriage to Eleanor Clark endured happily for the rest of their lives, giving them two children—Rosanna, a poet, and Gabriel, a sculptor.

I hope your grant comes through. I wrote promptly. And my thanks to you in the Guggenheim matter—but from what I have heard about the present board's dislike for criticism, I am taking nothing at all for granted.

I suppose that Caroline has by this time left for the U. of Washington. I hope that she will find it pleasant. Bob Heilman, I am sure, will do all that he can to make it so.

Do plan to see us and stay with us as long and as often as you can. Tinkum joins in love to you both.

Cleanth

[OH]   University of Minnesota
College of Science, Literature, and the Arts
Minneapolis 14
Feb. 17, 1953

Dear Cleanth:

This must be only a note—a poor return for your fine letter; but I am just back from three days at Iowa and face a mountain of detail.

I've written Norman my acceptance of the invitation from the Elizabethan Club; but I've not [received] word from Fr. Lakas. I do hope that Norman can fix the date for March 20.

Please send your PBK speech *now.*

I've heard rumors of the Bill Williams row but know nothing about it. I very much fear that senile egomania has overtaken him.

I really prefer the auspices that I shall come under to the Bergen. My main desire is to visit you all.

Affly.
Allen

[OH]   University College
Oxford
July 25 1953

Dear Brookses,

I'm here for fine week at the Fulbright Conference on American Studies lecturing the British on the New Crit and American poetry. Caroline arrives by boat Aug. 3. Sept. I will proceed to Rome.

Love,
Allen

[OH]   Villa Aurelia
                                    Fargo di San Pancrazio, #1
                                                    Roma, 28
                                               Oct. 6 [1953]

Dear Brookses:

We hear from Red that you all are coming to Europe next Spring. May we bribe you to come here with an offer of a tour in our new Austin? Caroline is practically delirious with pleasure. Esse la involato a catacombe in osso di pelvi. d'un martire!

                                         Love from us both,
                                                   A & C.

                                                Forest Road
                                          Northford, Conn.
                                           [February 1954]

Dear Caroline and Allen—

We hope to be sailing for Europe on March 20th. Unfortunately we can spare only two months or so for the trip. But we have decided to spend most of that all-too-short time in Italy and England.

We land at Cherbourg on the 25th and plan to come immediately to Rome and thence to Sicily. We would like to stay in Sicily something like a week and then work our way up the peninsula. Is there a chance that you all might join us for the Sicilian jaunt? It would be lots of fun seeing the Greek temples and the cathedrals together.

But whether or not you can come to Sicily with us, we are looking forward to seeing you all during our few days in Rome. Our best time I think will be on our way *back* from Sicily, probably about the end of the first week in April. I hope that this will be a good time for you all too, but we both are very hopeful that you all can come on down to Sicily with us.

                                              All our best,
                                                    Cleanth

                                   American Academy in Rome
                                          Via Angelo Masina 5
                                         (Porta S. Pancrazio)
                                                    Rome, 28
                                              March 3, 1954

Dear Brookses,

That's wonderful news. We will be expecting you all shortly after March 25. I think now that we can make it to Sicily. I shall only have to be back here by April 10 to start a new series of lectures. I was in Sicily only four days and saw almost nothing; so I welcome another chance at it. Caroline hasn't been at all.—We have an Austin. Shall we go in the car? It's a tremendous advantage once we get to Sicily. But it means that we can't get there as fast as by train. We can decide these matters after you arrive.

I will also save our meager news for your arrival. It can be summed under three heads: 1) a wonderful time, 2) constant indigestion, and 3) no work.

Our love to you both,
Allen

[OH]

University of Minnesota
College of Science, Literature, and the Arts
Minneapolis 14
January 2, 1955

Dear Cleanth,

When your good letter arrived it seemed that I might have to give up the trip to New Haven; as I delayed answering until I could be sure. I now definitely plan to come. The trouble, as usual in the past two years, is my teeth. I can't afford to take off a month or six weeks after having *them all* out at once; so I sacrificed one or two at a time; and the dentist makes temporary adjustments. The latest crisis is about over: the dentist says that he will have me in shape for the trip.

Caroline would love to come but she fears to leave the novel. She has within about 20,000 words of the end.[1] Then there's the expense. God knows when we'll recover from the year in Italy!—I expect to arrive in New Haven around 3 or 4 on Friday afternoon. I'll telephone you from N.Y. Friday morning, the exact hour. I must leave around noon on Saturday, or as soon as possible after the committee meeting, in order to get to Princeton to spend that night with Nancy. I must take a plane at 5:00 on Monday. You will be able to judge better than I whether there will be time to go out to your house—which I should love doing—or whether I must follow Mr. Babb's instructions and stay at a college.—All best wishes from this New Year; and love to Tinkum.

Affly.
Allen

1. Gordon was at work on *The Malefactors*, published in 1956.

University of Minnesota
College of Science, Literature, and the Arts
Minneapolis 14
January 26, 1955

Dear Cleanth,

I'm really ashamed to bother you about a trivial matter. I'm in a real jam with my 1953 income tax, and I need all the small sums I can raise to keep out of trouble. Jim Babb has not sent my expense money, and I'm a little embarrassed to remind him. I sent him a note about it immediately after I got back. Would it be too much trouble to speak to him about it?

I won't repeat here in detail what a fine time I had. We look forward to seeing you all early in the summer.

Affly.
Allen

University of Minnesota
College of Science, Literature, and the Arts
Minneapolis 14
March 14, 1956

Dear Cleanth,

I'm awfully glad you are our moderator at the Fugitive Reunion. I've just had a letter from Randall Stewart[1] asking me to tell you my ideas about the program. At the moment I haven't any. The public part of it won't be too hard, but the Rockefeller Foundation seems not to be interested in that. I suppose the Foundation wants us to talk for the tape, but that will be hard because we shall be talking for posterity. I feel rather stumped. But I know you will have some ideas. Please pass them on to me. I look forward to a lot of fun, but there *is* a ludicrous side. We shall be living documents. And I could do without meeting the Board of Trust.

I plan to fly from here to Kansas City, where I will pick Caroline up. We expect to stay with the Cheneys at Smyrna. We hope that Tinkum

---

1. Randall Stewart (1896–1964), the chairman of the English department at Vanderbilt, organized a reunion of the Fugitives in 1956 as a conciliatory gesture toward the group of writers who had placed Vanderbilt on the literary map and then been badly treated by the university. See *Fugitives' Reunion: Conversations at Vanderbilt, May 3–5, 1956*, ed. Rob Roy Purdy (Nashville: Vanderbilt University Press, 1959), and Louis D. Rubin Jr., "The Gathering of the Fugitives: A Recollection," *Southern Review* 30 (autumn 1994): 658–73.

will be along too. Randall's program seems to leave us little time for real conversation, but we can work it in somehow.

Love to Tinkum,

Affly.

Allen

[Telegram] Branford, Conn.

April 8 1957

PROFESSOR ALLEN TATE

DEPT OF ENGLISH UNIV OF MINNESOTA MPLS

CAN YOU GIVE PAPER ON PROBLEM OF BELIEF ENGLISH INSTITUTE THIS SEPTEMBER 3 THRU 7 HAVE FINE PROGRAM BUT NEED YOU TO COMPLETE IT IF CHANCE OF YOUR SAYING YES WIRE ME COLLECT AND I SHALL MAIL FURTHER DETAILS

CLEANTH

Forest Road

Northford, Conn.

April 9 [1957]

Dear Allen,

Thanks for your wire which gives me hope that perhaps you will accept a place on the English Institute program.

As you may remember from 1941 (or was it 1942?), the English Institute has each year four programs, each of which has four papers which are given on successive days. The fact that the audience is around 150 people and that the same audience, pretty much, hears all the papers make for a real continuity of discussion. I think that I can promise you a real fine audience and good talk—though unfortunately there is no fee and no expense fund. It would have to be charity on your part—though I hope that an interest in the topic and business or pleasure near New York at the end of the summer may induce you to come any way.

The phrase "the problems of belief" comes from I. A. Richards, but I am expecting the speakers to interpret it pretty much to suit their own interests. What *I* have in mind is the amount of acceptance of the poet's political, sociological, or metaphysical assumptions that we must share in order to participate fully in his work. Is there a clean severance possible between our evaluation of the work and its reflection of our "values," or if not, then what is the relation?

The topic is a worn one, but restatements and revisions may be useful—even a consolidation of positions, if that is possible. Or maybe the question of belief has from the first been badly asked, and what we need is a restatement of the question. At any rate, this is a topic that the members of the Institute, in effect, asked for, and my choices of speakers have been made with proper regard for a variety of points of view. But there is not a dud or freak among the lot, and the amount of silly or aimless discussion ought to be nil. I do hope—for a whole variety of reasons—that I may secure you. *Do* say yes if it is at all possible. In any case, I should appreciate your wiring me collect, for I have let matters get a little behind.

The English Institute meets Sept. 3 through 7, and at Columbia University as usual. But we would hope to have you here before or after for as long a visit as we might induce you to make. Tinkum joins in all cordial regards.

Cleanth

The University of Minnesota
College of Science, Literature, and the Arts
Minneapolis 14
April 10, 1957

Dear Cleanth:

Many thanks for your letter. I see what it is all about now, and I am of course interested. But since you need to get the matter settled at once, I'm afraid I'll have to say no. If I could be sure of writing the paper between now and June, I would say yes. I should have to be sure of that because I shall be too busy this summer to count on enough free time to write a letter. I am doing two courses at Brandeis and the International Seminar again at Harvard: grinding my bones to make my bread. I shall be through by August 20th but there would not be enough time left to do the paper. If I could even do a first draft before June . . .

A few days ago I received *Literary Criticism: A Short History,* which I have been reading around in with growing admiration. It is a brilliant job which will more and more seem indispensable. When I got back here in January from India and Europe, I found a set of the galleys, but it was obviously too late to do anything about them at that stage. I'm sorry about this because you went to a good deal of trouble to have them sent. The book is the first to make it possible to teach contemporary criticism with an intelligible historical perspective.

In any case, I shall hope to see you and Tinkum somewhere this summer. Affectionate regards to you both,

Allen

[OH]   Farwell Place
                                                       Cambridge 38
                                                       June 27, 1957

Dear Cleanth:

I was two days late leaving Princeton; so, I had to come here direct, resisting the pull of Northford. But I do hope that Jim Cunningham[1] is right in thinking you will come to Brandeis for a colloquium. I have a guest bed (for 2, so bring Tinkum), and would love to put you all up.

                                                       Affly.
                                                       Allen

                                                       Forest Road
                                                       Northford, Conn.
                                                       July 2 [1957]

Dear Allen,

We are sorry that we missed you on your way up to Cambridge. After getting your card, Tinkum tried to telephone you on Friday in the hope that you could just possibly come down last weekend. But we could only try at Brandeis and had no luck in reaching you.

The pressure is that we leave for the South and Far West this very week. But you are to be at Harvard during August, aren't you? Please save some time for us. I expect to return for August 1st; Tinkum, a little later in the month. Ideally, we want you to pay us a real visit while both of us are here, but if that is not possible, do plan to visit here anyway— and for that matter the more the better—early in August *and* then again later. We have much to talk over.

                                                       In haste,
                                                       Cleanth

All mail addressed here or at 1315 Yale Station will be forwarded to me promptly.

[OH]   Prince George Hotel
                                                       East 28th Street
                                                       New York, N.Y.
                                                       January 19, 1959

Dear Cleanth:

Your good letter of the 6th followed me around the lecture circuit (which began two weeks ago in Austin, Texas), and I got it only the day before yesterday. I return to England this Wednesday (21st), to Leeds

1. J. V. Cunningham, an essayist and poet, taught at Brandeis.

this time, for six weeks; then around mid-March back to All Souls. I shall look up your friends. I have greatly enjoyed Nevill Coghill and David Bolsdon; and I like David Cecil.[1] It has somewhat disconcerted me that his part of our anthology has taken a beating in England, and mine universally praised.[2]—Oxford is tepid but pleasant.

I shall be at Harvard again, and this time will have a seminar three times a week, instead of the *ten* lectures of last summer. I shall thus have greater mobility and shall count on seeing you and Tinkum.

I am trying to finish up the long poem, and until I do—no more prose, of which I am a little tired.—Is Tennessee Williams worth your attention?

My love to you both.

Ever yrs.,

Allen

[OH]

235 Harvard St.
Cambridge 38
7/22/59

Dear Cleanth,

I was mighty sorry to miss you at Georgetown. I had to take over one of Andrew's[1] courses, and in the first two weeks I had to read about 24 hours a day to get it going. Towards the end of August I'll be heading west, and I want to stop to see you and Tinkum. Monroe [Spears] informs me you have written something about me. Guess I'll have to wait to see it—a sort of surprise birthday party. Love to Tinkum.

Affly.

Allen

[OH]

533 W. Elm St.
Inglewood, California
July 28, 1959

Dear Allen—

Your welcome postcard of the 22nd has just been forwarded to me in California. (We are on our annual summer family visits—Tinkum in New

1. The Chaucer scholar Neville Coghill (1899–1980) had been one of Brooks's tutors at Exeter. David Bolsdon was a fellow of Exeter College whom Brooks had met when he was a student there. Lord David Cecil (b. 1902) was the Oldsmith Professor of English Literature at Oxford. He and Coghill were both active members of C. S. Lewis's circle known as "The Inklings," which also included Owen Barfield, Charles Williams, and J. R. R. Tolkien.

2. *Modern Verse in English, 1900–1950*, ed. Cecil and Tate (New York: Macmillan; London: Eyre and Spottiswoode, 1958).

1. Lytle had a serious operation in June that forced him to cancel his summer lectureship at Harvard.

Orleans; I, here.) But we will be back at Northford early in August—by the 9th, and we shall get in touch with you then. It will be so good to have a visit from you and some talk. It's been a long time since we have had any.

My piece on you is still, alas, an aspiration rather than an accomplished fact.[1] But I have not given up hope of getting it in. (I have never been so busy in my life as during the past year: the pressure exerted by Yale has been heavy—and two other commitments have vacuumed up such little time as I have had left. I must find a way to reorganize my life. I have three books in various stages of completion that I cannot get round to finishing.)

The Georgetown Conference was interesting without being in the least exciting. I hope that all goes well at Harvard. Do save some time for us before you go west.

As ever,
Cleanth

[OH]   Wellfleet, Mass.
                                                          10th Sept. '59

Dear Tinkum and Cleanth,

Many thanks for your nice telegram. I want you all to meet Isabella.[1] I wish it seemed possible for us to run in on you, on the 17th, when we drive to N.Y. But we must be there by 4:30 to meet Nancy and Percy. Therefore, I trust it won't be too long till we meet.

Love,
Allen

                                                      1315 Yale Station
                                                      New Haven, Conn.
                                                      October 16, 1959

Dear Allen,

We were sorry that we were not able to have you and Isabella here last month. Maybe we can catch you on some trip fairly soon, or maybe we can devise something to bring you East.

---

1. Brooks was asked to contribute an essay to a special issue of *Sewanee Review* in honor of Tate's sixtieth birthday. Due to other commitments he was unable to complete the project.

1. Isabella Stewart Gardner (1915–1981) was Tate's second wife; he and Gordon had been divorced for the second time earlier in 1959. Gardner was a poet and a member of a prominent Boston family; the Isabella Gardner who founded the Isabella Stewart Gardner Museum in Boston was her godmother.

I am thoroughly ashamed of myself for failing to get something into the birthday number of the *Sewanee,* but it has been the most harassing late summer and fall that I have ever been through. In addition to all the usual tasks, two that I had not counted upon hit me at the last minute and simply soaked up every moment of free time that I have had now for weeks. The special number of the *Sewanee* will be no worse for my having failed to get in it—I have no illusions about *that*—but I regret that for my own sake I can't be among those who are paying you honor on that particular occasion.

I do have an opportunity, however, to say something on the subject of Allen Tate's work in the record of your poems that I am editing for Yale.[1] I have heard the tapes—beautiful reading it is—and want to prepare my selections and then my jacket copy shortly. I would like to send what I propose we use to you in the next few days in the hope that you will express your own judgment on my selections. But let me ask you one or two questions here and now: Did you decide not to record "The Seasons of the Soul" or did I simply miss that in playing the tapes the other day? You do want me to use, I am sure, parts of the big unfinished poem, "The Buried Lake," certainly, but what about the other two sections? Do you hold the copyright for these or should I apply to the *Sewanee* and the *Partisan*? I assume that I should apply to Scribners for nearly everything else.

We are going in to New York tonight to see the first performance of Red's play.[2] I haven't read the present version and of course what a New York audience will do is the last thing that one can predict. We wish that you were to be along with us.

Tinkum joins me in love to you both.

Cleanth

University of Minnesota
College of Science, Literature, and the Arts
Minneapolis 14
October 19, 1959

Dear Cleanth:

I'm mighty glad to get your letter. Since September I've been uneasy lest our telegram saying we couldn't stop off with you and Tinkum hadn't arrived. We left the Cape two days late, and had to make time.

---

1. Brooks wrote the liner notes for *Allen Tate Reads from His Own Works,* Yale Series of Recorded Poets (Carillon Records, YP 300, 1960).
2. Warren's *Brother to Dragons* had been dramatized for the stage.

Couldn't we get together the week-end of Nov. 7th—or rather for the evening of the 6th—in New York? I have to be there to attend the Senior Fellows' meeting, and Isabella will be along too. I'm very anxious for you all to meet. Come in for dinner. We'll be at the Hotel Dryden on East 39th Street. Or if lunch would suit you better, come on Sat the 7th.

Lee Anderson wrote me you were to be my "editor" for the Yale recording, and I was delighted. I am surprised that you didn't find the tape of "Seasons of the Soul." It is possible, of course, that Lee didn't record it. If he didn't, please let me know, and I'll suggest that he come to N.Y. the week-end of the 7th to do it; for I'd very much like to have it included. In Boston, in September, I recorded The Buried Lake; but on reconsideration I believe it would be more suitable to use "The Swimmers" (Hudson Review). But you are the Doctor, and I want the selection to be yours, especially since you are doing the commentary.

I understand your problem and I am only sad that I couldn't see what you might think of me for the birthday issue of the Sewanee. I've seen an advance copy, and I am paralyzed by it. They are all talking about somebody else disguised as Tate. It has given me deep satisfaction and consternation. And I simply don't know how to thank them all for their generosity.

Please let us know about coming to N.Y. Love to Tinkum.

Affly.
Allen

All permissions except for the parts of the long poem are controlled by Scribner.

[OH]
Dept. of English
Univ. of Minn.
Mnpls. 14
11/28/59

Dear Cleanth,

Could you please persuade the photography department of the Poetry Recording to send us some selected proofs of the pictures the young man took of us out here?

It was wonderful seeing you all, and we look forward to next summer, perhaps to[ward the] end of February when we come East again. Love to Tinkum.

Affly.
Allen

1315 Davenport College
Yale University
New Haven, Conn.
Dec. 6, 1959

Dear Allen,

I was glad to have your postcard of the other day. I telephoned Elliot Kone at once, and he assures me that you will be hearing from the photographer soon. (But I know that there is a slip-up sometimes in these matters: therefore, if your proofs haven't arrived soon, don't hesitate to let me know and I will investigate.)

Kone tells me that he is about ready to press the record. It includes "Mother and Son," "Winter Mask for Yeats," "The Wolves," "Last Days of Alice," "The Meaning of Life," "The Meaning of Death," "The Cross," "Death of Little Boys," "Ode to the Confederate Dead," "The Mediterranean," "Aeneas at Washington," "The Seasons of the Soul," "The Buried Lake," and "The Swimmers." (This is not necessarily the order in which the poems are arranged on the record.)

I have written to Scribner's for permission. I hope to have a clearance from them any day. If there is delay, I may wire you to use your good offices with them. I have also written to the *Sewanee* and to the *Hudson*. I take it that you sold them only first serial rights, and that no permissions from them is *technically* required, though a courtesy acknowledgment may be in order. Am I wrong about this?

As soon as we have the permissions, we can press the record and our office here is still hopeful that it may have your record and one other ready for Christmas.

I turned in the jacket material sometime ago. I hope that you will like what I have written—but one can't say too much in 900 words! I noticed as I typed the last bit that I was finishing on your birthday— Nov. 19. Anyway, I hope that it may be acceptable as my birthday offering.

I do hope that you and Isabella will be able to pay us a visit this winter—the longer the better, but at least briefly, in any case. At the moment we are trying to get ready to leave here on the 17th—I to fly to California; T., to take train for New Orleans. This is absurd, in a sense— two people regularly separating at Christmas time, but California and Louisiana are simply too far apart, and our mothers have learned to expect the visits.

If we are held up by Scribner's, I may wire you or telephone. Your word with them should make the difference.

Tinkum joins in greetings to you both.

Cleanth

Everyone here who has heard the tape that has been now readied for recording thinks that the readings are excellent—the voice clear, resonant, and in good tone. We have had to eliminate everything but the poems themselves—all comment upon the poems—in order to get in as much material as we have. I hope that we have been wise in this. If not, it is not too late to change. Moreover, [if] there are poems that ought to be dropped, or added, again it is not too late to change. I am anxious that *you* be satisfied.

1315 Davenport College
Yale University
New Haven, Connecticut
December 9, 1959

Dear Allen,

The tapes for your record sound very fine and the record is just about ready to be pressed. We have been waiting to get permissions clear. Yesterday I had a letter from the permissions clerk at Scribners. Scribners is perfectly willing to collaborate but claims that under its contract with you it has a right to share in the royalties—goodness knows they are small enough!—and thinks that it ought to be a partner to the contract with Yale and that royalties should be paid to you *through them.* I get the impression from Miss Youngstrom's letter that it is not money but a matter of principle that is involved. (Louis Martz[1] had reported her a little touchy on the general subject of our approaching authors directly in some earlier letters from her.)

I think that there is nothing for us at Yale to do except to assume that her interpretation of the contract, which she says is that of Scribner's legal counsel, is correct, and accede, provided of course *that you agree,* to her request that Scribners be a party to the contract as well as you. Not much money is involved in any case, since we do not expect to make a profit, and our three percent royalty to the author was stipulated for the sake of principle rather than in the hope of actually fattening the poet's pocketbook. But we shall suggest to all such publishers as take the line that Scribners does that they waive their own percentage of royalties and pass on the whole small amount to the poet. Please let me have your thoughts on this matter when you conveniently can, for we are still hoping to get your record out in time for Christmas sales.

In great haste, but with all cordial regards.

Cleanth

---

1. Louis Martz was chair of the English department at Yale at this time.

I have not yet heard from the Hudson and Sewanee about "The Swimmers" and "The Buried Lake," but I am assuming that neither magazine will hold us up.

[OH]
1315 Davenport College
Yale University
New Haven, Connecticut
Dec. 11, 1959

Dear Allen—

I have just talked with Miss Youngstrom of Scribner's permissions department on the phone. She tells me that Scribner's is waiving its rights and that she is mailing us the contract. Lee Anderson had talked to her in New York the other day—and evidently had talked very persuasively. I hurry this off so that it may reach you as quickly—or nearly as quickly—as the letter I posted to you this morning, and thus save you from writing to her.

Cordially,
Cleanth

[OH]
2019 Irving Ave. So.
Mpls. 5. Minn.
12.15.59

Dear Cleanth:

Forgive card. Very harassed getting settled into new house.—But thanks for your three letters. A letter from Charles Scribner today confirms the most favorable arrangement. I do hope I can get the record to give to friends for Christmas. Many thanks for your kind offices. Eager to see your 900 words. Love to Tinkum.

Allen

1960s

[OH]

2019 Irving Ave., South
Mpls. 5, Minn.
1.11.60

Dear Cleanth,

Christmas and trip to Florida intervening, I'm a little hazy about the progress of the recording. Is mine ready? I wrote to Mr. Martz, but no answer. We'll be in N.Y. on Feb. 24–25; Providence 26th; Boston 27–29. Any chance of seeing you all? Love to Tinkum.

Allen

1315 Davenport College
Yale University
New Haven, Connecticut
Jan. 15, 1960

Dear Allen,

I apologize for being so poor a correspondent, but I was in California from the middle of December until last week and now I am trying to catch up with classes, papers, and correspondence.

The first four records which Yale is issuing, including yours, are supposed to be ready within a matter of days. I am sorry that your record was not ready before Christmas day—I was urged to make every effort to finish my part and we were assured, until the very end, that there was a fighting chance for us to make the deadline. But I should have known better.

It may be that the record is already on the way to you. I shall check again with the Audiovisual people here and if there is any further delay I shall let you know. By the way, we think the record is excellent. Everyone who has heard the tapes shares my feeling that the recording is really nearly perfect and that you were in particularly good form in your reading. I do hope that you will like it.

It is good news to know that you and Isabella are to be in the East next month. We certainly want to see you and count on having you stay with us. Tink is writing Isabella.

Cordially,
Cleanth

I've just talked to the A-V people and they say the records will be out the last week in January.

2019 Irving Avenue South
Minneapolis, Minnesota
March 5, 1960

Dear Cleanth,

This is an appeal, and I fear a nuisance for you; and if you can't do something for me by merely picking up the telephone, please ignore this letter.

Scribner's are reprinting my poems this spring (with a few new ones added) and they are getting up a new jacket for which they want a photograph.[1] Weeks ago I wrote to Mr. Martz on this subject, and he passed my letter on to Mr. Kone. Mr. Kone answered but did not reply to my question about the photograph. I telephoned his office a few days ago. He was away and the rather harassed young man who talked to me seemed vague on all fronts. I know that I can't use the picture which will appear on the jacket of the recording. I asked for half a dozen proofs of some of the others (the photographer took about 50), and also of the pictures he took of Isabella. I have no other pictures, and if I can't get one of these I'll have to get a picture taken elsewhere, which means more expense and more delay. If you can help by telephoning, won't you please do so?

I might add that I heard in New York that Mr. Kone is doing six jobs all at once—which explains the long delay of the appearance of the recordings.

We were mighty sorry not to see you all on this last trip. The pace was exhausting but we had a very good time everywhere.—We're going to Monteagle in June. Nancy and Percy and the Lytles will be there too. Love to Tinkum.

Yrs.
Allen

---

1. *Poems* (New York: Charles Scribner's Sons, 1960).

1315 Davenport College
Yale University
New Haven, Connecticut
March 12, 1960

Dear Allen,

I am mortified to hear how derelict our people have been in failing to send you the picture proofs. I saw your man Elliot Kone the day I got your letter and he registered surprise and mortification too, claiming that the photographer had let him down. The next day he told me that the proofs had been dispatched to you, but I am taking nothing on faith until I have heard from you that they have arrived. If they have not arrived by the time this letter reaches you, please say so by air mail and I will blow the place up.

You can imagine the kind of situation we have been in now for weeks, but the first records have finally arrived from the manufacturer and they sound very fine, and the printing on the folders that hold them is beautifully done. Unfortunately—there seems a perverse fate in this—your record, out of the first four, did not arrive with the others. A pressing machine had broken down at the last moment. But we expect copies of your record at the first of the week and some will be dispatched to you at once. The only consolation to be found in this long comedy of errors is that the photographic work, the printing, and the recording are all of really superb quality.

Let me know if the photo-proofs have not arrived.

As ever,
Cleanth

2019 Irving Ave. So.
Mpls. 5, Minn.
3.14.60

Dear Cleanth,

The photographs arrived in the same mail with your letter, for which many thanks. Sorry to have put you to all that trouble. You may imagine I am eager to get my record, and the others, too, of the first four. But I am most eager to see your "program notes"! Of course, I *would* jinx the pressing machine, but I trust it has recovered.—We would like to get at your convenience your summer schedule. We'll be coming by New Haven around June 26th. Love to Tinkum.

Yrs.
Allen

[OH]

2019 Irving Ave. So.
Mpls. 5
4.3.60

Dear Cleanth:

The photographer sent a glossy print, at last, to Scribner's—thanks to your intercession. But, alas, I have not yet received my record. I understand that Lee Anderson has!—We go to Sewanee for the wedding of Andrew's daughter Pamela on June 11th. Will be coming through Conn. around June 18th. Will you all be there?

Yrs.
Allen

2019 Irving Avenue South
Minneapolis, Minnesota
April 12, 1960

Dear Cleanth,

How can I thank you enough for your fine commentary on the jacket of my recording? Quite apart from the laudatory tone—though I am not for a moment forgetting it—your exposition of my work is just about perfect, if I can let myself judge such a matter.

Red leaves this morning after a fine visit of four days. Last night he gave a splendid lecture. We enjoyed having them very much indeed.

Please forgive the haste of this note. Tomorrow we leave for ten days in Washington and Virginia.

Affly.
Allen

1315 Davenport College
Yale University
New Haven, Connecticut
April 19, 1960

Dear Allen,

Your letter of the 12th with its comment on my jacket piece was most gratifying to me. You know how much I have always depended upon your suggestion and advice and how much I am always buoyed up by your commendation. I am sorry that I hurried the little essay as much as I did—but that was because I thought we were going to get a record to you by Christmastime! Had I known what was to occur, I might have made a number of revisions. But I am glad that the record is out and pleased that you like it. It seems to me a beautiful and skillfully done recording and I think that the picture is fine.

I hope in this new decade to devote more and more attention to the literature of the South. There are a number of books that I would like to write and a number of writers that I find I want to talk about. The little piece on you reminded me of how much I wanted to say certain things and how exhilarating it was for me to get back to such topics. My sabbatical begins this summer and I mean to get back to writing again. I am so far behind!

It is good news that you and Isabella expect to be in this neighborhood toward the latter part of June. Please save a generous amount of time for us. We have so much to talk about and it has been so long since we have had a real visit. At this writing, we expect to be here all through June. I'll write promptly if our plans *do* change—the possibility is remote—and in the meantime, you all do plan to give us a good visit.

As ever,
Cleanth

I am sending this on to the Minneapolis address though I know you are to be away. Virginia in the spring ought to be beautiful. Have a nice trip!

1315 Davenport College
Yale University
New Haven, Connecticut
June 17, 1960

Dear Allen,

Won't you and Isabella be in the East this month? And won't it be possible for you all to pay us a visit?

Our plans have finally jelled—we leave for California and New Orleans on the 29th of this month, to be away for some three weeks or so. I describe our plans in some detail so that we may hope to have you all for a visit in the latter part of the summer if we should miss you this month. But we do hope that you will be able to come—and to stay for a real visit—sometime in the next week or so.

In haste,
Cleanth

I am sending a carbon of this letter to you at Monteagle in the hope that it may reach you there or nearabouts and thus save some of the time that it will take for the original to reach you by forwarding from Minneapolis.

Wellfleet, Mass.
July 7, 1960

Dear Brookses,

We lingered in the chambers of the sea at Sewanee and got here four days late; so it was impossible to stop off. But we will definitely do so, you all being willing, around Sept. 1st. This is my first summer off in four years and I'm trying to get some writing done. Any chance you all could come here for a visit! That would be wonderful.

Affly.
Allen

2019 Irving Avenue South
Minneapolis, 5, Minnesota
February 26, 1961

Dear Brookses,

We've just had a note from Lee Anderson who says that you have gone or are going very soon to Europe. Where in Europe? Here's our itinerary in outline:

April 11, arrive Plymouth
April 12, arrive London
April 12 to 26, England (Oxford, Cambridge, Yorkshire, but mostly London)
April 26, to Paris
April 29, to Florence
May 1 to 6, Hill Towns
May 7 to 10, Rome
May 10 to June 13, Urbino
June 14, Genoa to NY on Leonardo da Vinci.

Please let's get together somewhere. It would be great fun. We are still sad at not being able to stop to see you last summer.

Affectionately,
Allen

[OH]   Syracuse, Italy
March 13 [1961]

Dear Allen—

I am delighted to hear from you and to know that you and Isabella are headed this way. We certainly must try for a meeting. The only complication is that we are just reversing each other's routes. We came on the "Leonardo"—you all are going back on it—(and curiously enough, both of us sail for home on June 14). We are going on to Greece, then return to Italy, pick up a car, and drive through France and end up (for our last month) in England.

Our only chance of meeting, it seems, is in France, for we can't get to England before the middle of May. We shall be in France in mid and late April though our plans are still very fluid.

I notice from the itinerary that you were so thoughtful to send that you will be in Paris only for a day or so—26 to 29. Let's try for it, anyway, though I can't be sure at this moment whether we can be near Paris on the 27th and, what is worse, I am afraid that you all probably will have a very crowded schedule for your day or so in Paris.

Let me have an address in England where I can reach you around the middle of April so that we can be in touch. Our address until April 7 will be Hotel Olympic, Athens (we sail for Greece on March 17) and until April 10, Hotel Splendide Suisse, Venice.

Sicily is wonderful just at this moment—temples in sunshine and all the fruit trees on the island in bloom. I hope that your good luck on weather holds during the next week in Greece.

I am hard at work on a book on Faulkner—a book I am convinced needs writing—and am now well into it, perhaps more than half way.[1] But I am treating this European excursion as pure holiday. I simply won't try to do more writing—though I hope that distance from America and the South will help my perspective and improve the book.

We have much to talk about—a very great deal indeed, for I need your counsel about a number of things, including some future things that I hope to do, once the Faulkner is finished, on Southern literature. We must try for the Paris meeting—and whether we arrange that or not, a real visit a little later on when we both return.

We hope you and Isabella have a wonderful trip.

Cleanth

[OH]   2019 Irving Ave. So.
                                                                       Mpls. 5
                                                                        3/25/61

Dear Tinkum and Cleanth:

Yours from Syracuse just rec'd. We *must* meet in Paris. We arrive on April 26th and *may* stay till 30th. Hotel is Hotel Burgogne et Montona (near Palais Royal); but a card a few days ahead to American Express would be more certain. Should you be delayed in Italy, try us care of

1. *William Faulkner: The Yoknapatawpha Country* was published by Yale University Press in 1963.

H. Brewster, Piazza San Franceso di Paola 3, Florence. Have a good time. Love to you both from us.

Allen

[OH]

2019 Irving Avenue South
Minneapolis 5, Minnesota
October 5, 1961

Dear Cleanth and Tinkum,

We shall be in New York on Friday November 3rd, and we hope you all will come in and join us for dinner. (Place to be selected later.) We are also inviting Red and Eleanor, and John Palmer if he is there, to join us.

We hope this may make up for the frustrations of last summer.

Love from us both,
Allen

[OH]

Mpls.
10/24/61

Dear Brookses,

That's fine. We had invited the John Hall Wheelocks too, and now Phyllis [Wheelock] has taken the entire party over, and we are to dine at their house. You will hear from her right away. We can't very well invite John [Palmer] now, as her table seats 8 only. But later.

Affly,
Allen

University of Minnesota
College of Science, Literature, and the Arts
Minneapolis 14
[November 1961]

Dear Cleanth:

I understand that Keith Fort, one of our teaching assistants, has applied formally to your Department for an instructorship for the academic year 1962–63. I write this letter in support of his application.

Mr. Fort came here in the fall of 1958 and has done extremely good work. Last year he shifted to comparative literature and will have his Ph.D. this June. The only course he has had with me is my graduate Seminar in Writing. In this course his work was brilliant. He is, in fact, a very gifted writer, and his first novel is being seriously considered by Houghton-Mifflin. His record as a teacher is excellent.

It was wonderful seeing you and Tinkum and I am sorry we were late and there was no time for serious conversation but we shall hope to remedy that before too long.

Ever yours,
Allen

1315 Davenport College
Yale University
New Haven, Connecticut
Nov. 28, 1961

Dear Allen,

Just a note to acknowledge your good word about Keith Fort. If you recommend him, he ought to be good, and I shall check at once with our department head. It was very fine seeing you and Isabella for even the little time we had together. I do hope we can land you here for a longer visit and have an opportunity for some talk. I must stir up my young friend who is at work on the Bollingen committee, or if that is set by this time, we shall think up something else.

Cordially,
Cleanth

[OH]   2019 Irving Ave. So.
Mlps. 5, Minn.
12.5.61

Dear Cleanth,

Thanks for your card. We expect to arrive in New Haven after lunch on Jan. 5th. Mr. Johnson writes me that *you all* are putting us up! Can you? Love to Tinkum.

Affly,
Allen

[OH]   [Minneapolis]
1/2/62

We'll be delighted to stay over Saturday night with you.—Red telephoned to say they would work out the program for Sat. evening with you all.—Will telephone from N.Y. Friday morning what train we'll [arrive] on that afternoon.

Affly,
Allen

2019 Irving Avenue South
Minneapolis 5, Minnesota
March 1, 1962

Dear Cleanth,

I need some confidential information which I think and hope you may be able to give me. Henry W. Wenning, the New Haven rare books man, writes me that he thinks he can sell the earliest typescript of my Ode to the C[onfederate] D[ead] and the typescript of *The Fathers* (the printer's copy) for about $1,000. I am anxious to pay off the balance on Caroline's mortgage in Princeton.

Is Wenning thoroughly reliable? I like the tone of his letters. He offers to sell the mss. on a commission of 30%.

If you can tell me anything useful without making enquiries, I'd appreciate it.

Love to Tinkum.

Ever yrs,
Allen

1315 Davenport College
Yale University
New Haven, Connecticut
March 6 1962

Dear Allen,

I did not answer your letter by return of post, because, though I know Wenning slightly, I wanted to ask others about him. One of the senior people in our library who buys rare books constantly for the library tells me that Wenning is capable, reliable, solvent, and responsible. I am sure that you would not go badly wrong in letting him have the MS material to sell. (Wenning is one of three rarebook dealers who have their offices in New Haven—the youngest of the three, I should say.)

But Tinkum thinks that $1,000 seems mighty little for the earliest typescript of the "Confederate Dead" and the typescript of *The Fathers*, and I think that I agree with her. Still, I don't know the details of this market, and what I pass on to you is simply a hunch. As for the 30% commission, that sounds like a lot; but then it may not be. I suppose that such commissions do run high. (I wish that these treasures might come into our library, but I have no special "in" with the library—and shall not even mention that they may be up for sale unless you tell me that I can.)

Tinkum joins in warm regards to you both.

In haste,
Cleanth

[OH]   2019 Irving Avenue South
                                              Minneapolis 5, Minnesota
                                                        April 4, 1962

Dear Cleanth:

I take this opportunity to thank you for your letter about my mss. After much correspondence, the Princeton Library stepped in and pointed out that my original agreement gave them an option. They are buying the two mss for the sum fixed by Mr. Wenning.

Love to Tinkum.

                                                                Yrs.
                                                                Allen

                                              2019 Irving Avenue South
                                              Minneapolis 5, Minnesota
                                                        Dec. 28, 1962

Dear Tinkum and Cleanth,

Here's another cheque, Cleanth's share of the latest earnings of *The Language of Poetry*. If the four essayists live to be 100, they will get rich!

We're terribly sad that you all will not be in New Haven next week. But we're hoping for a reunion early next summer.

                                                    Love to you both,
                                                                Allen

Professor Cleanth Brooks
Professor I. A. Richards
The Executors of the Estate of Wallace Stevens
Professor Phillip Wheelwright

Gentlemen:

I have received from the Princeton University Press a cheque in the amount of $30.35, in payment of royalties earned by the paperback edition of an ancient book entitled *The Language of Poetry*. After consulting several presumably reliable reference books, I find that you, gentlemen, contributed each an essay to the volume, and that I was the editor of the symposium.

The sum of $30.35 divvied by four yields to each of you the princely sum of $7.58, my cheque for which is enclosed. The odd three cents I am retaining for services performed.

                                                    Very truly yours,
                                                            Allen Tate

1315 Davenport College
Yale University
New Haven, Connecticut
January 19, 1963

Dear Allen,

Thank you for your letter and the check. We are indeed sorry that we had to be out of town just at the time that you all were here. We must definitely plan ahead this time to make sure that we can get you here for a real visit this summer.

I am trying to finish up my Faulkner book during the next two weeks. If I can complete the MS. by February 1, it will be scheduled for October publication.

I have just read with interest and admiration your obituary note on Faulkner in the current *Sewanee*.[1] I expect that I shall be making some allusion to it in the course of my book.

Tinkum joins me in all good wishes to you and Isabella.

Cordially,
Cleanth

[OH] Mpls.
Jan. 24, 1963

Dear Cleanth,

Thank you for your letter, and for your kind word about my Faulkner obituary. Your essay on *Sanctuary*[1] is the best thing on F. I have ever seen: *what happens,* not vague talk about guilt and slavery. I look forward to the book. Love to Tinkum.

Yrs,
Allen

2019 Irving Avenue South
Minneapolis 5, Minnesota
January 11, 1964

Dear Cleanth,

Your Faulkner is a very fine book, I should never have seen certain things in *Sanctuary,* for example, without your guidance. But even more important, you do a first-rate critical job in the course of your exposition

---

1. "William Faulkner," *Sewanee Review* 71 (winter 1963): 160–64.

1. "Faulkner's *Sanctuary:* The Discovery of Evil," *Sewanee Review* 71 (winter 1963): 1–24.

and analysis. I had no idea that your treatment would be so detailed; it will remain the definitive work. You are the only critic, except Red, who has seen him from the inside.

It seems that the reviewer in the NY Review of Books does not agree with me.[1] I liked that sheet at first, but now I'm turning sour. In the current issue there's a review of Arthur Mizener's book on the novel that turns me into acid. I am used to beat[ing] Arthur over the head. I believe the reviewer is the same as yours.

I had hoped that you and Tinkum might be at the Ransom reading last month. Anyhow, we hope to see you next summer. Love to Tinkum.

Affly.

Allen

1315 Davenport College
Yale University
New Haven, Connecticut
Feb. 7, 1964

Dear Allen,

Thank you very much for your kind remarks about my Faulkner book. As you see, I have been banged at very sharply twice, and am quite sure that I'm in for some hard knocks before things are over. But I have garnered some complimentary reviews too, and if the present ratio of good to bad will hold for the next several months I shall be well satisfied.

The New York Review people showed their hand, I thought, rather promptly in the reviewers that they assembled. Some of the reviews have, of course, been excellent, but a good many of those who write for the N.Y.R. are much more interested in being bright themselves than in illuminating the works that are discussed. But then, I suppose that this is a temptation to any writer, and I can't except myself: I suppose that at one time or another all of us have found the temptation to score off a book more than we could resist.

I wish the Tates and Brookses could get together. We've not had a real conversation for a couple of years—much too long. Are you likely to be in the East this winter or spring? Maybe we can cook up something to

1. In "The Over-Wrought Urn" (*New York Review of Books*, January 9, 1964, p. 8), Marvin Mudrick, among other things, accuses Brooks of "tub-thumping zeal for 'traditional,' Southern Protestant Christianity" and suggests, "After decades of the bowler-hat and furled-umbrella litcrit that made his academic reputation, Cleanth Brooks has reverted with a rebel whoop to the Confederacy. His Faulkner book is a Southern blend of vitriol, tart courtliness, regional piety, genealogies back to Adam, the stupefying trivia of life in a small town, and uninhibited hero-worship."

bring you this way. We are to be in Europe, I believe, for the next year. Just how or where—or why—has not been determined, but I've been granted the year off and there are at least two ways in which I might finance my stay. But I hope we won't have to wait for another meeting until we both land up somewhere in Europe. Tinkum sends her love to you both.

Cordially,
Cleanth

2019 Irving Avenue South
Minneapolis, Minnesota
March 19, 1964

Dear Cleanth,

I have just received a copy of Lon Cheney's letter of March 15th to you—and in the same mail one from Margaret Haferd at the US Embassy in London informing me that you will be there next year as cultural attaché.[1] That's wonderful news. I hope I may have had something to do with a change of policy, for I told them several years ago that they ought to get a distinguished person; and not an academic hack like that man [Carl] Bode who was there a few years.

Now about Vanderbilt and Andrew. In 1960 I got Henry Alexander and my brother Ben—both trustees—interested. (This was just before Andrew left Florida.)[2] I think they would have raised the money, but Randall Stewart was lukewarm, and it all evaporated. Poor Randall's illness has virtually incapacitated him—and the department. I hope you will find it tactful to raise the question again when you are there in April. Andrew ought to give up the SR, even though this would mean a loss to all of us.

They will have a hard time finding the right chairman. I'm sure you wouldn't take it. Now they imagine they could interest Arthur Mizener. What has Vanderbilt to offer that anybody should leave Yale or Cornell? I have suggested Leonard Unger, but Don [Davidson] seems only moderately interested.

When do you go to England? We sail for Italy on June 13th, and will go to London around July 20th for three weeks. Please you all be there.

---

1. Brooks served as cultural attaché to the American Embassy in London from 1964 to 1966. He had originally accepted a Fulbright to the University of Bordeaux, but the opportunity to live in England while serving his country was too appealing to pass up.

2. Lytle taught fiction writing at the University of Florida for many years before returning home to Sewanee in 1961. His Florida students included novelists Madison Jones and Harry Crews.

I am going to Sewanee to see Andrew this spring, and I will try to make it coincide with the Vanderbilt festival and take Nashville in too.

Love to Tinkum from us both.

Affly.
Allen

I was glad to see that good review of your Faulkner in the TLS.

1315 Davenport College
Yale University
New Haven, Connecticut
April 2, 1964

Dear Allen,

I hope that you got my wire when you were in New York a few days ago. It was unfortunate that we were just headed South at the time that you and Isabella were in the vicinity, for otherwise we should have tried to get you to stop off with us. But my one chance to get another look at the Faulkner manuscripts was the spring vacation, which coincided almost exactly with your trip east.

I am to go to Washington on June 1 for some orientation work and briefing, but I am told that this will be cut rather short and that I will probably be arriving in London about the middle of June. There are so many things to be done here with regard to leaving the house and packing that Tinkum may have to delay her departure until a little later. But at the worst, she should be there well before July 20, when you and Isabella are to arrive. I do not mention your staying with us there since we shall house-hunt after we arrive and it's unlikely that we'll be settled within the month. But we must plan to have a lot of visiting and talk. Our visits with the Tates have been all too brief and infrequent for the last years.

I have heard a second time from Lon, and have written to the Chancellor[1] asking for an appointment with him when I come to Nashville toward the end of this month. Any notions that you have on the subject of a chair for Andrew, or for the department generally, I hope you will communicate before I see him. And I do hope you can time your visit there to coincide with the symposium.

Tinkum joins me in affectionate greetings to you both.

As ever,
Cleanth

1. Alexander Heard (b. 1917) was chancellor of Vanderbilt University from 1963 to 1982.

[OH]
Minneapolis
April 9, 1964

Dear Cleanth,

Thanks for yours of Apr. 2nd. We did get your telegram and appreciated it, but were sorry to miss you. I fear I can't be in Nashville when you are there: I'm going down on May 8th. But we'll get together in London: I'll let you know exact time of arrival well in advance.

Yrs. ever,
Allen

1315 Davenport College
Yale University
New Haven, Connecticut
May 5, 1964

Dear Allen,

I have just got back from Vanderbilt where I took part, as you know, in the Literary Symposium. The schedule was too tight for me to get to Sewanee to see Andrew, but I did see a lot of Lon and Fanny Cheney and I had a good deal of conversation with Don Davidson.

When I wrote for an interview with the Chancellor, Rob Roy Purdy replied that the Chancellor would be out of town just at the time of my visit and that he (Purdy) would be glad to talk with me. Then just before I left New Haven I had a nice note from Heard saying that he would return to Nashville a little sooner than planned and hoped to see me on my final night there.

I had a long talk with Purdy at lunch and one that was more satisfactory from my standpoint than I had thought it would be. He opened up, was engagingly frank about the condition of the department, and seemed to take seriously some of the advice that I pressed upon him. But I didn't know him well enough to open the matter of Andrew's appointment—especially since Lon indicated that the early proposal about Andrew had bogged down in that quarter and that he thought I might well confine myself to generalities with Purdy. Thus I confined myself to the problem of the department, making basically these points: that the department would be sensible to try to get someone like, say, Arthur Mizener—and I named one or two other people of that stature—but that my prediction was that Vanderbilt would be unable to secure such a person. I pointed out that a big salary was not enough, since Cornell, Princeton or whatever university would meet the salary at once, and that a man in his fifties, with his own books to write and his visits to Europe to make, would not feel the prospect of rebuilding the department in a section of the country to which he had no ties would be a valuable way in which to spend his prime. I argued that the choice would probably have to be a Southerner eventually, and that it would probably have to be a man somewhat younger and at the moment of less reputation than some of the names that Vanderbilt had been thinking of. My point was that if a really good younger man could be found, his own reputation and the reputation of the rebuilt department might be expected to flower ten years hence.

I meant all of this, but I was also laying the groundwork for the argument to the Chancellor later, that if this were the prospect, all the more need to bind to the department a distinguished person like Andrew who, in addition to his own sterling qualities, would add to the department some much needed glamour and a tie to the old Fugitive group during this transitional period.

I could not see the Chancellor until Thursday night at the reception at his house after my lecture. He was very cordial, but there was no opportunity for a long talk. I did give him a brief summary of what I told Purdy, referred him to Purdy for a more extensive account, and then spoke about Andrew. After our talk, Heard suggested that I talk to Dean Field; so we got off in another part of the room and I gave him basically the same material with again a strong emphasis on Andrew. Here I am confident that I got some answering response.

When you are in Vanderbilt I hope you will talk to the Chancellor about this. There is no point in my telling a diplomat as finished as you how to approach him, but of course an obvious way would be to say that I had written to you, telling you that I had proposed Andrew to him and asking you whether you would not talk to him in more detail about it.

This is too long a letter already, so I shall simply say that Tinkum joins me in affectionate greeting to you both.

Cleanth

You can imagine how busy we both are. I must report [to] Washington on June 1 and we both expect to be in London by the third week in June.

2019 Irving Ave. So.
Minneapolis 5, Minnesota
May 30, 1964

Dear Cleanth,

I've been back from Tennessee about a week. Andrew seemed in good shape, was up and about his business; but of course will have to wear that mechanical contraption the rest of his life. But he was in good spirits. I didn't go into the Vanderbilt matter with him, for the obvious reason.

Cancer of colon

The day I left [I] saw Chancellor Heard, and was greatly taken with him; and the Dean too. I talked to the Chancellor about half an hour, and he was extremely responsive to both my suggestions; i.e., a head for the Department and Andrew. So was the Dean. But they both still feel that a big salary may attract almost anybody they want, even after you and Arthur faded out. They are now trying Meyer Abrams. I warned them that they were wasting their time, and only delaying the solution of their problem.—I lunched with Don [Davidson], and came away with a rather depressing conclusion; which is that Don *wants* the Department to collapse, so that he can blame the past couple of Administrations for letting the Great Vanderbilt English Department go down the drain. After Don, the Deluge, etc. He has not done one thing to solve the problem, and he didn't even mention Andrew's name, not even a reference to his illness! A strange man, as we've always known.—Nevertheless, I believe that your conversation with the Chancellor, followed by mine, may have done some good. We must remember that an obstacle to inviting Andrew to Vanderbilt is Walter Sullivan,[1] backed by Randall Stewart who has now reached the point where he cannot make any sort of decision. Well, we'll see.

You and Tinkum are leaving shortly for London; so don't bother to answer this. We'll see you in London towards the end of July. Our love to you both.

Ever yrs.
Allen

[OH]
Pensione Annalena
Via Romana, 34
Florence
July 7, 1964

Dear Cleanth,

What I'm about to write is, for us, very sad news. We are not coming to London, alas, and are staying on here till July 28th, when we sail from Genoa to N.Y., two weeks ahead of our original schedule.

The work hasn't gone as fast as I'd like, and too much travel is certainly not good for it. We land in N.Y. on August 7th and will go at once to Wellfleet, Mass., until about Sept. 20th.

---

1. Walter Sullivan (b. 1924), a professor of English at Vanderbilt University, taught southern literature and fiction writing and was a close friend of Lytle's. Presumably the problem had to do with the possibility that they would both be teaching fiction at Vanderbilt. Sullivan is the author of *Allen Tate: A Recollection* (Baton Rouge: Louisiana State University, 1988).

It would have been great fun to see you and Tinkum in London, doing that job for the first time as it should be done. Are you in the job for the full academic year?

When you've got your bearings, please write us views and impressions. Good luck. Love to you from both of us.

Ever yrs,
Allen

Please give our love to Maggie Haferd.

You *must* see our dear friend Muriel Spark: 13 Baldwin Crescent, Camberwell, S.E. 5.

American Embassy
Grosvenor Square, W.1.
July 13, 1964

Dear Allen:

We are indeed disappointed to hear that we shall not be seeing you all in London this summer. We are not likely to be back in the United States for a good while and so you and Isabella must definitely plan on your next trip across the Atlantic to save some time for us. I hope all goes well with your work for both of you.

I have told Maggy Haferd all this disappointing news. She sends greetings to you both.

I have not yet met Muriel Spark and I think that she may still be in New York. But we do mean to see her as soon as we can.

Tinkum joins in all cordial regards.

Sincerely yours,
Cleanth

American Embassy
Grosvenor Square, W.1.
January 27, 1965

Dear Allen:

I am very glad to learn that you are planning to edit an Eliot issue. In my present state of affairs, the prospect of writing something for it seems slim. But I shall try and shall hope to make your deadline of September 1.

I had only one meeting with Eliot before his death. He was very frail but we had some good talk.[1]

---

1. Eliot died on January 4, 1965. The essays compiled by Tate for the special Eliot issue of *Sewanee Review* (winter 1966) were published as *T. S. Eliot, the Man and His Work: A Critical Evaluation by Twenty-Six Distinguished Writers* (New York: Delacorte Press, 1966).

We are delighted with the thought that you and Isabella will be here this summer. Unless there are cataclysms, now unforeseen, we shall be here in July and actually plan ourselves to go to Ireland in August.

Tinkum joins in fond greetings to you both.

Sincerely,
Cleanth

American Embassy
Grosvenor Square, W.1.
May 4, 1965

Dear Allen:

A young British scholar has showed me a copy of his piece on "Petronius and *The Waste Land.*" Whether or not it will take us further into the meaning of the poem, it is very interesting in itself and I think that it convincingly shows that Petronius was bobbing about in Eliot's mind as he worked on his poem.

I have been told that you will appear at the Edinburgh Festival. I am delighted to hear it. T. has had a rather heavy operation but the surgeon gives her now an absolutely clean bill of health and she is recuperating nicely. We look forward to seeing you and Isabella in July.

In haste,
Sincerely,
Cleanth

American Embassy
Box 444,
London, W.1.
March 17, 1966

Dear Allen:

It is very good to hear from you and you speak a very handsome word indeed about my Eliot piece.[1] I hardly need say that praise from you is praise that I have always particularly valued. It is good to know that *M[odern] P[oetry] and the T[radition]* still holds up in your opinion.

We won't see you in New York this month, for my time at the Embassy here does not end until June 1 and we shall hardly be home before mid-June. But I do hope that we can have a meeting, with time enough for a

1. A talk on Eliot that Brooks gave in his capacity as American cultural attaché was published as *T. S. Eliot, Thinker and Artist: A Lecture by Cleanth Brooks Given on December 10th, 1965, to Members of Eliot College and Their Guests* (Canterbury: University of Kent at Canterbury, 1965) and included in *T. S. Eliot, the Man and His Work.*

great deal of talk, soon after we get home. It's really been years since we have had a long conversation.

Someone told me that you were buying a house at Sewanee. Is there anything in it? And, if so, will you be in Sewanee this summer?

The Eliot number of the Sewanee has come in and looks to be a very fine job indeed. I have stayed much too busy to do more than sample it, but the sampling tells the story. I. A. Richards, by the way, wrote to me very warmly about it saying that only Allen could have got together such a fine set of tributes. I am glad it is going to be published as a book a little later.

In great haste, but with all cordial regards from us both.

Sincerely,
Cleanth

Forest Road
Northford, Conn. 06472
Nov. 8, 1966

Dear Allen,

How are you? Is there any chance that you will be in our neighborhood some time this winter? It's been so long since we had any conversation that I am anxious that I don't let any opportunity slip. I shan't, however, try to put any of that hoped-for conversation in this letter. I'll simply say that we are glad to be back even though the London experience was exciting and interesting, and that we are trying to get our house back in order and are caught up in a dozen enterprises, including a couple of books on which I am far behind.

I do, however, have something of immediate consequence to put to you in this letter. I have nominated Bob Heilman (Robert Bechtold Heilman) for membership in the American Academy of Arts and Sciences, and several of Bob's friends are seconding the nomination. Would you care to do so? If so, the only catch is that it must be done quickly. Through my own fault, I got the nomination in only shortly before the deadline. But I am told that if seconding letters can get in promptly, the fact that they arrive after the deadline would probably not be allowed to matter.

In any case, do let me hear from you. Tinkum joins in all cordial regards.

Cleanth

[OH]

2419 Hawthorne Street
Greensboro—27408
Nov. 13, 1966

Dear Cleanth,

I am getting a letter off today to the A.A. of A. & S. in support of Bob Heilman's nomination. I don't quite know what this society does for us, but anyhow, I didn't decline the invitation to join!

I too am eager for a reunion. I shall be in New York Dec. 8–9. Could you and Tinkum come in for dinner either day? You have surely heard that Isabella and I were divorced and that I have married Helen Heinz of St. Paul.[1] I want you all to meet her. She is half my age and very beautiful.   ϒ-30-66

I am just starting the sort of book I never thought I'd write: a literary mémoir.[2] I need to ask you some questions and to use your memory to help mine.

And I want to hear about London. I *have* heard rumors. The firing of Maggie Haferd and the State Department vandals' destruction of the Embassy Library are first-rate scandals.

Let me know about New York.

Love to Tinkum.

Affly yours.
Allen

Forest Road
Northford, Conn. 06472
Nov. 17, 1966

Dear Allen,

It is indeed good to hear from you. That fact is best of all, though I am also glad to know that you have written so promptly in support of Bob Heilman's candidacy for the American Academy. (I received from their secretary just this morning a note saying that they had received your seconding letter along with the others that were required and that Bob will be considered during the next year.)

We had indeed heard rumors, though rather vague ones, about your marriage, but as you will guess from the fact that my letter had to be forwarded to you from Minnesota or from Vanderbilt—I sent copies to

1. Gardner and Tate were divorced on March 28, 1966. Tate married Helen Heinz on July 30, 1966.
2. Tate never completed these memoirs; however, finished chapters, combined with a selection of his later essays, were published as *Memoirs and Opinions, 1926–1974* (Chicago: Swallow Press, 1975).

both places—that I really didn't know where you were and badly need to be brought up to date on a great many things.

We do look forward for a visit and some talk. Tinkum suggests that we make a counter proposal. Can't you and Helen plan to come in from N.Y. and stay the night with us on either Dec. 8 or 9? We should love to have you. If this proves impossible, then of course we shall hope to come in and have dinner with you on one of those two days. But we much hope that you all can visit us instead. For one thing, it would give us, I'm sure, a great deal more time for some real talk.

Tinkum joins in all cordial regards,
Cleanth

2419 Hawthorne Rd.
Greensboro
November 22, 1966

Dear Cleanth,

Many thanks for your good letter of the 17th. I wish it were possible for us to come out to Northford, but I fear it isn't. Since I wrote you I have heard from Jack Wheelock (now 80) and we must dine with them on the 8th. We must leave New York early (around 8:30) on the 10th; so do please try to come in to dine with us on the 9th. We can dine early so that if you must get back home that night it will not be too difficult. We shall be at the Princeton Club; so you can let us know there, at the last minute.

I was up in Ithaca recently and had a good visit with the Mizeners. Arthur was wondering to just what degree you were frustrated by the job in London. I want to hear all about that.

Love to Tinkum.

Yrs.
Allen

3313 Hobbs Road
Nashville 37215
June 2, 1967

Dear Cleanth,

Please glance at the enclosed form, which is largely self-explanatory. I want to get a grant for the year after my retirement, but I must apply this year, by July 3rd. The Senior Fellowships offer $15,000.

My "project" is my long literary memoir, which I believe I told you about when we saw you all in December. I feel a little embarrassed at my age asking for testimonials, but that is the procedure; so if you can say a good word about my chances of writing a good literary memoir (cir. 125,000 words) I shall be most grateful.

I have just finished up the spring semester. I have never had better students anywhere—Minnesota, Princeton, Chicago. I couldn't possibly have made them as good as all that in four months; so I infer that they have been well-taught, and infer further that the Vanderbilt English dept. couldn't be as bad as it was reputed to be, even though there are now no "nationally famous" teachers here. I am sorry to say that Russell Fraser has made a complete flop of his job as chairman. He came here with the familiar Eastern condescension towards a Southern university, and then proceeded to insult the entire Department. He is a very able scholar (I've read some of his essays) but he has neither humility nor common sense. He has an offer from Ann Arbor which he will probably accept. Vanderbilt will have to start all over again the search for a chairman.

We are about to start building a house at Sewanee for my retirement in June 1968. In fact, I'm expecting the contractor to come here today for the final arrangements. We hope to break ground next week.

Well, I'm addressing the assembled alumni on June 10th, on "The Decline of the Liberal Arts." I've faced audiences in England, France, India, Belgium, and Italy, but never before have I had that sick feeling in the pit of the stomach. Pray for me.

Love to Tinkum.

Affly yours,
Allen

1315 Davenport College
Yale University
New Haven, Connecticut
June 6, 1967

Dear Allen,

I am delighted to hear of your proposed literary memoir and have got off a letter to the National Endowment for the Humanities at once. Unless their committee has lost all sense, the Fellowship will certainly be awarded. I look forward—and all of us will be looking forward—to its publication.

Your news about the Vanderbilt department and Fraser's probable departure from it is interesting. I am inclined to write the Chancellor on the subject. Last time I thought that I was both consulted and not consulted—to be specific, that I wasn't consulted until almost too late and then when my opinion was solicited it was interpreted rather literally and naively. Anyway, it's a shame if the whole process of finding a new chairman has to begin over again.

No time for a real letter. Tink and I plan to fly to London on Friday and then by way of the Scandinavian capitals to Helsinki, where I am to give a paper late this month. But we expect to be back in Northford in early July. I do hope that all goes well with both of you. Please remember me to Andrew and the Cheneys, and my other Tennessee friends. In haste.

Cordially,
Cleanth

[OH]

Smyrna, Tenn.
Sept. '67

Dear Tinkum and Cleanth:

Born at the V.U. Hospital August 30, 1 1/2 months premature, fraternal twins: John Robert Allen Tate and Michael Paul Tate. Michael had a bad time but is pulling through. John and mother in fine condition.

Love from Helen and Allen

accidental death in 1968 *See p 235*

Forest Road
Northford, Connecticut 06472
July 2, 1968

Dear Allen,

How are you and Helen and the boys? Have you moved into your new house? What are your plans for the summer? I hope that things have gone on apace and that the house *is* finished or nearly so, and that you all are set for a pleasant summer on top of the Mountain.

Tinkum and I are looking forward to a summer of alternate mowing and hard work on a couple of books. Northford is, on the whole, a good place to spend the summer, though yesterday was and today is very hot and humid—up into the 90s. I am on sabbatical leave for the next year and expect to be here until some time early in 1969. Then we shall be in Louisiana for the late winter and spring. I do hope that we'll have a chance for a meeting during this year.

I have just finished up a brief article on the furnishings that Poe gives to the typical houses in his tales.[1] I am quoting from your fine essay ("Our Cousin, Mr. Poe")[2] and I am also making references to a most interesting book by Siegfried Giedion (*Mechanization Takes Command*)

---

1. "Edgar Allan Poe as Interior Decorator," *Ventures* 8, no. 2 (fall 1968): 41–46.
2. "Our Cousin, Mr. Poe," *Partisan Review* 16 (December 1949): 1207–19.

which appeared in 1949. He is not writing about Poe, never mentions him in this book, and for all I know, has never read him. For that reason, some of his comments about nineteenth-century interior decoration are startling when one applies them to Poe's stories. Giedion is also making—at least very generally—some of the points that you make in your criticism of Poe. What I want to ask is whether you know the Giedion book. I am assuming that you don't and that if you don't, the convergence of Giedion's interpretation of the significance of Poe's interior settings with what you say about Poe's "dead furniture" is all the more interesting.

Do—but of course at your convenience—let me have a word on this point. Much more important, let us have a little news from you and Helen and the children. Tinkum joins me in affectionate regards to all of you.

Cordially,
Cleanth

Running Knob Hollow Road
Sewanee, Tennessee 37375
July 8, 1968

Dear Cleanth,

We were delighted to get your letter. We had heard rumors. One that you were leaving Yale for good, and going back to LSU; another that [you] would be at Vanderbilt next year. I wish sectional patriotism would bring you to Vanderbilt for the rest of your teaching career. Vandy hath need of thee.

We are "settled," that is in the main part of the house; the boys' room drags on. The workmen leave and don't return for ten days. I try to explain to Helen that this is the Southern rhythm. But whenever you come down, you must come via Sewanee. The guest room will be ready for you.

I am trying this week to get back to my memoir. The move from Mpls was horrendous, and getting a new house organized no less so. But the house is charming.

I learned a few days ago that the Univ. of Minn. Press has asked Cal to organize a volume of essays in my "honor," and that he has consented to do it. I don't disguise my pleasure. I should think that Cal would try to use the best things from the beginning.[1] I suppose you know that the

1. Robert Lowell was unable to pursue this project. Radcliffe Squires assumed responsibility for editing *Allen Tate and His Work: Critical Evaluations* (Minneapolis: University of Minnesota Press, 1972).

first extensive treatment my verse had was the section on me in Modern Poetry and the Tradition. It's as good as it ever was. If your permission is asked I hope you will let Cal use it.

The twins are flourishing. Helen is well, but very thin. She is on her feet all day and into the night. Let us hear more of your plans.

No, I have never read Giedion. I always meant to, but didn't, as with many other things. I look forward to seeing your article.

Our love to you both.

Ever yrs,
Allen

Forest Road
Northford, Connecticut
July 12, 1968

Dear Allen,

Thank you for your good letter of July 8. Tinkum and I are delighted to know that you all are in your house and on the way to finishing up the rest of it. We had the same experience in Connecticut of workmen disappearing for weeks at a time and nothing is more frustrating.

I won't go into much detail about the reasons for my deciding to go to LSU for the second term of next year. Part of my reason is to live again in the South for some period of time so as to see how it is changed and how much I have changed and to get closer to a feeling for it, especially for the sake of my second Faulkner book.[1] Part of the motive is family: Tinkum has lots of family still left in New Orleans and the opportunity of being near them (but not too near) is one that she rather cherished. An additional, though slight, motive is a kind of curiosity to see what [it] is like teaching again in the university in which I started. (I suppose a further reason is simple greed: a very pleasant combination of pay in relation to work which will make the second half of my sabbatical year profitable both financially and as to conditions for writing.) But I am certainly not burning my bridges with Yale and I expect to finish my teaching career here—unless something very special indeed happens to persuade me to do otherwise.

As for Vanderbilt, I did get a feeler of a sort this spring—indeed, a very cordial inquiry from the present department chairman. But I frankly don't know how I would fit in to the "new" Vanderbilt and, honestly,

---

1. *William Faulkner: Toward Yoknapatawpha and Beyond* (New Haven: Yale University Press, 1978).

when I look back at the last forty years, I am a little surprised to see how tenuous my whole connection with that place has been.—Part of the fault's lying on my side, but, I feel, far from all of it. Anyway, I have very fond feelings about the "old" Vanderbilt and a real concern for its present reputation. But there is a great deal that I don't know about what goes [on] there. This is one of the many things I'd like to have a chance to talk with you about some time in the months to come.

I'm delighted to hear about the volume that Cal means to get up in your honor. Naturally I hope that I'm asked to have some part in it. The occasion is a fine one and I think that a very special volume could be put together. Cal is the man to do it.

We both send best love to you and Helen and the boys. Please remember us to Andrew. We had hoped we might see him here this winter. (He had written that it was possible he might come up, but we heard no more.)

As ever,
Cleanth

[Baton Rouge]
May 24, 1969

Dear Allen,

Will you and Helen be in Sewanee on the evening of Tuesday, June 3? If you will be, Tinkum and I would come that way to spend the evening with you.

We've been in Baton Rouge all this term, are leaving now for a week in New Orleans, and will leave N.O. on Monday afternoon for the drive back to Northford. We think that we can make it to Sewanee by the evening of Tuesday.

We won't be able to linger, since we are already leaving later than we had planned, and therefore will be up and off early the next morning. So we would plan to stay the night at the Holiday Inn there. Let's say that we'll be there by about 6, and that if we're going to be much later than that, we'll phone from the road.

I'm dropping a note to Andrew too, hoping that he can join us for the evening. I hope it will be convenient for all of you—we're really eager to see you all.

To save us all time, I'm enclosing a card addressed to me in N.O. so that you can let us know while we're there.

All the best from us both,
Cleanth

[OH]

598–5849
Sewanee 37375
May 28, '69

Dear Cleanth,

We're looking forward to seeing you and Tinkum next Tuesday June 3rd. This is great news. Just telephone when you arrive at the Holiday Inn. We'll take you all to dinner.

Yrs,
Allen

1970s

[OH]

Forest Road
Northford, Connecticut
March 25, 1970

Dear Allen,

It was with deep pleasure that Tinkum and I heard some time ago of the birth of a new baby, a little boy. I am at fault for not sending you our good wishes immediately. I know that you and Helen—to whom our fond greetings—have been made very happy.

Someone has told me that you are going to Europe this summer. Is there any chance that you and Helen and the children could break your journey here before you take off. We have, as you know, plenty of room and it would be wonderful to see you all and have some talk. It's been many a day.

regimen?

We have little more to report except that we stay unbelievably busy but seem to thrive under the regime. But we don't see enough of our friends, don't have time for the things that we would really like to do, and don't have enough time to travel.

I am promising myself to extricate myself from the textbook mill as soon as I reasonably can and if I can manage it to make an early retirement. There are so many things that I would like to do that seem to me more important than many of the things that occupy me.

I much enjoyed my five months in Louisiana last year. I'd like to talk with you about the experience some time and to talk with you about many other things.

Tinkum joins in affectionate greetings to you,
Helen, and the children,
Cleanth

[OH]   Sewanee 37375
                                                           March 31, 1970
Dear Cleanth and Tinkum,

Many thanks for your fine, cordial, and hospitable letter. I wish we could stop off at Northford on the way to London. There is now an Atlanta-London flight, and we must go that way, on June 21st.   *1969*

Our little boy Benjamin was born in Nashville on December 18th. Why at my age I'm giving so many hostages to fortune I can't explain; nor do I try; I merely accept what happens, and rejoice.

Is there a chance that you all may come South this summer? We'll be back from Europe on July 16th. You can see what a *flying* trip it will be, confined to London, Rome, and Florence.

It will be Helen's first view of Europe. I thought it sensible to have a week in each of the three cities, instead of one day in each of twenty-one cities! We have a very good woman to leave the boys with.

Why not retire to Sewanee? The winters are rough but the summers are delightful.

                                                      Love to you both,
                                                               Allen

                                                           Forest Road
                                                       October 17, 1970
Dear Allen,

We hope that you and Helen had a pleasant visit to Europe this summer and that all of you are thriving in your beautiful house in Sewanee. We had bits of news of you last June from Andrew when we saw him in Florida and recently from Cecil and Marie Wood[1] when they were here, but it's too long since we saw you and I wish we could persuade you up here for a visit.

I should have written about a number of things long ago, but the pressure here remains constant. In addition to the university work, Red and Dick Lewis and I are trying desperately to finish up our American literature anthology—which is really better described as a rather heavily illustrated brief history of American literature.[2] One of my assignments has been to prepare a long section on Southern literature

---

1. The Reverend and Mrs. Cecil Wood were longtime Sewanee residents. Reverend Wood had studied English with Brooks at Yale as a graduate student in the late forties.

2. Cleanth Brooks, R. W. B. Lewis, and Robert Penn Warren, *American Literature: The Makers and the Making*, 2 vols. (New York: St. Martin's Press, 1973). Lewis was a longtime friend of Brooks's and a colleague at Yale University, where he taught American literature.

from about 1870 to the beginning of the Second World War. The assignment has, among other things, given me an opportunity to reread your poetry and prose, as I try to put down on paper something to the purpose about it. I've enjoyed this immensely. How fine your work is and how well it holds up—as poetry and as perceptive comment on our culture.

My special occasion for writing just at this time is to ask you a question about the "Ode to the Confederate Dead." As you know, I've always adopted as a working principle the notion that it is the text that counts, and I've therefore always been chary about asking the writer what he meant to say. Yet, in a work of this kind, I don't want to be foolishly doctrinaire, and so I am asking you whether I have interpreted correctly lines 21–41 of the "Ode." I am stating that I disagree with John J. Stewart who, in his *Burden of Time,* regards "Parmenides and Zeno . . . as early representatives of the 'scepticism and the habit of abstraction' which have brought modern man to the situation in which he 'knows only what animals know and in the animal way. [The man at the gate] is terrified by the darkening forms in the twilight and by the sudden call.'" My view is that: "He is not terrified, just as the Confederate soldiers were not terrified. For he has imaginatively entered into their world and, like them, knows what it is to possess the 'twilight certainty of an animal' and to be sustained by 'midnight restitutions of the blood.' The dead Confederate soldiers shared something of the certainty of the animal, who is not wracked by doubt and scepticism. That certainty is 'twilight,' whereas the consciousness of the intellectual, suffused with rational light, is multiple and uncertain. The soldier's knowledge is closer to a blood knowledge."

Please forgive my blundering if I have blundered, but as you see, I have interpreted the "rage of muted Zeno and Parmenides" as a rage against a world of change. I take them to be philosophers who had argued that whatever possesses "true being" is eternal and is not subject to change, "apparent change being no more than a delusion."

I'm not a good correspondent. Letters, I find—at least the letters that I have to dash off—are not an adequate substitute for real conversation. How fine it would be if we could get together more often in the future for visits and talk. How are the memoirs coming on?

Tinkum joins me in affectionate greetings to you and Helen and the children.

Yours,
Cleanth

[OH]   Running Knob Hollow Road
                                          Sewanee, Tennessee 37375
                                          October 21, 1970

Dear Cleanth,

It is a delight to get your letter.

First, Zeno and Parmenides. As usual, you are right and Stewart is wrong. *Nuf said*. Go ahead.

We expect to be in N.Y. Dec. 9–11. I am giving a joint reading with Jack Wheelock at the Morgan Library on the 9th. I suspect that Mrs. Kray will ask you to introduce us. If she does, please accept.—I say *me:* I'm not yet sure that Helen can come. The baby-sitting problem here is most difficult. We shall have to decide at the last minute.

The memoir is stalled. Scribners is rather luke-warm about it, and that scarcely cheers me on. But I'll get back to it after I return from Greensboro: I go there this week-end for two weeks—my old stomping ground—Oxford (London) is to bring out my *Essays* and a larger *Selected Poems* this month, the books appearing simultaneously.[1] There's been a lot written about me recently. Radcliffe Squires has finished a book for spring publication.[2] When I consider the small bulk of my work, I am more than pleased with the fact that it continues to get attention. I have never been able to feel "neglected."

If you can't introduce us at the reading, perhaps you and Tinkum could come in for dinner on Dec. 10. And Red and Eleanor too, I hope.

Affectionate greetings to you both.

                                          Ever yrs,
                                          Allen

My longhand is now worse than Red's. Arthritis is the approximate cause.

[OH]   Forest Road
                                          Northford, Connecticut
                                          Oct. 31, 1970

Dear Allen,

When Mrs. Kray called me by telephone some weeks ago to ask whether I would be willing to introduce you (and Wheelock) at the American Academy of Poets, I was prompt to say yes, not because I can promise an adequate job but because I was flattered to be asked and

1. *Essays of Four Decades* (Oxford: Oxford University Press, 1970); *The Swimmer and Other Selected Poems* (London: Oxford University Press, 1970).
2. Radcliffe Squires, *Allen Tate: A Literary Biography* (New York: Bobbs-Merrill, 1971).

eager to make a further testimony to my regard for your work. I do look forward to seeing you—and I hope to [be] seeing you *both.*

Can't you and Helen plan to pay us at Northford a visit before or after the occasion? (I write for us both since Tinkum is so tied up today that she can't write to Helen herself.)

We would deeply love to see you both. Do try to find a way to accept. Even if you can't know until the last minute, that will not put us to any inconvenience. A last-minute telephone [call], saying yes, will be most welcome.

I write in haste,
Cleanth

Thanks for your recent letter with its reply to my questions about the "Ode to the Confederate Dead."[1]

[OH]
Running Knob Hollow Road
Sewanee, Tennessee 37375
November 12, 1970

Dear Cleanth,

I was, of course, delighted to know that you will introduce Jack Wheelock and me. I shall see you before the reading at Mrs. Bullock's dinner party.

Alas, Helen just can't come. Last summer we left both boys with a reliable woman whom we imported from Minneapolis. But there's nobody in Sewanee Helen is willing to leave them with for as long as three nights. She is at present a prisoner, and will continue to be until we can find a suitable baby-sitter who is more than that, really a mature woman who has had experience with children.[1]

I admire your essay on *Soldiers Pay,*[2] and it goes without saying that you are Faulkner's best critic. The new *Southern Review* gets better all the time, and is rapidly making the *Sewanee* our no. 2 review. Poor Andrew has withdrawn into fantasies of genealogy and the Old South, and he doesn't know what is going on in the literary world.

I'm looking forward to seeing you and Tinkum on Dec. 9th.

Affectionate greetings.

Ever yrs,
Allen

1. See Brooks's "On the Poetry of Allen Tate," *Michigan Quarterly Review* 10 (1971): 225–28.

1. One of the Tates' three sons, Michael, John's fraternal twin, had died in a tragic nursery accident in 1968.

2. "Faulkner's First Novel," *Southern Review,* n.s. 6 (1970): 1056–74.

I see that I haven't responded to your invitation to come to Northford. I must go to an Institute committee meeting on the 10th, and fly home that afternoon. But many thanks.

[OH]   Running Knob Hollow Road
                                            Sewanee, Tennessee 37375
                                            November 25, 1970

Dear Cleanth,

I know you are dining tomorrow with the Spearses in Houston; but I am sending this to Northford. So this note is written in the hope that you and Tinkum can come to N.Y. on the 9th in time for lunch. I shall arrive at La Guardia at 10:50, and should be at the Princeton Club by 12:00. We could meet there, say, at 1:00. There will not be much of a chance for a real visit at Marie Bullock's dinner party, though it will be extremely pleasant.

I have not congratulated you on your election to the Institute and I am not doing so now. The Institute should be congratulated, and I would see that this was done if I were still President.[1] We are not supposed to tell the new members the names of his sponsors, but I think this is absurd. Malcolm Cowley, Howard Nemerov, and I did it; and I think you did us a favor to accept an "honor" which should have been done you twenty years ago.

By the way, Monroe's *Dionysus and the City*[2] seems to me to be a masterpiece of historical criticism. I hope it will be so received.

                                            Love to you both,
                                            Allen

[OH]   Forest Road
                                            Northford, Connecticut 06472
                                            Dec. 3, 1970

Dear Allen,

A hasty note to say that we will be most happy to have lunch with you at the Princeton Club on the 9th. Expect us there at 1:00.

The Texas visit was pleasant and a welcome break in a too hurried Autumn work season. But five days is too much to take out and I have been paying for the break ever since. Hence the lateness of this note.

1. Brooks had been elected to the National Institute of Arts and Letters. Tate had served as the group's president in 1968.
2. Monroe K. Spears, *Dionysus and the City: Modernism in Twentieth-Century Poetry* (New York: Oxford University Press, 1970).

But before I sign "In much haste, Cordially," I must tell you that I had rather assumed your good offices in the matter of my election to the Institute. Many thanks to you and my other friends.

Cleanth,

P.S. We are sorry that Helen can't come with you on this trip. We must plan on a real visit soon. Our affectionate greetings to her and the children.

P.S.S. I agree with your opinion about Monroe's book and I have said as much to his publisher.

Forest Road
Northford, Connecticut 06472
Feb. 9, 1971

Dear Allen,

Greetings from the frozen North—it has been a vile winter ever since mid-December. I understand that the South, and certainly the Cumberland plateau, has been suffering too.

I write to ask for your help with a program which Louis Rubin and I are trying to arrange for the Modern Language Association meeting to be held in Chicago this December, just after Christmas. I am, for my sins, this year's president of the Society for the Study of Southern Literature, and we plan to ask the MLA to join us as co-sponsors of a program on Southern literature. We plan to take as our topic your fine essay, "A Southern Mode of the Imagination."[1] We are trying to assemble a distinguished panel, including Southerners and non-Southerners, to talk about it. I can't imagine that there will be very much quarrel with your general reservations and qualifications. But I think that there are many aspects of this seminal essay that could be explored further and tested against literary outbursts in other cultures. (I am thinking here of some remarks that you have made on the Elizabethan renaissance and the nineteenth-century New England upsurge.)

Anyway, we obviously want you there in the flesh if we can lure you, to answer questions or to make any comments you like or—as the *Congressional Record* puts it—to extend your remarks. But you won't be asked *to do anything*, and the only set pieces we are asking of our other panelists are five or ten minute prepared statements and then any further discussion in which they would like to join.

---

1. "A Southern Mode of the Imagination: Circa 1918 to the Present," *Carleton Miscellany* 1 (winter 1960): 9–23.

A Society so young as ours doesn't have very much of a treasury, but we can offer you traveling expenses and furnish a hotel room in Chicago. I do hope that you can see your way to say yes. A number of your friends would be delighted and it would be a fine chance for some visiting and talk.

Tinkum joins me in affectionate greetings to you and Helen and the boys.

Yours,
Cleanth

Don't hesitate to call me collect for further information at Area Code 203, 489–9770—my home telephone. I hope that you can say yes at once, but please at least say "maybe."

[OH]
Running Knob Hollow Road
Sewanee, Tennessee 37375
February 14, 1971

Dear Cleanth,

Your program for the M.L.A. meeting promises to be most interesting, and I should like to be there. And of course I am pleased that you want me to be. It's a little hard for me to see that far ahead, and my acceptance of your invitation must therefore be conditional. We may be in Florida next Christmas; we don't want to be in Sewanee another winter. December to April is unbearable here. From Florida it's a long way to Chicago. Another reservation that occurs to me is my possible embarrassment at having to answer questions concerning an essay that I wrote thirteen years ago. But these are not serious obstacles to my going to Chicago. So let's assume that I'll be there, God willing.

For six weeks we struggled with a virus that I brought back from New York in December. We're all "well" now, but with crossed fingers.

Love to Tinkum,
Ever yrs,
Allen

[OH]
Forest Road
Northford, Conn. 06472
Feb. 20, 1971

Dear Allen,

I'm delighted to have your word that you will try to make it to Chicago this December. Naturally, we'll understand if something untoward comes up and you have to cancel. But we hope that you will be there.

We've already assembled an excellent panel. You will be among friends and admirers. And you can say as much or as little as you care to. (We'd prefer the former but will happily settle, if need be, for your simple presence.)

If you all are in Florida next winter, the jet plane has made it almost as quick and perhaps even easier to get to Chicago from there.

I'm sorry you've had a hard winter. We've heard that from the national weather reports. We've had a hard winter too—colder and snowier than usual. Though we will be here until after Xmas, we too may be in the South for the late winter and spring of 1972. I shall have half a year off.

Perhaps I can catch up with projects then. I'm still woefully behind with everything—including letters to my friends. That's another reason for you to come to Chicago. Perhaps we can get in a lot of talk.

Tinkum joins me in affectionate greetings to you, Helen, and the children.

Cleanth

[OH]
Running Knob Hollow Road
Sewanee, Tennessee 37375
November 16, 1971

Dear Cleanth,

I've been in the doldrums or I would long ago have thanked you for the fine essay in the Michigan Quarterly. Last month I went on a three week jaunt to Harvard, Greensboro, and Chapel Hill, and returned with a wicked virus which still hangs on. Helen is now down with it; so is John Orly. Benjamin seems to defeat it.

I am trying to decide about the M.L.A. meeting. I talked to Louis Rubin when I was at Chapel Hill, and he made the schedule seem easy. Will it be? My hesitation is due to fear of getting another virus on top of my chronic emphysema. What *will* the schedule be—the date, the hour, etc.?

I ask because I understand you are in charge. I could hope that the program I'm on will be in the morning in the same hotel where we would stay—the Palmer House, I believe.

I've done little work since September. Not only the trip and the virus, but a quarrel with Charles Scribner has taken up a lot of time and worry. I've now succeeded in moving my poems from Scribners to the Swallow Press, so that all my books in print will be with one publisher.

I hope you and Tinkum are well. We all join in love to you both.

Ever yrs,
Allen

[OH]   Running Knob Hollow Road
                                        Sewanee, Tennessee 37375
                                        November 30, 1971

Dear Cleanth,

It was good of you to telephone, and I'm sorry I was not at home. But Helen passed on the schedule: Thurs. Dec. 30 at 9 to 11. Louis Rubin made a reservation for me at the Palmer House. I expect to arrive in Chicago around noon on the 29th. I suspect I'll be with the Swallow Press people that afternoon, but I'll hope to see you that evening.

Helen *might* come, and then go on to St. Paul to see her mother, if we can arrange the children. If she thought Tinkum would be with you, that would be an added incentive.

                                        Affly but in haste,
                                        Allen

John Ransom has now "revised" and ruined his "Old Mansion."[1]

[OH]   Forest Road
                                        Northford, Connecticut 06472
                                        Dec. 14, 1971

Dear Allen,

My plans for the end of the month have now taken firm shape and I hurry off this note to say that I expect to get to Chicago on the 28th, probably by mid-afternoon. I'm to be at the Palmer House. I need to get back here as soon as I can and so expect to leave Chicago soon after lunch on the 30th.

Won't you have dinner with me on the 29th? If you are engaged for that time then save what other time you can. I do want to get more than simply a glimpse of you and I will keep clear of engagements from late afternoon of the 29th on until I leave. The people that I have to see are few and I'll try to meet them before you arrive.

I do hope that Helen can come. Tinkum can't. We're having some family here through the holidays and she will have to stay at Northford— but she detests MLA and other such meetings and couldn't be persuaded to come in any case.

This morning I've just finished putting the final touches to The Literature of the South, 1914–45, a section of the textbook on American

---

1. Ransom had a habit deplored by some of his friends and critics of reworking his earlier poems for each new collection. His "Old Mansion" went through five different revisions. Tate once described Ransom's constant fidgeting with some of his most beautiful elegies as a "last infirmity of the noble mind" and ascribed it to Ransom's dependence on logic as his guide.

Literature that Red, and Dick Lewis, and I hope to bring to a close this month (publication next year).

You bring up the rear—place of honor, chivalric position, and all that—of the section. I hope you will like what we have done when you see it. We've really ended up by doing, not an anthology but a highly illustrated short *history* of American literature and not so short at that—400,000 words of history, I should guess.

I must stop and hurry this scrawl into the mail. It's already overdue.

T. joins in greetings and holiday wishes to you and Helen and the children.

Cleanth

[OH]
Running Knob Hollow Road
Sewanee, Tennessee 37375
Dec. 17, 1971

Dear Cleanth,

Thank you for yours of the 14th.

I am arriving—with Walter Sullivan—at O'Hare at 10:25 a.m., the 29th. The Swallow Press is meeting me. We will go direct to the Palmer House, although my reservation is not until 6:00 p.m. May I use your room, if necessary, to wash up, etc.? I may have to lunch with the Swallow people, but *dinner* that evening is open, and I'll be delighted to dine with you.— Helen is not coming either!

In haste,
Allen

[OH]
Forest Road
Northford, Connecticut 06472
Dec. 20, 1971

Dear Allen,

I hasten to reply to your note of the 17th, which I picked up an hour or so ago. You are indeed welcome to my room when you arrive at the Palmer House on the 29th. It is possible that I shall be out at an official lunch (1–3 p.m.) nearby. But if I have had to leave the room before you arrive, I'll leave written instructions with the hotel that you are to be given a key to my room.

A telephone call from Louis Rubin the other day would indicate that he thinks all the members of the "panel" shall dine together on the evening of the 29th and without seeming selfish and possessive, I saw no way to [tell] him no. After all, he is the person really in charge and he has made most of the arrangements—though I suggested the topic. Anyway, it will be good to see you even sharing you with two or three others and we will try to get a promise to get you and Helen and the boys here for a real visit this spring or summer.

See you in Chicago,
Cleanth

T. joins me in wishes for a blessed Christmas for all the Tates. PLEASE EX-CUSE THIS HASTY SCRAWL. MY H-WRITING HAS JUST ABOUT DISINTEGRATED.

[OH]

Running Knob Hollow Road
Sewanee, Tennessee 37375
January 14, 1972

Dear Cleanth,

I am not sure who was my host in Chicago—you or Louis Rubin; perhaps both. In any case, I enjoyed *all* of it, and regret only that my participation was rather thin.

I can't refrain from reporting to you a long-distance call I had a few days ago from a master at Choate School. He identified himself as a Sewanee alumnus ('63), and forthwith invited me to fly to Connecticut on January 26 to join you and Dick Lewis at a dinner in honor of James Dickey.

I declined as politely as possible under the circumstances. After I had hung up the receiver I remembered what Dick Wilbur[1] wrote to the organizer of a writers' conference: he would be glad to attend but *only* during the week that James Dickey was *not* present.

I am now trying to finish up one of the pieces in *terza rima,* and beginning a new essay, or rather section of my memoir to give at Michigan as the Hopwood Lecture.[2] I should be back in teaching harness Feb. 1st, with a seminar here.

Love to Tinkum,
Ever yrs,
Allen

[OH]

Forest Road
Northford, Connecticut 06472
Jan. 19, 1972

Dear Allen,

I tried to see you after our forum on Dec. 30 in Chicago to express my particular thanks for your consenting to be with us and for the part you

---

1. The reference is to Richard Wilbur, a poet and notable translator of French literature.
2. This was "A Lost Traveler's Dream," published in the fall 1972 issue of *Michigan Quarterly Review.*

took. But the time filled up—what with checking-out delays—quicker than I had expected, and since I had to get out to the airport early, there was nothing to do but ask Walter [Sullivan] to convey my thanks to you.

Your presence and your comments made the occasion. For one thing, it gave us our good crowd—remarkably large in view of the fact that we were the last thing on the program. Many people had told me they would have to leave before we got started.

I hope that you felt the session was successful. I was much pleased. The talk seemed to me good and pertinent. Besides, it *was* a forum—not three long papers that used up all the time so that one heard one question or two and then everyone shuffled out.

I am grading examinations and getting ready to wind up the term. I have the spring semester off. We expect to be abroad most of April. Otherwise we shall be right here trying to catch up with various things that have had to be postponed during past months.

I hope that T. and I can have a trip or so South this spring and summer. Is there any chance that you and Helen and the little boys could come to see us here this summer? We have a sandy brook for the children to wade in, some meadows around the house to play on, and complete safety away from traffic. Do think about it.

T. joins me in affectionate greetings to you and Helen and the children.

Cleanth

p.s. I do hope you will like our American literature book when it achieves print. St. Martin's Press promises bound copies by December.

[OH]   Running Knob Hollow Road
                                                        Sewanee, Tennessee 37375
                                                        June 27, 1972

Dear Cleanth,

Just a note. Could you do anything for the lady whose troubles are described in the enclosed letter? In other words, are you still in touch with the Embassy in London? It's really a desperate situation.

Please tell Red that I will write him in a few days.

Love to Tinkum.

Affly,
Allen

[OH]   Forest Road
                                                        Northford, Connecticut 06472
                                                        July 16, 1972

Dear Allen,

I'm just back from a week in Oxford, Mississippi, attending a kind of writers' conference. The weather was pleasantly cool for this time of the year there. I had originally hoped that we might come by car, stopping at Sewanee briefly if we could catch you there. But circumstances came up that made that impossible. In the end, I flew to Oxford alone and T. remained here.

I should have written earlier that I have appealed on Mr. Paschell's behalf to the man at our Embassy whom I know best. He is fairly highly placed—he is a Counselor for Public Affairs—And I am sure that he will go to the Consular section and do what he can.

My own experience was that I could sometimes help in such cases but sometimes not. But I hope for the best: my friend (William Weld) has much higher rank and seniority than I had and he is a decent person of intelligence and real good wit.

I trust that you and the children and Helen are all well. I'm reading proof on the American literature book and busy with several other commitments. My semester off didn't do me much good—I was too far behind. But I mean to take the spring semester off in 1973. Perhaps I can some day get to a resting place and the opportunity to see some of my friends. Is there any hope of you all being able to come this way in the summer or early fall? Tinkum joins in affectionate greetings to all the Tates.

Cleanth

p.s. Red seems to be thriving. He was with us here for some two weeks after he was able to leave the hospital and before that Eleanor was here with us some two or three weeks while Red was in the hospital. He had an operation on his liver, but the surgeon found nothing amiss. He then went on to recover rapidly without medication! His jaundiced condition has been clearing up nicely. All very mysterious, but the liver specialist here says that this sometimes happens. Red and Eleanor are now in Vermont (West Wardsboro, Vt.)

RPW's illness 1972

[OH]   Forest Road
                                              Northford, Connecticut 06472
                                                          August 2, 1972

Dear Allen,

I enclose a letter from the Embassy in London which speaks for itself. I'm sure that your friends in Sewanee have already received the good news.

How are matters with the Tates? We remain much too busy here, what with proof-reading, promised articles and reviews to complete, and a dozen other things. But now that our hot and humid air has been blown away by breezes from Canada, it is really pleasant once more.

Red was here for the weekend to have a check-up on his condition from the New Haven doctors. He looks fine—there is no evident trace of jaundice, and he says he feels well except for getting tired more easily than he used to.

Is there any chance of you all coming this way in the late summer or early fall? I believe that I wrote that we had hoped to be able to call by Sewanee early last month but ultimately had to alter our plans. We must, however, plan to get together, here or there for some talk. Our Chicago meeting was pleasant for me but it simply was too brief and crowded.

T. joins me in affectionate greetings to you and Helen and the boys.

Cleanth

[OH]   Sewanee 37375
                                                              17 Aug. '72

Dear Cleanth,
    Thank you for writing to Bill Weld, and for the letter from the Consul. Bill Weld "managed" me in Paris in 1956!—Excuse this card. I'm just back from ten days in the Vanderbilt Hospital: bronchitis, etc. Much better now.

Affly,
Allen

[OH]   Sewanee 37375
                                                                3 May '73

Dear Cleanth,
    Could we, after all, lunch at the Gotham? I don't like forfeiting your hospitality at the Yale Club, but I don't see how I could get there before 2:30. My plane arrives at Kennedy at 12:50, usually a little later. Could you and Tinkum meet me at the Gotham at approximately 2:00?

In haste,
Allen

[OH]   Forest Road
                                           Northford, Connecticut 06472
                                                             May 4, 1973

Dear Allen,
    How good it was to hear your voice on the telephone the other day. It's good to know that we shall be seeing you on the 15th with a chance for some real talk with you.

A second thought about our plans however: if you are free for dinner on the 15th, let's shift our date from a luncheon meeting to a dinner meeting. But if you already have plans for dinner, then let's keep the luncheon engagement by all means. We don't want to miss the opportunity for a visit with you and retention of our first arrangement will simply mean that we will be coming in from New Haven somewhat earlier than we could for a dinner date.

I am eager for you to see our Allen Tate section in *American Literature* (Brooks-Lewis-Warren). I hope that what we have selected from your poetry and prose will meet your approval and that our account of your place in Southern (and American) letters as given in the introduction to your work and the headnotes will please you.

Our second volume may be out in time for May 15. If not I shall get you a copy of the Tate section in a xerox copy—if that is possible.

T. joins me in affectionate greetings to you, to Helen, and the little boys.

In haste,
Cleanth

p.s. Just drop me a card or, if you prefer, call me at (203) 484–9770.

Red is still out of town. I'll speak to him about dinner on the 15th as soon as he gets back.

[OH]   Running Knob Hollow Road
                                       Sewanee, Tennessee 37375
                                                  May 9, 1973

Dear Cleanth,

Yrs. of May 6th [*sic*] just received. Alas, I had already accepted Jack Wheelock's invitation to dinner on the 15th. Could you all stay for dinner *after* the ceremonial on the 16th? I'm not flying back till next morning.

In any case, I'll hope to see you & Tinkum at lunch on the 15th. I hope you got my card suggesting change to Gotham for lunch.

Yrs. in haste,
Allen

p.s. yes, do please bring xerox of A.T. section of book if possible.

[OH]   Running Knob Hollow Road
                                       Sewanee, Tennessee 37375
                                                  May 21, 1973

Dear Cleanth,

I forgot to give you the galleys at the Academy. Here they are. I am still dazed by the brilliance of your commentary.

Let's elect Austin.[1] I'll get to work on it soon. Won't you ask Red if he will join us?

I am swamped. Forgive brevity. Love to you both.

Affly,
Allen

[OH]   Forest Road
Northford, Connecticut 06472
June 7, 1973

Dear Allen,

Our dilatory publisher finally managed to bring out Vo. II of our American Literature book. I checked at once and the Squires' books (both of them) are included in the list of Further Readings. I had supposed so; but when I first heard from you, I couldn't be sure. (The proof I showed you was indeed an early one.)

As soon as I can acquire an entire copy of the book, I'll send it along. There are some sections that I believe you will be particularly interested in seeing and certainly many sections that I want you to see and on which I'd like your comments.

I was much heartened by your kind words about the introduction and the notes to the selections that we use from your own work. Needless to say, you figure very often elsewhere in the two volumes—on Poe, on Hart Crane, on MacLeish, etc., etc.

It was pleasant seeing you in New York. I said that you and Helen could make plans to bring the children up and have a real visit with us. Failing that, T. and I may be able to call by Sewanee. But when? It looks as if my summer [is] already filled with things to finish and still other things to begin.

Tinkum sends affectionate greetings to you and joins me in love to Helen and the little boys.

As ever,
Cleanth

[OH]   Forest Road
Northford, Connecticut 06472
June 13 [1973]

Dear Allen,

It was nice to be able to talk with you a few minutes yesterday morning. I am hurrying off to you this afternoon (herewith) the form

1. Tate and Brooks supported the candidacy of Austin Warren to join the National Institute of Arts and Letters, and in due course he was elected.

that you have kindly agreed to fill out for me. I'm sorry that I have cut the time so short, but as I indicated over the telephone, this notion of applying for a Senior Fellowship came to me late in the day. Anyway, I hope that I am not being too much of a nuisance in applying for your help on such short notice. Many thanks.

Cleanth

[OH]
Running Knob Hollow
Sewanee, Tennessee
Wed. 20 June '73

Dear Cleanth,
   The form arrived last Friday. I mailed it on Sat. the 16th. Hope it reached the bureaucrats on Mon. 18th, the dead-line.—You complimented me by asking for testimonial!—am looking forward to the Brooks, Warren, Lewis book.—Have you read Lewis Simpson's *The Man of Letters*, etc.?[1] A fine book.

Yrs.
Allen

[OH]
Running Knob Hollow Road
Sewanee, Tennessee
30 June '73

Dear Cleanth,
   I have not, alas, received a copy of The Book, though I hear from several people that they have! I'm eager to see it.

Yrs.
Allen

[OH]
Forest Road
Northford, Connecticut 06472
July 3 [1973]

Dear Allen,
   Your card (of 30 June) has just come in and I hasten to reply. St. Martin's has not been expeditious in getting out copies of *American Lit,* and I am

---

1. In *The Man of Letters in New England and the South: Essays on the History of the Literary Vocation in America* (Baton Rouge: Louisiana State University Press, 1973), Lewis P. Simpson, a critic and historian of southern literature, considers Tate's southern essays, especially "The Profession of Letters in the South" and "A Southern Mode of the Imagination."

still not certain whether they have sent out the gift copies from the list we sent them.

But a few days ago I did get a number of copies of the hard-cover edition direct from New York and one will be on its way to you before the week is out. I'm flattered that you really want to see it and we are, of course, on our side, extremely eager to have your opinion of it.

Many thanks for your prompt response to my appeal for help in the matter of the NEH.

Love to Helen and the boys from us both,

Cleanth

[OH]   Running Knob Hollow Road
July 13, 1973

Dear Cleanth,

You have distracted me from four days of work: I've been immersed in the Great Anthology. I simply couldn't put it down. Not that I've read all 2970 pages in four days. Who could? But I've sampled much of it. I am awed at the *rightness* of the entire two volumes. Think of the versatility and the *vast* erudition. Who did Henry James and Henry Adams? I think I know who wrote certain introductions; but how could you three men know enough to write as well on Adams as on Faulkner? The introductions are complete critical-biographical essays, and could stand separately in a magazine or book.

I suspect that Dick Lewis did Adams; you did me; Red did Hawthorne, Melville, Whittier, Dreiser, etc. You did Caroline [Gordon] and K. A. P[orter] and Faulkner. But these are guesses. Who did the fine introductions to the Blacks?

My one criticism is that all three of you have hidden your lights under a bushel.

Audubon is a very fine poem, but it is not enough to represent Red. Where are you under your own name, even though you are ubiquitous anonymously? Couldn't you, without immodesty, have included an essay like the one on Marvell's Cromwellian Ode?

Red's "Thomas Wolfe" is as good today as when it was written.— Dick did Adams, obviously, and it couldn't be better.—The historical introductions to the various sections read like the work of professional historians.

I could go on indefinitely. The work as a whole is a masterly job.

Ever yrs.
Allen

p.s. I haven't said that your treatment of me is perfect—the introduction as well as the selection of poems.

I would think that Peter Taylor should have been included.

[OH]   Sewanee 37375
                                                                      16 July '73

Dear Cleanth,

I need *urgently* to know where & when we first met. I know it was in Paris. Pip arranged the meeting. Was it Xmas vacation '28 or '29? And where was it—a café?[1]

I'm still dipping into *American Lit.* again: how could three men, individually and collectively, know so much?

                                                                           Yrs.
                                                                           Allen

[OH]   Northford
                                                                     July 21, 1973

Dear Allen,

I hasten to answer your card of July 16. We met as nearly as I can remember in Paris, at the Deux Magots Café in the autumn of 1929 or was it in early spring in 1930? It could not have been 1928, for I did not get to Oxford until early October 1929. I was in Paris briefly in December(?) on my way to the south of France and, again, at the end of Hilary Term, about the end of March, 1930, on my way to Italy. If you had left Paris by 1930, then it must have been in the late fall or early winter 1929. Otherwise, I'm inclined to believe that our first acquaintance dates from the Spring of 1930. How are the memoirs coming along? T. and many another person look forward eagerly to reading them.

And now for something approaching a proper answer to your letter of the 13th. I was much gratified and elated to read those two pages and my impulse was to sit down at once and express my delight and appreciation. But I let myself be put off by the press of work—we are now trying to cut *American Literature* to a one-volume edition for one-semester courses and Red and I are also revising two other text-books, revisions long delayed for the past several years in which we were trying to finish the full edition.

---

1. Tate was working on "What I Owe to Cleanth Brooks," which was published in Lewis P. Simpson, ed., *The Possibilities of Order: Cleanth Brooks and His Work* (Baton Rouge: Louisiana State University Press, 1976).

I have sent a copy of your letter to Red (now at his summer place in Vermont), for I know that he will be as happy to read your handsome comments as I have been. I mean also—since I can't believe that you will object—to send a copy to Dick, still in Florence, Italy. Dick worked manfully at this job and, as you know, he is a great admirer of your work. Like me, he will consider your commendation the final accolade.

Your surmises and guesses at the authorship of the various essays and introductions are very shrewd. Red was responsible, as you have sensed, for Hawthorne, Whittier, and Dreiser. You are right also about my contributions: Caroline, K.A.P., Faulkner, and you. In fact, I did all the Southerners, beginning with Jefferson and Poe and coming on down the line with the exception of Thomas Wolfe. As for John [Ransom]: Red turned over to me a long essay that he had recently done and I reworked it.

There was a certain amount of this kind of swapping and reworking. For example, I turned over to Dick an unpublished essay I had done on E. A. Robinson and a good deal of material on Frost and Dick worked that up with his own stuff and then passed it back to me for a few touchups.

You ask about Crane. Red, I believe, did Stephen Crane. (As I look back over the Introduction at this moment, it seems to bear Red's stylistic trademark.) As for Hart Crane, Dick did the original draft but turned it over to me for some additions and some reworking. I don't know how to balance accounts: perhaps 60% Dick's, 40% mine? But though each always submitted his own work to the other two for suggestions, additions—or cuts—and a general cosmetic treatment, nearly all the introductions are substantially from one pen. The Hart Crane and Frost pieces are somewhat exceptional. Dick did nearly all the 17th century figures, and Franklin, Woolman, etc. of the 18th century. He did Emerson, Melville (the fiction, that is), Whitman, Dickinson, Henry James, and many another.

Red did Melville's poetry, Henry Adams, William James, Santayana, and most of the material on the Blacks. I thought I knew Red's mind and abilities long ago, but I had not realized until the last six years how much he knows about American history and the American literature of the nineteenth century.

I did the section entitled "From Imagism to Symbolism"—(pp. 1043–1202) needless to say, with some very important suggestions from Red. I was especially delighted to read your good word about the general historical introductions. These came closer to being collaborative efforts—at least to the extent that all three of us proposed additions and modifications and helped in the reworking. But here, too, one individual was basically responsible for the general layout and the style. Dick did the first one (1620–1743). I did (1743–1826). Red did the third and fourth (1826–1861) and (1861–1914); and I did the last one, (1914–72).

.With a book already busting at the seams, it seemed to us extravagant to publish literary essays and critical pieces that we had done in the past. Red—as a poet and novelist—was a very different matter. Dick and I beat down his objections finally but we were, even so, strictly limited as to what Red would allow us to use. No fiction—because of the space required and the great difficulty of using a section of a novel—and no poetry before 1945. In short he agreed to appear only as a poet and in the one section in which we sampled, with no historical or critical comment, the literature of the last quarter-century. We thought (Dick and I) that *Audubon* complete could register with more impact than a handful of miscellaneous poems, however fine.

The omission of Peter Taylor is distressing. The truth is that we had hoped to include him and a short introduction had already been written for him when we realized that by the rules we had adopted for ourselves, his relative youth would force him into the crowded Post-1945 section and he was a victim of the intolerable squeeze. (But this explanation is for your eyes alone: I hope that Peter will understand our problems about space but I had rather [he] see it in these terms simply rather than to learn that we had gone as far as we had, and then had to drop him. If the book prospers and should take another form at some stage—say four volumes, each of smaller compass—we might be able to print one of his excellent stories. I like, by the way, his recent book of plays.)

This letter has turned out to be too long and I've perhaps been tedious in detailing who wrote what—but I've been tempted to run on, in view of your evident interest in the book and the very knowing quality of your guesses at the distribution of authorship.

I hope the summer is going well for you and Helen and the children. I would think that Sewanee would be a marvelous place in which to spend the summer. We've had a good summer here, but we are too busy: we never have time for simple leisure, taking a ride, going to see a play, or taking a trip. But I hope to retire from the textbook business after this year and since I expect to retire from Yale early in 1974 or, at the latest, in 1975, I am looking forward to a much more flexible arrangement, more travel, and even time to lie in a hammock and read a book simply for the pleasure of reading it.

With all best wishes, in which T. joins me, to all the Tates, including the little ones.

Cleanth

p.s. I don't believe I ever sent you a copy of my last collection of essays, *A Shaping Joy*. It was published in London in 1971 and last year by

Harcourt.[1] It was received not unfavorably in the N.Y. *Times* weekday review but, in company with John's *Beating the Bushes*,[2] butchered in the N.Y. Times Sunday Review of Books. I send it, not only because I hope you will have time to look at some of the essays, but because it contains an essay that indicates how much I think of Peter Taylor. See "The Southern Temper," pp. 198–215.

p.s.s. I hope that you can read this scrawl. I've chosen tablet paper so as to keep my script large so that it will be more nearly legible.

[OH]   *lst mtg*   ✗

Sewanee 37375
28 July '73

Dear Cleanth:

It was Xmas vacation 1929. C[aroline] and I left France New Year's Day 1930. Many thanks—I'm so hard-pressed that I must merely thank you for your *very* fine *A Shaping Joy* (but more on it later). Your long letter about the anthology is most illuminating. (If you do a one-volume edition, please cut me down *only a little:* the selections, introductions, and analyses are the best I've ever read!) Love to you both.

Allen

[OH]

Running Knob Hollow Road
Sewanee, Tennessee 37375
August 14, 1973

Dear Cleanth,

I've sent the enclosure to Lewis Simpson. I've hesitated to send this copy to you, but I do so in case I've made some errors of fact regarding our first meeting and your later sending me parts of *Modern Poetry and the Tradition.*

I have long awaited the chance to speak my mind on this subject, lest I be accused of Southern log-rolling. Now I don't care. Let the accusations come!

Ever yrs,
Allen

p.s. Who wrote the hateful review of *The Shaping Joy*? J.C.R.'s *Beating the Bush* is very weak, and should not have been published. Poor old

1. *A Shaping Joy: Studies in the Writer's Craft* (London: Methuen and Co.; New York: Harcourt Brace Jovanovich, 1972).

2. John Crowe Ransom, *Beating the Bushes: Selected Essays, 1941–1970* (New York: New Directions, 1972).

John—all his life chasing the phantom of philosophical aesthetics! But a great poet!

[OH]   Forest Road
                                                  Northford, Conn. 06472
                                                      August 23 [1973]

Dear Allen,

I have put off answering your last communication because I literally lacked the words—the proper and appropriate words, that is—to express my sense of gratitude for the handsome things that you set down on paper about me and my work. Part of my difficulty in making a response comes from my consciousness that you have been much too generous in your praise. But I am too much moved and, indeed, deeply touched to feel like quarreling with your commendations. Instead, I'll turn to another aspect of the matter: praise from you—even when I know that it is [in] part an effect of your generosity—means a great deal to me and always has.

Why shouldn't I say it now—we are both old enough—that from a very early period you were my special hero as man of letters and that you remain one of the three or four people from whom I have learned most. I have always thought of you as the man of insight, the man of the shrewdest judgment, the truly orthodox man. I would not apply the last objective to many people—even to the few that might deserve it— for fear that they would suggest that I was really sneering at them. In a relativistic age, the notion that there is such a thing as *the* truth has become unthinkable. But I am confident that you will understand what I mean by "orthodox." It includes literary values, of course, but much more.

You have asked me to point out errors of fact in what you have written about me and the answers to certain matters about which you were unsure. Here goes, though all the matters are trivial or of very little importance.

Pip was a Rhodes scholar and had been at Oxford early in the 1920s. Through a series of accidents, of happy consequences for me, Red and I had met in the fall of 1924 during my freshman and his senior year at Vanderbilt. We did not see a great deal of each other but he was very kind to me and when I arrived in Oxford in October of 1929, he looked me up at once.

I decided to read the English Honors School at Oxford and took my B.A. in 1931. I got my B. Litt. in the summer of 1932 and just managed to land a job at L.S.U. a few weeks before the start of the new school year in September, 1932. It was in the Depression, jobs were scarce, and I am sure that without Pip's help I could not have got the place. (I had applied some months before from Oxford and had been turned down.)

I probably began sending you chapters of *MP and the T* in 1937 or 1938. I owe Bill Couch's acceptance of the book at the North Carolina Press to your generous help. It was still the Depression era and it was very difficult for an unpublished author to place a book of this kind. You have, Allen, all your life, been concerned to help the younger men to get a hearing. Your deeds of this kind must be many.

T. and I have stayed home and worked away all summer. We've had good weather and quiet but I am wearied out with revising textbooks and doing other work of this kind. I hope that in the years just ahead we can relax a bit, travel a great deal more, and have a little fun.

I teach the fall term at Yale but plan to teach the second semester at L.S.U. in Baton Rouge. I did this for the spring semester in 1969 and T. and I both enjoyed it very much as a change of scene and a break in pace. I wish that we could persuade you and Helen to come down for a visit in Baton Rouge and New Orleans. Think about it.

T. joins in affectionate greetings to all the Tates including the little ones.

Cleanth,

[OH]   Sewanee 37375
                                        28 Aug. '73

Dear Cleanth,

Many thanks for your fine letter. The corrections have been sent to Lewis Simpson.

Forgive this card. I'm swamped!

Yrs aff.
Allen

[OH]   Running Knob Hollow Road
                              Sewanee, Tennessee 37375
                                        Nov. 1, 1974

Dear Cleanth,

Again, you're going to great trouble to please an old friend. I can never express the depth of my gratitude.

We hope Tinkum is coming. She is always indispensable! And good to know that Bill Wimsatt is coming with you.

Now: my doctor at Vanderbilt says I may go to the dinner on the 15th but not to Donoghue's[1] lecture before, nor to yours after dinner. *I will be in a wheel chair.* My breath is short, shorter than ever these past few days: bronchitis on top of emphysema. All this leads to a request: may I see a carbon (or xerox) of your lecture before your arrival? I want to know what people who heard you are talking about.

We are looking forward also to seeing you (and Tinkum) for lunch at our house on Saturday the 16th.

                                                          Affectionately,
                                                          Allen

p.s. You will be as amused as I was moved, by Ivor Richards' response to the invitation. He wrote a long, longhand eulogy (his letter), which enclosed a sequence of three sonnets, "norce teipoium, to honour Allen Tate." The sonnets are as involuted as Hopkins! I hadn't known that Ivor "admired" me. I supposed he thought of me as a friend of his friend T.S.E.!

                                                          A.T.

I hope Red can come. I believe he will try. But he isn't too well himself—though he always look vigorous.

[OH]   Forest Road
                                                 Northford, Connecticut 06472
                                                          Nov. 7, 1974

Dear Allen,

Your letter of Nov. 1 came in the other day and it was delightful to hear from you. I am looking forward to my visit with a very real and deep anticipation. My concern—and it is a very real one—is that I may not be able to say all that I would like to say and say it in a way befitting the occasion. For it is truly a great occasion for all of your many friends—and for American letters in general. I will truly like to have my talk measure up to the occasion. But enough of that. All of us who are scheduled to speak must share the same anxiety because we share the same regard for our celebration of you and what you have accomplished.

Tinkum has decided most regretfully that she had best not try to come. She has a hundred things to do and will have to content herself with sending her love and affectionate wishes. Bill Wimsatt will be on the plane with me.

----

1. Denis Donoghue, the Irish critic and professor of English at New York University, was at that time teaching at Trinity College in Dublin. Donoghue's lecture launched a two-day celebration of Tate's seventy-fifth birthday held by the University of the South.

I'll definitely get a xerox or carbon copy of my paper into your hands—if not by mail beforehand—then at least immediately after my arrival. I hope that you will like what you see, and I do stress "hope," for I am far from sure that it will properly express what I would have it do.

In haste,
Cleanth

[OH]   *75th birthday*
nov. 19, 1974

Running Knob Hollow Road
Sewanee, Tennessee 37375
November 26, 1974

Dear Cleanth,

Your lecture—if I may use a political metaphor—was the "keynote speech." If I represent one-third of the high merit you credit me with, I shall be content.

In short, many thanks, for all your trouble.

Affectionately and gratefully,
Allen

[OH]

University of South Carolina
Columbia, S.C. 29208
April 20, 1975

Dear Allen,

Sometime ago the people at the Swallow Press were kind enough to send me page proofs of *Memoirs and Opinions, 1926–1974.* I read it—and *re*read it (for of course I know well some of the essays of time past—at once). Now I find that I have let too much time elapse before sending you my thanks and appreciation. I was gratified and deeply touched to find that you had dedicated the "Opinions" section to me. This is a high accolade. (I believe I tried to tell you at Sewanee, last November, for how many years you have been my literary hero.)

I have been made very happy, too, by the letter you sent me last fall after my return from the celebration of your birthday. The letter is, and will remain, one of my most treasured possessions.

I hope that next month I may be able to say some of these things to you in person, for I hope to be in Sewanee. The University of the South has invited me to receive an honorary degree on May 25. (I do not know whether they have made yet any public announcement.) Naturally, I hope that circumstances will allow you to have some time for a visit from me—a few hours of talk at the least.

Tinkum feels that she had better not try to come with me though I'd still like to persuade her. In any case, my visit to Sewanee will have to be short, for we will not get back to Connecticut until May 3 and there will be a hundred things to do in getting the place in running order—as well as literary comments that I have promised to fulfill.

Be, therefore, candid, Allen about whether a short visit with you will be entirely convenient and just when. After having heard from you, I'll then work out my travel plans as to time of arrival and time of departure. I am assuming that I will put up at the Sewanee Inn for at least one night—possibly two.

Please give our affectionate greetings to Helen and the little boys.

Cleanth,

[OH]

Forest Road
Northford, Connecticut 06472
May 28, 1975

Dear Helen and Allen,

How fine it was to have a long, fine evening of talk together! My special thanks to you, Helen, for arranging it so pleasantly with a quiet and intimate meal together.

I also feel so much gratified that Allen felt strong enough and well enough to give me the many hours of talk that he did. I could have happily gone on much longer but I was concerned not to tire Allen out.

I wish that we lived much closer together so that we could visit more often. That, of course, can't easily be done. But I will try to be a better correspondent than I have been in the past. Let us really try to keep in touch. And, Allen, please don't hesitate to ask me to perform any services that you think I am competent to perform for you nor hesitate to lay upon me any special commissions. It will be a pleasure to carry them out.

It's a beautiful morning here in Conn. T. is working *in the ground*, as she likes to do, trying to solve a drainage problem. I am in my outside study, getting ready to settle down to an afternoon's work. (I've just labeled a notebook "The Influence of Gnosticism on Anglo-American Literature"—not a good title for a book but a sufficient one for a repository of notes looking forward to such a book. I hope some day to write it.)

I've spoken to Red about seeing you. He is happy to have good news of you. So is Tinkum who sends her best love.

Cleanth

[OH]

Running Knob Hollow Road
Sewanee, Tennessee 37375
May 28 [1975]

Dear Cleanth,

Your visit lifted my spirits no end. I cannot tell you how much I enjoyed your company. What you said about the ending of the *Fathers* inspired me to revise it at once. I enclose a copy of my revision. I hope you approve. Please come again soon.

Our love to you both,
Allen

Forest Road
Northford, 06472
June 9, [1975]

Dear Allen,

I am much flattered that you have taken seriously my query about the last sentence of *The Fathers*. I do prefer very much your revised ending. If that revision itself still leaves certain mysteries unresolved, maybe the mysteries ought to be left unrevealed—or not fully revealed. (I am not forgetting what is said on p. 272: "You remember what you cannot understand.")

Last night I reread the last section of "The Abyss," and I am moved again to exclaim: "What a wonderful novel it is!" It *is* intricately wrought —rich, massive, and full of wisdom about the human predicament.

Having reread it, I can see that the failure to understand Lacey's final attitude toward George Posey was basically my own fault. But you do put a heavy load on your reader's powers of comprehension; hence, my plea for a little more help with the last sentences. That is to say, Lacy is writing his account of the events many years later, and he has come to understand so much of what is essentially wrong with George—has isolated so clearly George's part in the family disaster—that the reader, unless he is very discerning indeed, may find it hard to believe that Lacy now, a half-century later, can still say "I love him more than I love any man." Your version "I loved him more than I could love any man" has proved accordingly very helpful to this admiring, almost persuaded, but still fumbling and puzzled reader.

By the way, you deal out a very even-handed justice in this novel as between George the impulsive man and Semmes the logical man, as between George, obsessed with his personal problems, and Major Buchan who is too tightly locked into the rituals, ceremonies, and ethics of an ordered family society. I could go on and on with this; but I won't.

It's a busy morning for me and I am sure that you have more important things to read than the long and rambling letter that this one threatens to become.

It *was* good to have the long talk with you. Tinkum joins in love to you, to Helen, and to the little boys.

Yours,
Cleanth

p.s. I must not close this letter, however, without writing my more and more confident prediction that *The Fathers* is going to turn out to be one of the great novels of the twentieth century. It contains, in [my] opinion, the finest intellectual analysis of the clash of cultures in the War Between the States—you show how it was truly a conflict between states of mind—and yet the ideas are never allowed to "violate" the human drama.

p.p.s. I enclose a letter from a Yale student (with whom I am not acquainted) rather than supplying him with your address. It occurs to me that this way of handling the situation may be easier on you. If you can't help, for whatever reason, you can simply let the matter drop. I'll simply write him a note that I am relaying his request to you and that if you are able to help, he'll probably hear from you in due time.

[OH]

Forest Road
Northford, Conn. 06472
Sept. 23, 1975

Dear Allen,

I had a note from George Core[1] this morning in which he said, among other things, that you had to return to the Vanderbilt Hospital. I hope that by the time this letter reaches you, you will have made a good recovery and be at home once more. I hasten to write to you not only because of my concern for your health but because Tinkum and I are just on the point of hurrying over to London—we are expecting to fly tomorrow morning—to have a short holiday.

We've had a pleasant but crowded summer—too crowded, even hectic, as Red and I have been seeing through the press the fourth edition of *Understanding Poetry*. Red and Eleanor departed last week for Paris, but will be making their way down to the Chianti country south of Florence, Italy, where they will spend the autumn in John Palmer's country house. Our trip is more modest in goal and length of stay. We hope to spend about two weeks in London, seeing some plays and ballet and talking

1. George Core became editor of the *Sewanee Review* in 1973.

with a few friends. For the third week we will try to get up to Scotland to see one friend and out to Wales to see another; then home and back hard to work. We are both tired and need a change of scene and a little *dolce far niente.*

Though we have longed to get back to England for a visit, we have been dismayed by the price of London hotels. Indeed we had about given up hope of going when T. got through a friend the address of a small flat, where good friends of ours had in the past stayed satisfactorily for a reasonable price.

The flat is just north of Baker St.—to be exact, 48 Balcombe St., NW1. It's in a part of London we don't know well, but close to a good station on the underground and hence not far from theatres, galleries, etc.

I recall with very real pleasure our more recent meetings, particularly the long four-hour talk we had last May. I was fearful of tiring you and finally suggested that it was time for me to leave, but I did so very reluctantly. I hope that we will have some more such visits in the weeks and months to come.

T. joins me in affectionate greetings to you and to Helen and to the children.

Cleanth

[OH]

Forest Road
Northford, Connecticut 06472
30 August 1976

Dear Allen,

I was sorry to be able to be of no more help than I was when you telephoned about the Swallow contract. My memory is not my strongest faculty these days. I find that I am beginning to get into that state where one remembers very vividly scenes from fifty years back, some of them at least, but that more important things of very recent vintage have disappeared without leaving a trace.

The incident in question did leave a vague trace—that is, I do remember being asked to witness something, but whether the witnessing included a contract for your collected poems,[1] I could not and cannot remember.

I hope that it can, however, be settled satisfactorily and amicably. If there *has been* any hanky-panky, a copy of the signatures might well show that.

1. Tate's final *Collected Poems* was published by Farrar, Straus, and Giroux in 1977.

We are leading a very monotonous but generally satisfactory summer here in Northford. The Faulkner book goes moderately well.[2] It has picked up during the last three months and moves ahead. I expect to have a MS by Christmas. But I tire out early with steady reading and writing. When the weather is fine, as it is most of the time, I ride my mower close to ten acres these days. At the moment, it all looks very pretty, a little like an English park. Tinkum sometimes asks why do we do it? For whose benefit? We stay so busy, both of us, that we don't see much of our friends or have them out often enough. And we stay too busy to travel. Maybe such work is its own reward.

Tinkum is now working on her house—painting, scraping, staining, and repainting. At the moment she is superintending a crew of four people. It's a little hard on her, but I think that she truly enjoys it. I tell her that she should have been in sole charge of a large plantation in Mississippi or Georgia in the 1840s—that she would have had a wonderful time—and she is inclined to admit that I am right. Thus, what with her work at Recording for the Blind and her constant typing for me, she stays busier than I do.

The Warrens in Vermont were almost washed away by Hurricane Belle. We got a good deal of Belle's wind but not too much rain. Their luck was to get not much in the way of gales, but inches and inches of rainfall.

They return to Connecticut on the 13th or 14th of this month. I believe that the condition of Eleanor's eyes is essentially unchanged. She is a good stoic and doesn't complain. Rosanna [Warren], who has not been really well for months, seems now to be on the mend and expects to leave for Paris at the middle of the month. I think she is to be there for a good many months.

T. and I fly out to Arizona for a family visit to my elder brother's ranch. He has been a cowboy and then a rancher in Texas and Arizona since 1920 or earlier. It has been the life he really wanted. He is a good amateur taxidermist and has a fine knowledge of botany—especially the wildflowers of the southwest.

We expect to return on the 13th, however, and mean to slog along until my book is finished.

I hope that the move to Nashville did not prove too strenuous and that all of you are well settled. Tinkum joins me in affectionate greetings to Helen and the little boys.

Cleanth

2. *William Faulkner: Toward Yoknapatawpha and Beyond.*

p.s. I had a pleasant letter from Austin Warren a few days ago. He seems in good spirits. He lives not really terribly far away but we have been able to lure him over for a visit only once since he moved to Providence, R.I. We see Margaret Wimsatt[3] from time to time. Indeed, had dinner with her last night.

113 Groome Drive
Nashville, TN 37205
September 29, 1976

Dear Cleanth,

Your letter of August 30 was much appreciated. I have waited to answer until I got the results of the conflict with the Swallow Press. Yesterday I received a letter releasing me from the contract of *Collected Poems*. Bob Giroux will publish the book next spring.

There was a real contract. I had completely forgotten it; nor could a copy be found at the Princeton Library nor in my papers here. I have written an apology to the Swallow Press for suspecting fraud on their part. My memory *is* faulty and I should not have relied upon it.

When you and Tinkum are at Chapel Hill you must come over and see us.

I am sure you have seen that dreadful issue of *Time Magazine* about the South. I am a little ashamed to have been quoted in the wrong place for the wrong reason. The Fugitive Group is not mentioned nor are you and John Ransom. Since when did the present Chancellor become Vanderbilt University?

Love to you both,
Allen

3. Margaret Wimsatt was the widow of Brooks's old friend and colleague William Wimsatt.

See p. 110 ref

"Anony reader" [Date]
AA 111–112

Appendix written approx 1944 ?
app. pub. — SR 1946

The Maelstrom, by Cleanth Brooks

of Faulkner's
S & J Quentin

"At first I could not make out what he meant—but soon a
hideous thought flashed upon me. I dragged my watch from
its fob. It was not going. I glanced at its face by the moonlight,
and then burst into tears as I flung it far away into the ocean.
*It had run down at seven o'clock! We were behind the time of the
slack, and the whirl of the Ström was in full fury!*"

—From Poe's "A Descent into the Maelstrom"

Graham's Magazine May 1841

     Then when the terror is at its height, you hurl
The useless watch away, fling time away,
Having no more to do with time, and watch
The scudding circles of the empty spray
That are not empty—are competent and clutch
The abandoned rudder, and firm it to their whorl.

Geared to the whirlpool now, destruction's dial,
The fool can read—the fool that runs, that speeds
On the dial's hurrying face, knows what's o'clock,
Himself the second hand, at first hand reads
The timepiece Braille-wise past strained eyes' denial
Like the scared mouse that climbed inside the clock.

The gleaming funnel into nothing shines
As black as mahogany, as brittle as ice,
Down which the fluid moonlight steadily pours
Past spinning flotsam, past concentric lines
Of ordered wreck, to spill on what far floors
Beneath. You wipe the spindrift from your eyes.

But now, committed to time's enterprise,
Your boat itself can teach the sought-for poise,

As, neatly tilted to the spinning walls—
Adjusted in an instant to hell's laws—
It rights itself before your dazzled eyes,
And like a delicate water-fly clings and crawls.

And tranced by the murderous organ-roar, or cleared
By the monstrous centrifuge, the chilling brain
Is hardened to a screen across which run
The pretty patterns: spar, green branch, broached tun,
Smashed dory, orange-crate, each carefully steered
And keeping like a racer, each his lane.

And you, the railbird, loll and eye the track
That's lightning fast, the field of wreck that's slow.
You back the rakish derelict to beat
The bluff Dutch brig. And lose! But win the heat,
For your own boat, now on her easiest tack,
Creeps past both downward toward the spume below.

And then you see! Prepare to abandon ship,
Explain to the frantic brother, your clumsy hands
Futilely gesturing physics. But the leap
Asks too much of his mind; the tilting boat
Is the sole formula he understands.
He shouts you down with screams from the mute throat.

But hands keep up their argument until
Your brain, now tingling like the rat's gray fur
Alive with prescience, hauls them from the craft
Onto the polished water that does not spill
Or foam like water, is darker and thicker far
Than the thinned blood that rides your crazy raft.

But is the expedient desperate enough?
You have abandoned everything but hope
That scuds too fast—that would anticipate
The last gyrations down the nether slope
And after, when the spent vortex shall slough
Its fury off, and like a flower dilate.

Yet hug hope to you like the empty cask
And strictly purge the brain as dry as cork
That it may bob, dry-shod, outside the gates
Of the abyss, may bob, and dip, and lurk

Above the false rainbows of spume that mask
The final gyres of Dante and of Yeats.

Who knows the whirlpool's season or the hour
That ripens it to peace? Who thinks to catch
Time's phoenix on her nest? Not even the fool
With the fool's luck. Yet stare; prepare to watch—
Since nothing's left but staring—the calm floor
Ascend, the surge become the stagnant pool.

Index

Matthews, Tom: with *Time Magazine,* 86, 88

Matthiessen, F. O., 32, 32n2, 51, 143, 151

McCarthy, Cormac, 34n5

McGhee, Paul, 146

McLuhan, Marshall, 124n3

McMurphy, Robert, 136

"Meaning of Death," 199

Mechanization Takes Command, 226

"Mediterranean," 199

Mediterranean and Other Poems, 118

Melville, Herman, 118, 123, 249, 251

Memoirs and Opinions, 223, 234, 257

Memoirs of Hecate County, 130

Meredith, William, 162

Mesure Lectures, 2, 74, 77, 94

Metaphor, 41

Metaphysical poetry, 38, 52

"Metaphysical Poetry and Propaganda Art," 64n7

Michigan Quarterly, 239

Milton, John, 27, 111, 135, 137–38, 179, 181

Mims, Edwin, 21n2, 75–76, 75n1

Mind of the South, 77

"Miss Emily and the Bibliographer," 63, 63n3, 65

"Mrs. Colum and Mr. Jones," 118, 125

"Mr. Kazin's America," 102–3

"Mr. Kenneth Burke and the Historical Environment," 33

Mizener, Arthur, 61–62, 65, 61n2, 67, 81, 88, 93–94, 110, 166, 176, 215, 217, 224

MLA, 61, 132, 145–47, 171, 185, 237–39

Modernism, 2

"Modern Poet and the Tradition," 41

Modern Poetry and the Tradition, 39, 45–46, 48–52, 56–60, 228; work on, 41–42, 45, 54–55, 58, 64, 221, 253, 255; dedication to Tate of, 50–51, 58–60; acceptance for publication of, 57

"Modern Southern Poet and Tradition," 23n3

"Modern Southern Poets" (Fletcher), 23

Modern Verse in English, 195

Modest Proposal, 157

Moe, Henry Allen, 88, 88n2, 100–101

Monk, Samuel Holt, 69, 69n4, 146–47

Moore, Merrill, 1, 148, 148n1, 150

"More Sonnets at Christmas," 103

Morrison, Theodore, 163

"Mother and Son," 199

Mudrick, Marvin, 214n1

Muller, Herbert J., 154

Nash, Ogden, 55

Nashville Group. *See* Fugitives

Nation, 163

National Endowment for the Humanities, 225

National Institute of Arts and Letters, 236–37

Naturalism, 116–18, 123

Nemerov, Howard, 236

Newberry Library, 139

New Criticism, 2, 4–6, 111n2, 157–58; biases toward, 4–5; definition of, 5; method for reading poetry, 6

New Masses, 19

New Republic, 17, 22

New York Critics, 18

Nietszche, Friedrich, 108

Night Rider, 34, 58

Nixon, Herman Clarence, 58n2

None Shall Look Back, 31, 37n2

"Note on the Limits of 'History' and the Limits of 'Criticism,' " 147–49

"Notes for a Revised History of English Poetry," 41, 52

"Notes on Marxian Criticism" (Cowley), 22

"Notes Towards the Definition of Culture" (Eliot), 154

Novel and the Modern World, 68

Noyes, Alfred, 95, 95n2

"Ode to the Confederate Dead," 199, 233–35; typescript of, 211

O'Donnell, George Marion, 48, 48n1

"Old Mansion" (Ransom), 240

"Old Red" (Gordon), 97

On Native Grounds, 102n1

On the Limits of Poetry, 144

"On the Poetry of Allen Tate," 235n1a, 239

"Open Letter on Critics and Criticism" (Krutch), 98

Order and History, 108n5

"Our Cousin, Mr. Poe," 226

"Over-Wrought Urn," 214, 214n1

Owsley, Frank, 55–56, 55n1

Oxford University Press, 46

Palmer, John, 80, 80n1, 130–33, 182, 209, 260

AU tel 7-5-99 ✓
202 - 546 - 7009
213 1/2 6th St. NE
Wn DC 20002

Cleanth Brooks 1906 - 1994 at 87

Edith Amy Blanchard Brooks
"Tinkum" 1911 - 1986 (n) A 27

Allen Tate 1899 - 1979
d in Nashville

Andrew Lytle

Tate
Poe essay 1949
Brooks comA (?.)
"Maelstrom" 1944
pub SR 1946